TWENTIETH-CENTURY BRITISH AUTHORS
AND THE RISE OF OPERA IN BRITAIN

To Richard, Sheila, Roy, and Lenore Morra.

Twentieth-Century British Authors and the Rise of Opera in Britain

IRENE MORRA
Cardiff University, UK

ASHGATE

Published by
Ashgate Publishing Limited
Gower House
Croft Road
Aldershot
Hampshire GU11 3HR
England

Ashgate Publishing Company
Suite 420
101 Cherry Street
Burlington, VT 05401-4405
USA

Ashgate website: http://www.ashgate.com

British Library Cataloguing in Publication Data
Morra, Irene, 1975–
  Twentieth-century British authors and the rise of opera in Britain
  1. Opera – Great Britain – 20th century 2. Music and literature 3. Libretto
  I. Title
  782.1'0941'0904

Library of Congress Cataloging-in-Publication Data
Morra, Irene, 1975–
  Twentieth-century British authors and the rise of opera in Britain / by Irene Morra.
    p. cm.
  Includes bibliographical references (p.   ).
  ISBN 978-0-7546-6063-7 (alk. paper)
  1. Opera—Great Britain—20th century. 2. Music and literature. 3. Libretto. I. Title.

ML1731.5.M67 2007
782.10941'0904—dc22

2007017962

ISBN: 978-0-7546-6063-7

Printed and bound in Great Britain by MPG Books Ltd, Bodmin, Cornwall.

Contents

Preface

Twentieth-century Britain saw literary figures become extensively involved in the writing of opera libretti and in the formulation of musical aesthetics. This involvement has so far been under-explored, and calls for more critical attention from literary, cultural, and musical scholars. Through some contextual analysis and selective close readings, this book aims to expose a new field for critical investigation, and to stimulate further studies.

My key aim is to isolate the extent to which the twentieth-century "renaissance" of opera in Britain was particularly defined and influenced by literary aesthetics, assumptions about literature, and literary figures themselves. The literary celebration of music and musical collaboration was in turn strongly informed by assumptions about musicality and musical effect; these assumptions also demand further interrogation.

The relationship between key figures in music and literary "development" says much about the evolution of opera as a hybrid form. Furthermore, it points to the complexity of the interaction in any celebrated dialogue or collaboration between the arts.

Irene Morra

Acknowledgements

This project originated some years ago, at the University of Toronto. I am extremely grateful to Linda Hutcheon, for her constant support, constructive advice, and unflagging enthusiasm in those vital early years. Thank you also to Sam Solecki, David Townsend, Caryl Clark, Judith Herz, and Brian Corman.

Many friends, colleagues, and loved ones have endured and supported this project in various stages. Thank you to Tatjana Chorney, Aparna Halpe, and Robin Norris, whose friendship and solidarity made the entire experience enjoyable and refreshingly human. Flanny Alamparambil, Paul Eros, Iwona Piotrowska, and Dawn Tam suffered manic emails and inarticulate expostulations with humor and friendly concern. Thank you also to those colleagues and friends at Cardiff University who helped to support and enrich the project in its later stages. I am particularly grateful to Carl Phelpstead and Sean Purchase, for their choice nuggets of constructive criticism, and to Judith Pryor, for offering a constant critical ear to my unending musings about Britishness.

For their unwavering presence and gentle companionship: Giuseppe and Papagena Morra. Always, forever, my family.

The generous financial support of the Social Sciences and Humanities Research Council of Canada sustained this project through its early years. Some of the early attempts to think through the ideas in Chapter Three were published as: "'A Song Not Without Words': Singing Billy Budd," *Literature and Musical Adaptation*, ed. Michael J. Meyer (New York: Rodopi, 2002), 7–27.

Introduction

The English forte is words, and words are the key to modern opera ... Now that the Word is with us again, English opera comes into its heyday, and there may be said to be a literature of librettos, a poetry certainly. (Mordden 285)

The involvement of literary figures in the definition and creation of modern British opera offers a glimpse into the aesthetic anxieties and projects of modern writers and composers. As we shall see, collaborations and interactions between such artists as Benjamin Britten, E. M. Forster, Michael Tippett, W. H. Auden, and Harrison Birtwistle have indeed contributed to a "literature of librettos," and represent an increasingly synthetic movement between literature and music. Such collaborations have redefined the genres of opera and the opera libretto in modern Britain, and necessitate a new critical language. The opera libretto is a literary as much as a musical form, and its development as such demands a reconsideration of traditional critical narratives about dramatic, poetic, and narrative aesthetics in the twentieth century.

British opera did not fully emerge to assert itself internationally until the twentieth century. In 1944, W. J. Turner claimed that "since the beginning of the twentieth century there has been a genuine renaissance of music in England" (qtd. in Stradling and Hughes, 45). Since then, however, Benjamin Britten's *Peter Grimes* (1945) has been generally recognized as having initiated the rebirth of British opera. The success of *Peter Grimes* "went far to break down the inferiority complex under which English opera had laboured for so many years" (White, *The Rise of English Opera* 168), asserted a modern operatic idiom for British opera, and ensured the prediction that "English is likely to become of increasing importance as one of the key operatic languages" (White, *A History of English Opera* 437). Most important to this recognition of twentieth-century British opera is the perception of Britain as the site of one, if not two, concerted renaissances of opera in the twentieth century.

Despite this international emergence, however, British opera suffers from a lack of specific critical consideration within the context of international operatic studies. A possible explanation might be found in the fact that British opera has no distinct national musical idiom from which developments can be traced. Purcell, generally considered England's most important opera composer, did not exert such operatic staying power as to determine twentieth-century operatic developments. Although Gay's *The Beggar's Opera* (1728) was influential in ensuring the decline of baroque *opera seria* in England, it was constructed as a pastiche of popular song, and offered no alternative operatic idiom through which a national musical style could be developed.[1] Due in part to a lack of government patronage and concert

---

1   While Gay's work was a prominent "British meta-opera" (Gilman 545) in its time, it did little to influence identifiably British operatic developments until the twentieth century,

venue, British composers did not by and large play an international part in eighteenth or nineteenth-century musical creativity. English audiences preferred to import their music, insisting that operas based upon the novels of Sir Walter Scott be sung in Italian, preferably to tunes adopted from *The Marriage of Figaro*. "Serious" secular music was left to select venues in London that ensured profits with international works and international performers. If asked to name a prominent and respected English composer, the average concert-goer would have been hard-pressed to offer a name other than that of Handel or Mendelssohn, two adopted foreigners whose repertoire continues to dominate English concert performances to this day. Furthermore, "representative" British operas are sufficiently distinct from each other musically as to inhibit any generalizing of a twentieth-century British musical idiom. One need only contrast the conservative tonal idiom of Williamson with the experimental solo instrumentalism of Tippett, or the focused lyrical text-setting of Britten with the vocal acrobatics of Davies, to recognize a diversity of compositional styles and priorities.

Despite this apparent lack of a national musical idiom, critics and composers refer frequently to modern British opera as a distinct genre. In part, this is because of the sudden international respect enjoyed by particular composers from Britain in the twentieth century. More important, however, is another unifying element to these operas that renders them recognizably representative of a British operatic idiom.

Defining the British operatic idiom

In 1902, William Johnson Galloway, MP, expressed the frustration felt by many: "things have come to such a pass that one may well wonder whether there is any room at all for an Englishman, and whether the time has not arrived for a voice to be raised on behalf of native artists and native art" (12). The first decades of the twentieth century witnessed a birth of nationalist interest in founding a British musical tradition. The emergence of Sharp, Parry, Stanford, Butterworth, and Vaughan Williams coincided with a general nationalist movement in European musical composition. Wagner, Bartók, Grieg, and Smetana had turned to their national traditions in narrative and music to express emancipation from foreign musical and cultural influences, and to celebrate the individual myths of evolving nations. Often, this nationalism led to the enthusiastic incorporation of folk song into a constantly developing classical idiom.

Composers of this first British renaissance were concerned primarily with celebrating the nation through the consistent representation of Britain in music. In 1882, the Prince of Wales provided a public manifesto for the first renaissance: "by inspiring among our fellow-subjects in every part of the Empire these emotions of patriotism which national music is intended to evoke ... [music will] strengthen a common love of country" (qtd. in Stradling and Hughes 30). The music that was to emerge would be an English music for Britain and the British Empire. Successful British composers were defined by their cultural awareness that "vital art must grow

---

when Britten and Auden expressed a renewal of interest in the work.

in its own soil and be nurtured by its own rain and sunshine" (Vaughan Williams 1963 qtd. in Whittall 15).

Unlike their European contemporaries, the composers of the first renaissance were not immediately interested in developing and challenging conventional musical structures through this nationalism; their primary focus was on celebrating the nation through folk song. Nonetheless, they faced considerable difficulties. England in particular did not really have a vigorous living folk song tradition akin to that of Hungary, Russia, or Finland. Furthermore, the folk songs of Scotland, Ireland, or Wales expressed an autonomous sense of culture that defied musical assimilation into ideas of the British nation, and validated increasing assertions of national independence and distinction. Attempts to make English folk song representative of either an 'essential' or a contemporary Britain generally came across as sentimental, whimsical, and culturally naïve, and the first renaissance was "haunted by the suspicion that the popular music of the Celtic countries was older, richer, more original and less corrupted than that of the Anglo Saxon homeland" (Hughes 205).

Furthermore, this awareness of the competing nationalist forcefulness to "Celtic" folk song could not be tempered with a confident English compositional style. Britain had no constantly developed classical idiom into which it could incorporate folk song. The difference between the original tunes as "collected" by the composer and the composer's final rendition was ultimately rhetorical; the musical piece had to remain inherently a simple folk song to ensure the recognition of its nationalist "modernity."

The answer to this difficulty emerged as the aesthetic marker of the British operatic tradition. Composers turned to literature to validate folk reference and structure, to ensure a greater assimilation of that reference within the ideal of a homogenous nation, and to point to the artistic sensitivities of their work. The British celebration of idealized folk traditions has found its strongest manifestation in musical settings and allusions to the romantic comedies of Shakespeare, pastoral literature, eighteenth-century poetry, and, somewhat ironically, the late nineteenth-century Irish celebration of the "Celtic twilight." Thus, songs from Shakespeare's plays and excerpts from *Lycidas* gave cultural respectability to folk song melody. The interest in pastoral tradition was often combined with an emphasis on myth and allegory inspired in part by Wagner and in part by traditions of the Renaissance masque, and resulted in such operas as Boughton's *The Birth of Arthur* (1909), Holbrooke's ill-fated Welsh operatic trilogy, *The Cauldron of Annwn* (1911–1920), and Easdale's "ritual opera," *The Corn King* (1935). Other early operatic hallmarks include Stanford's *Much Ado About Nothing* (1901), Napier's *Westward Ho* (1913), Holst's *At the Boar's Head* (1925), and Vaughan Williams's *Sir John in Love* (1929).

By rooting the subjects of their operas in the context of a recognizable national literary and cultural tradition, British composers defined the idiom of British opera according to the subject interests and origins of their libretti. In so doing, they unknowingly paved the way for the emergence of a distinct musical aesthetic tied to literary constructions of the nation and art. Yeats's early poetry epitomized the progressive-nostalgic aesthetic of these composers who wished to contribute a relevant modern music, but who defined this modernity by celebrating past literary and cultural achievements. When they devoted their settings so explicitly to the

Celtic twilight period, composers willingly ignored the validity of contemporary Irish culture and politics: Vaughan Williams set *The Lake Isle of Innisfree* in 1928, the same year in which Yeats had defined a new poetic interest in his publication of *The Tower*. His opera *Riders to the Sea* premiered in 1937, years after the play's debut and the "new" theatre of Sean O'Casey. In a derogatory recognition of these nostalgic, culturally assimilating literary tendencies, the critic and composer Constant Lambert asserted, "English composers have invented a species of synthetic Anglo-Irish melodic line which conjures up the weakest passages in Housman and Yeats at one and the same time" (154). Works of the first renaissance defined musical sophistication and nationalism by referring to literary works and ideals that had already been developed, challenged, and surpassed in modernist literature and modern politics.

This literary aesthetic had implications for literature as well as music. When Yeats ignored Philip Heseltine's request for permission to set some of his earlier poetry, the composer warned: "there is a method of publication by which—at some sacrifice to both poem and music—these songs may be published without affording ground for an action at law" (424). By associating their "renaissance" with a national project, composers were implicitly constructing a literary canon. As modernist poets, dramatists, and musicians increasingly noted, that canon derived from a fundamentally conservative literary aesthetic informed by a nationalist nostalgia. Such valuations often belied the concerns of the source, and ignored contemporary literary subjects, themes, and styles. In 1934, bewailing the current condition of English music, Lambert advocated a musical tradition that would mirror developments in contemporary fiction and poetry. He praised contemporary non-English composers for their ability to evoke the modernist spirit fully evoked in literature, and provided what was to be the rallying call of the second renaissance: "It is typical of the hiatus that exists between music and the other arts today that in England, the country where poetry and music have, in the past, been almost indissolubly linked, there are no musical settings of the more important poems of our time" (206). Although "there are magnificent settings of early Yeats ... there are none of later Yeats, let alone of poets more closely in touch with the contemporary *Zeitgeist*" (206).

Lambert articulates the central difference between the first and second periods of musical "renaissance" in modern Britain: the second musical renaissance aspired to emulate the modernist profundity perceived as already existing in contemporary literature and drama. By asserting the importance of their country first through folk song, and then more importantly through national narrative and literary text-settings, Vaughan Williams and his contemporaries had established the "musical" tradition that Britain lacked. Their successors differed from them primarily in their modernist literary tastes; these tastes also embraced a very different social and cultural philosophy. In defining this second movement by its literary and thematic interests, composers such as William Walton, Benjamin Britten, and Michael Tippett granted the author and the literary text a greater prominence than previously seen in musical composition. Furthermore, they more closely aligned the modern aspirations of music and literature with each other, ensuring a unique discourse in British musical and literary creativity.

The second renaissance

With *Peter Grimes*, the traditional exemplar of the second operatic renaissance, Britten granted the nationalist assertion of cultural heritage through music a contemporary artistic relevance. For the source, he used a poem by George Crabbe (*The Borough*), thus placing the work within the British literary folk tradition celebrated by Britten's predecessors. He collaborated closely with Montagu Slater, a self-consciously modernist librettist, to produce a work that refigured the original source and established itself thematically within a contemporary dramatic and literary aesthetic. While conforming to the perceived literary self-reflexivity of twentieth-century British operas which preceded them, Britten's operas declare their attempt to impart a sense of modern relevance to their subject matter. They simultaneously exemplify by their subject or original source a respected literary tradition, and provide Britten with a literary means to delineate his thematic concerns. This thematic, rather than nationalist, interest allowed Britten to explore the literature of other nations and cultures: his operatic sources include a Japanese Nōh play (adapted as *Curlew River*), and works by such writers as Thomas Mann (*Death in Venice*), Henry James (*The Turn of the Screw* and "Owen Wingrave"), and Herman Melville (*Billy Budd*). Britten's operas recognize a British tendency to adapt esteemed literary works, and conform that interest to a more recognizably modern aesthetic in both the choice and treatment of literary sources.

The use of literary works as sources for opera libretti is not of course unique to British opera, and reflects a curious trend since the beginnings of opera. What is significant about the use of literary sources in British opera after 1945 is the literary status of the majority of these sources, and the unusually consistent reverence paid to the source by a libretto that is typically either faithful to that source, or observably conscientious in its reinterpretation. No other national operatic idiom has so consistently defined its nationalism or modernity in relation to its proclaimed literary aesthetics.

This idiom was determined by the increased dialogue between literary and musical artists in twentieth-century Britain. Literary figures had long been involved in musical projects, but such an involvement in an implicitly lower art form had more often than not been considered (both by critics and the literary artist) to demand a lesser artistic role from the writer. By the twentieth century, however, assumptions about music's intellectual inferiority had been directly challenged. Thus, the composer Michael Tippett, himself the author of an anti-war play (*War Ramp*), corresponded with T. S. Eliot and Christopher Fry on the merits of his libretti. William Walton was for a long time a protégé of the Sitwells, Peter Warlock/Heseltine was a member of D. H. Lawrence's circle, and Britten fraternized with such writers as Christopher Isherwood, W. H. Auden, Stephen Spender, William Plomer, and E. M. Forster.

Such interaction was undoubtedly influenced by a larger cultural recognition of unprecedented affinities between literary and musical aesthetics. With the works and treatises of Wagner, opera in particular gained an intellectual (rather than purely aesthetic) reputation, demanding that serious artistic attention be paid to the ideas of both the composer and the opera itself. Opera became more directly involved in concerns of literary creation, conscientious dramatic presentation, and complex musical and textual expression. This emphasis introduced a seriousness of artistic intent that has remained to define the aspirations and apparent critical worth of subsequent operas.

By the end of the nineteenth century, Britain was the only European country to promote, perform, and critique opera without possessing its own clearly-formulated operatic tradition. As such, it was particularly open to the influence of modern re-valuations of the role and function of opera, literature, and music. This influence initially manifested itself in literature: many novels, for example, attempted to incorporate or represent musical effect. Huxley's *Point Counter Point* (1928) is structured according to a musical pattern, and Woolf's *Between the Acts* (1941) organizes narrative in musical rather than purely textual terms by creating verbal "leitmotifs." Forster's *Howards End* (1910) contains an extended narrative description of Beethoven's Fifth Symphony that constitutes an integral structural and thematic device. Indeed, in the same novel, Forster has his character Margaret Schlegel recognize this "new" relationship between the arts:

> [Wagner] has done more than any man in the nineteenth century towards the muddling of the arts … Every now and then in history there do come these terrible geniuses, like Wagner, who stir up all the wells of thought at once. For a moment it's splendid … But afterward—such a lot of mud; and the wells—as it were, they communicate with each other too easily now, and not one of them will run quite clear. That's what Wagner's done. (37)

Without the writings of Friedrich Nietzsche, George Bernard Shaw, Thomas Mann, and, indeed, Forster, the artistic philosophies of Wagner may not have achieved and maintained such aesthetic significance in Britain. This marked interest in the musical and narrative ideas of opera led to the emergence of the serious music critic, and the development of an intellectual respect and audience for innovative musical work. As we shall see, it also created in some musical circles a certain indebtedness towards the literary intellectual who could "validate" the artistic worth of musical endeavor. This rhetorical elision of musical and literary ideals further allowed writers to claim an authenticity to their representation of musical structure and effect in literature.

Unsurprisingly, the interest of literary figures in music, particularly opera, often resulted in the involvement of these artists in the creation as well as appreciation of musical works. Cocteau provided Poulenc with libretti, Edith Sitwell wrote the text of *Façade* for Walton, and Auden continued to compose works for Britten well beyond the point at which Britten considered their collaboration to have ended. This involvement of novelists, poets, and dramatists in the production, appreciation, and dissemination of music contributed to a noticeable shift in the narrative interests of twentieth-century opera. Where the nineteenth century saw countless operas based on the narratives of Walter Scott and Schiller, twentieth-century opera developed alongside literary innovation, and saw works based on such esoteric works as Joyce's *Ulysses*, Beckett's *Waiting for Godot*, and Apollinaire's *Les Mamelles de Tirésias*. In twentieth-century Britain, composers turned increasingly to literary works characterized by their introspection and dense and ambiguous narrative. This is not to say that such staple operatic sources as the plays of Shakespeare or popular nineteenth-century novels did not achieve operatic status. Increasingly, however, the more popular, plot-oriented and generally accessible the literary source, the more likely it was to be transcribed into the form of a musical (e.g., *Oliver!*, *The Phantom of the Opera*, *Les Misérables*, *Ragtime*) than an opera. This preference for the esoteric literary status of its original narrative source has helped to differentiate British opera in particular from other forms of musical theatre.

The music of the first British renaissance relied on literature to validate the national worth of its musical aesthetics. Towards the middle of the twentieth century, this tradition grew to acknowledge the increased intermediality of the arts, and to incorporate a self-conscious literary modernity. The consequent "second renaissance" therefore actively encouraged an unprecedented contribution from recognized British literary figures. The majority of modern British operas signal their intellectual aspirations through their subject or libretto, and evince a thematic concern for the position of the individual within a society defined by various political, social, sexual, and artistic authorities. At the same time, they tend to attempt to universalize the situation of their protagonists, rather than to confine themselves to overly specific narrative contexts.[2] Such a thematic focus demands a complex musical language, and a subject and libretto to provide an appropriate structure and dramatic context. Composers turned consistently towards librettists with considerable literary credentials to provide such a drama, usually from a pre-existent literary source.

The literary librettist

This involvement of literary figures in the composition of opera libretti says as much about literary aesthetics in Britain as it does about music. In "The World of Opera," Auden lamented what he observed to be the modern necessity for the poet to write in a "Drab style," that is, in "a quiet tone of voice which deliberately avoids drawing attention to itself as Poetry with a capital P" (116). Asserting that it is no longer acceptable to write poetry for reading or recitation in a "High style," he argued:

> Opera is the last refuge of the High style, the only art to which a poet with a nostalgia for those times past when poets could write in the grand manner all by themselves can still contribute, provided he will take the pains to learn the metier, and is lucky enough to find a composer he can believe in. (116)

For Auden, the opera libretto affords the poet an opportunity to write in a manner considered in other literary contexts to be overly performative; it is a "form of drama in which the poet may play a role, minor though it be" (115). Perhaps recognizing the "minor role" for the poet advocated by Auden, Robert Graves, Christopher Hassall, David Harsent, Ted Hughes, Stephen Spender, and Paul Muldoon all made

---

2   The archaic language and ambiguous depiction of the central character's motivations and actions in *Peter Grimes*, for example, combine to invoke Auden's ideal of the "secondary world" of artistic achievement, distinct from the "primary world" of everyday experience. The drama resists mimetic representation, apparently recognizing both that a secondary world must have "something significant to stay … about our present life" ("World" 95), and that no "secondary world can have a setting in the immediate present" ("World" 94). Auden's influence on the early Britten, himself very influential, was significant.

forays into Auden's "last refuge of the High style." The authorship of libretti was not restricted to poets, however; novelists and dramatists such as Arnold Bennett, Edward Bond, Forster, Iris Murdoch, and J. B. Priestley contributed one if not more libretti to the repertoire. This involvement invites a reconsideration of the traditional role of the opera libretto, as providing a narrative framework that allows music a certain transcendence over words. If the literary structure and devices of the libretto gain a greater distinction within the opera, they can challenge music's dominance. Furthermore, it questions conventional assumptions that it is primarily the composer who determines an opera's dramaturgical effect. Such literary involvement in British operatic creation points to the possible validation of the libretto as a literary and dramatic form.

One must ask why literary figures would agree to write a libretto unless they were able to perceive a literary, musical, or creative authorship to their participation which as yet remains unacknowledged. Although Auden claimed that the job of the librettist was "to furnish the composer with a plot, characters and words" and that "of these, the least important ... are the words" ("World" 89), he also saw the opportunity to write in a poetic style unsanctioned by contemporary literary trends. Similarly, the negative reception of verse drama in 1950s Britain coincided with the rise of the literary librettist. Verse dramatists such as Christopher Fry, Auden, and Ronald Duncan became among the most prolific authors of opera libretti. Their involvement hints that opera provided an alternative dramatic form through which they could manifest their verse aesthetic and dramatic themes. Likewise, the involvement of such contemporary dramatists as Edward Bond and Paul Muldoon in libretto writing suggests a potentially "regressive" appreciation for themes and modes of expression no longer valued on the spoken stage. Such an appreciation can very well act against any self-conscious literary modernity aspired towards by the composer.

In their novels, Woolf, Forster, and Huxley attempt to emulate musical effect through narrative structure and allusion to works and composers from earlier centuries. Such attempts come close to imposing narrative and text upon a hitherto independent art. In his description of Beethoven's Fifth Symphony in *Howards End*, Forster relegates the primary authorial role to the literary writer, who is capable not only of subsuming Beethoven's achievement within descriptive prose, but also of affirming in the novel's structure that "Beethoven's Fifth Symphony is the most sublime noise that has ever penetrated into the ear of man" (25). As they incorporate what they define as musical effect and appreciation within literary forms, such writers subtly assert their ability to create musically. In so doing, they implicitly deny the achievements of contemporary composers, and suggest for themselves an ability both to compose music, and to define musical achievement.

Ironically, such textual attempts to manifest musical effect and define musical value mirror the conservative literary tendencies of the "progressive" practitioners of the first renaissance. Unlike the music of the first renaissance, however, the opera of the second renaissance was characterized by a more concerted collaboration between musical and literary figures. Forster's role as librettist might very well have encouraged him to translate his musical appreciation of Beethoven into his own creative contribution. When librettist and composer actively interact, the tensions become even more pronounced.

As this project shall explore, such tensions define and characterize British opera, and are ensured by the presence generally of a composer writing within a musical idiom informed by literary aesthetics, and a librettist working with potentially conflicting, conservative musical ideals. These tensions are further complicated by the fact that most opera libretti are based upon pre-existing literary works, which are then rewritten by composer and librettist to define and explicate social and artistic interests. Often, the treatment of the source signals very different artistic agendas and attitudes towards literature, music, opera, and cultural achievement.

The following chapters will examine specific operas in order to isolate and address questions about the libretto's literary status and aspirations, and the relative role of music and literature in the creation of opera. Each chapter will examine one opera in depth, and contextualize that discussion with some consideration of another opera with which it might usefully compare.

Michael Tippett's adaptation of Homer's *Iliad* into *King Priam* (1962) offers an intriguing example of the extent to which composers were influenced by the literary re-definition of contemporary opera. Tippett's literary anxieties and aspirations signal his own re-valuation of the role of music in opera, and point to the increasing importance of the libretto as the marker of an opera's contemporary cultural worth. This approach compares nicely with that of Auden and Chester Kallman in their adaptation of Euripides' *Bacchae* as *The Bassarids* (1966), with music by Hans Werner Henze. This opera manifests the creative tensions that result from the heightened role of the British librettist. Tippett seems to use his source as a mere foundation from which to assert his own literary credentials. *The Bassarids*, however, aspires towards an interpretative fealty and musical dramaturgy determined by the literary confidence of its librettists.

The next chapter examines the role of the source in defining and determining an opera's construction. The use of medieval narratives in modern British opera ostensibly allows for a staged awareness of national culture and "modernity." David Harsent and Harrison Birtwistle's adaptation of *Sir Gawain and the Green Knight* (*Gawain*, 1991) attempts to recognize both the "postmodernity" of its narrative source and to emphasize the contemporary sensibilities of both libretto and music. The musical and textual means by which this is articulated point to the difficulties of transforming a text into two very different, self-consciously postmodern languages. In contrast, Christopher Hassall's adaptation of Chaucer's *Troilus and Criseyde* for William Walton (as *Troilus and Cressida*, 1954) offers a self-conscious response to resist comparison to Shakespeare's play. This opera is constructed as a much more self-conscious response to innovations in modern British opera. The choice and treatment of source underlines the collaborators' anxieties about signaling the opera's "modernity," and their awareness that such modernity is defined by the aesthetics and implicit social philosophy of modernist literature as celebrated on the British operatic stage.

The final chapter shall bring together this interest in the adaptability of particular sources and genres with a renewed consideration of tensions between composer and librettist, and librettist and literary source. Of the prose narratives chosen as sources for twentieth-century operas, few possessed a canonical status at the time at which they were adapted. Nonetheless, a number were written by authors considered canonical, or at the very least, prominent. This chapter will investigate the extent to which the operas offer a critical revaluation of the original authors by celebrating these lesser works. Furthermore, it will explore the literary implications to both source and librettist when prominent writers adapt what at the time would have been seen as relatively obscure works of literature.

Alun Hoddinott intriguingly aimed to assert the glory of Wales by adapting Robert Louis Stevenson's *The Beach of Falesá* (1974). Glyn Jones's libretto, however, is more involved in its artistic rivalry with Hoddinott's original choice of librettist, Dylan Thomas. The nationalist and artistic dialogue that results offers an indication of the struggle to assert Welsh nationalism through a British operatic idiom. The question of competing motivations can be explored more thoroughly in a primary discussion of E. M. Forster and Eric Crozier's adaptation of Herman Melville's *Billy Budd* for Benjamin Britten.[3] Like Auden, Forster brought with his literary status and musical appreciations a number of expectations and assumptions about creative authority. Furthermore, he clearly perceived in both the original source and the operatic form a sympathy with many of his own thematic and aesthetic interests. His collaboration with Crozier and Britten further complicated the adaptive project. A close examination of the opera reveals tensions among Britten, Forster, Crozier, and, ultimately, Melville: each collaborator works to realize his own literary, musical, and dramatic aesthetics.

By thus analyzing the dramatic and interpretive function of the very separate "components" of these operas, this study will reveal the extent to which literary and musical aesthetics have become competitively interdependent. The movement towards intermediality between the two arts reveals much about British opera, and even more about the theoretical importance of the dialogue between literature and music in twentieth-century Britain.

---

3   Despite the changes made to the original 1951 version in 1961, there is little discrepancy between the two operas in terms of thematic or dramatic emphasis. As all three collaborators regarded the revised version as a structural improvement, I will quote from the revised libretto. References will be to page numbers. For a consideration of the changes made to the original libretto and score, see Reed, "The 1960 Revisions: A Two-Act *Billy Budd*."

Chapter 1

Drama, Verse, and the Musical Libretto

The Bassarids and *King Priam* were composed at the height of literary involvement in operatic creation, and provide a useful critical basis from which to investigate the increasing involvement of literary and musical figures in music and literature respectively. Auden and Kallman attempt to stir the viewer (or reader) into an appreciation of what they declare to be a faithful adaptation; Tippett, however, distances himself from his source to assert the originality and literary status of his opera, both of which he isolates primarily in the libretto. *The Bassarids* is the product of collaboration in which the librettists occupy a creative domain distinct from the composer,[1] whereas *King Priam*'s score and libretto were written by a single creator. Nonetheless, all of the operatic creators—Tippett, Auden, Kallman, and Henze— demonstrate a tendency towards redefining the traditional roles of the composer and the librettist. Both operas point to the necessity for a revaluation of the function of words, music, and literature in twentieth-century British artistic endeavor.

Tippett, verse drama, and *King Priam*

King Priam, unlike many other British operas, does not lend itself to examination as a conscientious adaptation. Tippett was ambivalent about declaring any interpretative affiliation, and perceived the *Iliad* as a repository of narratives to be recreated, redefined, and staged according to his own creative impulses. In one instance, he speaks of needing to "pare everything away" out of "such rich material" to achieve his chosen dramatic emphasis ("Resonance" 234); in another he disregards the literary source by claiming that it was a visit to the historical Troy ("amazingly like what one imagines from Homer's story of the *Iliad*") which impressed upon him the domestic importance of the Trojan War to Priam's family ("Resonance" 231). The opera and Tippett's approach are significant for the way in which they reveal the composer constructing a reaction to literary influences on modern British opera. *King Priam* manifests the anxieties of a composer working in a cultural atmosphere that lends increasing importance to the role and literary rank of the librettist. The result of these anxieties challenges traditional assumptions about the boundaries between spoken and sung drama, and between literary and musical creativity.

---

1   The title "The Bassarids" was sufficiently uncommon as to make the composer himself request of Auden a program-note to explain "what the fuck the 'Bassarids' mean" (qtd. in Auden and Kallman, *Libretti* 682). Auden replied to Henze's request that the original title be retained by asserting, "Uncommon or not, *The Bassarids* is a genuine word and sounds well both in English and German. Also, slightly puzzling titles titivate public curiosity" (qtd. in Auden and Kallman, *Libretti* 682).

Borrowing from a modernist writer, Tippett articulates his operatic aesthetic: "My motto will tend also always to be the simple one of Ezra Pound's: 'Make it new.' Adventure will in the end take us further than repetition" ("Opera Since 1900" 203). A work cannot satisfy Tippett's operatic aesthetic merely by moderating between old and new musical tradition or by asserting a modernist musical idiom. While a work such as Menotti's *The Consul* achieves some modernity by bringing "the Italian tradition ... up to date," it is ultimately unsuccessful because it remains "fundamentally just exactly what it says" ("Opera" 202). In contrast, *The Rake's Progress* is worthy of being considered an operatic landmark because it contains "undertones and overtones of all kinds" that ensure that the opera "is not at all just what it says" ("Opera" 202). For Tippett, the depth of the modern opera and the ultimate determinant of its success seem to come from a self-consciously enigmatic libretto.

Tippett's framing of his aesthetic motto in a literary context is significant; the "adventure" upon which composers must embark to make an opera "new" is to be found in the subject and text of the libretto. Music is implicitly secondary to the intellectual interests of the drama as articulated in libretto and staging. In writing of his first opera, *The Midsummer Marriage* (1955), Tippett refers to having written a magic "musical veil" to "clothe" his "strange libretto so that the final product [had] the appearance of that indissoluble unity of drama and music that is opera" ("The Birth of an Opera" 49). The "strangeness" of the drama is to come from the libretto, and be discovered beneath the deceptive covering of the music. Adapting Eliot's belief that "for himself as a poet, 'the words come last'," Tippett composed his music only "when he had a clear concept of the structure and character of the piece in question" (Bowen, *Michael Tippett* [1997] 39). This unusual compositional approach (notably inspired by a modernist poet and dramatist) indicates the seriousness with which Tippett constructed his libretto as a drama containing themes and intellectual concerns assumedly to be highlighted (or disguised) by music. Tippett's comments suggest that music has disguised his libretto to give the illusion of a traditional opera. It is left to the discerning audience to separate the ostensible unity of music and drama, remove the "magic musical veil," and discover the dramatic truth of the opera in its libretto ("Birth" 49).

Tippett's reaction to criticisms of *The Midsummer Marriage* further points to his isolation of the libretto as the most important element of an opera. He notes delightedly that "the bulk of the serious criticism was directed in any case at the libretto": "it meant that critics, instead of ignoring what was being sung ... and simply talking about the quality of the singing and orchestral playing, now actually engaged with the drama" (*Those Twentieth-Century Blues* 219). Nowhere does Tippett equate drama with music; to him, the attention granted the libretto is not misplaced.[2] Indeed, Tippett suggests that if the libretto were to be ignored, critics would naturally next concern themselves with the opera's staging and performance rather than its music. Stage effects "enhanced" the music of *King Priam*; David Webster (General Manager of the Royal Opera House) "had watched the stage with such intensity" that "he had been mostly unaware of the music." Tippett asserts: "it was the effect I had intended for *King Priam* and it is an essential of the opera" ("Resonance" 233–4). He attributes a greater dramatic effect to staging than to music, and notably fails to mention critical reactions to his music, or to suggest that music might collaborate with the libretto to achieve dramatic effect. Such rhetoric ultimately disavows a position for music in any critical hierarchy.

For Tippett, then, the libretto provides an opportunity for musical embellishment of words, but more importantly demands consideration as serious and potentially autonomous drama. He emphasizes that the "newness" of opera must be found in the profound drama that exists *beneath* the aesthetic pleasure provided by music. A closer examination of his critical writings reveals assumptions about the role and function of the composer which further marginalize the aesthetic relevance of music.

Ever conscious of his motto to be "new," Tippett defines his modernity in intellectual, as well as literary terms. He rails against an "anti-intellectualism" in "English musical life in general," asserting, "As someone seeking to fertilize creative projects with intellectual ideas and perceptions, I was running very much against the grain of English musical life" (*Those Twentieth-Century Blues* 16, 188). His own artistic instincts are implicitly superior: he qualifies his assertion of having always had a strong "drive to make musical and theatrical artefacts" with, "but absorbed into that was an intellectuality which I could never refuse" (*Those Twentieth-Century Blues* 16). Tippett's writing constantly distinguishes between music and intellect, and ultimately prioritizes intellectual endeavor. He dismisses the "anti-intellectual" view "that if you composed, you didn't write"; such a view is nonsense "when there were so many composers who were also fine writers" (Bowen, "Tippett in Interview" 158).

Nonetheless, Tippett suggests that although composers are capable of demonstrating their intellectualism in writing, they cannot do so in music, an implicitly unintellectual form. While he criticizes the attitude that "the metaphor of music [is] ... disrelated to what one might consider a system of thought" (Bowen, "Tippett in Interview" 158), he does not identify such a "system." Instead, he again asserts the potential for a musician to possess creative and intellectual instincts, without defining the means by which those instincts can be achieved or articulated in music (Bowen, "Tippett in Interview" 159). Claiming that the cultural "reluctance to accept

---

2   This isolation of the libretto as the primary source of Tippett's operatic originality has been half-acknowledged by prominent Tippett critics. Whittall, for example, notes that "Tippett's references to Brecht's epic theatre, and also to the Claudel-Milhaud *Christophe Colombe* ... clearly did not imply any comparable, or parallel musical influences" (*The Music of Britten and Tippett* 188); we are left to assume that the influences must have been dramaturgical, thematic, or literary. Distinguishing Tippett from other British composers, Bowen states that if Tippett "relates to any English tradition it is to the pluralism of Shakespeare and to the strained imagery of the seventeenth-century Metaphysical poets" (Bowen, *Michael Tippett* [1997] 243).

the notion of the composer as thinker later dogged [his] reputation considerably" (*Those Twentieth-Century Blues* 16), Tippett nonetheless maintains that the intellect of a composer is best manifested in his writing and ability to appreciate written work, rather than in his music.

Tippett's "newness" lies in his rhetorical reinvention of the role of the opera composer as that of the literary intellectual. Throughout his writings, Tippett places himself in the ranks of contemporary writers, simultaneously referring to literary figures as mentors and intellectual artists, and asserting his intellectual (and implicitly literary) equality. He claims to have found solace from the anti-intellectualism of his contemporary musicians in the company of writers; Eliot was "the most rewarding of them—a true artistic and spiritual mentor" who guided his reading to help him develop "a profound love of Yeats" (*Those Twentieth-Century Blues* 188). Despite Eliot's role as mentor,[3] he could be "gently chided" by Tippett over "his retreat from the tone and technique of *The Family Reunion*" (*Those Twentieth-Century Blues* 272). Although he turned to Christopher Fry for help in writing madrigal verse (for *A Garland for the Queen*), Tippett qualified the choice by noting that Fry "had rather lost his way as far as writing poetry was concerned" (*Those Twentieth-Century Blues* 190). He speaks of being "accepted" by the Sitwells, yet asserts, "I had no illusions about this tiny group of upper-middle-class dilettantes: Edith was the only one who seemed to me to be producing work that would hold" (*Those Twentieth-Century Blues* 188).

Tippett is at pains to demonstrate the ease with which he was accepted and taken seriously by contemporary literary figures, all the while emphasizing his autonomous critical ability to appreciate and assess literary worth. His autobiography, *Those Twentieth-Century Blues*, is so replete with references to literary figures and works as to resemble more the life of a writer than that of a composer. On one page alone of an essay purportedly about opera, Tippett cites his knowledge of Chekhov's *The Cherry Orchard*, Shaw's *Heartbreak House*, Albee's *Who's Afraid of Virginia Woolf*, and Shakespeare's *Measure for Measure* and *The Tempest*, apparently to prove the prevalence of the theme of love in conflict with duty ("Love In Opera" 219).

Because Tippett assesses intellectual worth in terms of literary knowledge and critical ability, he tends to place his own works within a literary, rather than musical, dramatic tradition. He likens the construction and thematic interests of *King Priam* to those of *Hamlet*: "Since all is declamation rather than line, there are not arias in the opera so much as monologues—static moments of self-questioning, or the questioning of fate, formally somewhat similar to the monologues in *Hamlet*" ("At Work on 'King Priam'" 62). The only theatrical movement upon which opera should depend is "verse drama: the theatre of Auden, Eliot and Fry" ("Birth" 49), and he speaks of the aesthetics of opera and drama from the Camerata "to the time when verse drama returned in English theatre, through figures like Christopher Fry, W. H. Auden and T. S. Eliot" ("Love in Opera" 214). Finding it "perfectly right to accept the example of Shaw and Butler, and deploy the intellect as part of one's creativity"

---

3   He was "guided by Eliot," for example, to believe "that whatever words [he] had, the music [he] wrote would swallow up their intrinsic poetry" (*Those Twentieth-Century Blues* 189).

(*Those Twentieth-Century Blues* 16), Tippett likens *The Midsummer Marriage* to dramatic works by Auden, Eliot, Fry, and Shaw ("Birth" 52). Indeed, he insists that opera's primary influence be derived from spoken drama rather than the operatic tradition: "the opera, however much it seems to us a mainly musical experience, is always ultimately dependent on the contemporary theatre" ("Birth" 49).

With his writings prioritizing literary composition over musical endeavor, Tippett seems to marginalize the musical role of the composer. Even his valuation of verse drama, a form celebrated for the musicality of its text, disregards the importance of sound.[4] Indeed, in his writings, Tippett equates language with idea, and seems almost persistently to disregard the importance of musical effect in either score or text.

Tippett's valuation of literature is similarly problematic, however: he values words for their ability to articulate ideas and themes, but frequently obscures the difference between intellectual thinking and literary creativity. Although he and Eliot had agreed that his "second art" was literature, he never regarded himself "as a true literary artist." At the same time, Tippett writes of having resisted (to his financial disadvantage) "regular obligations in [the] domain" of literature (*Those Twentieth-Century Blues* 191). As an example, he cites the offer from Michael Astor of an opinion column in the *Observer* (*Those Twentieth-Century Blues* 191–2). For Tippett, both literary art and the expression of opinion in writing are intellectual pursuits, and subsequently of literary value. Much like the writers who claimed that they could be "musical" in their text, Tippett claims an artistic skill and specialization for himself by redefining the role and nature of "literature." Such a redefinition allowed him, as the writer of his own libretti, to equate his articulation of ideas in opera with the literary accomplishments of contemporary librettists.

This ideological focus is always evident in Tippett's operas. Indeed, he claimed that he only decided upon musical forms and dramatic narrative after he had determined what was to be the primary intellectual "stimulus" of an opera. Thus, *King Priam* was first and foremost a response to (French Marxist critic) Lucien Goldmann's book, *Le Dieu caché* (1955). Objecting to the book's claim that "tragedy in the Greek sense is not theatrically viable" in a world which must either be Christian or Marxist, Tippett set out to prove "that tragedy is both viable and rewarding" ("Resonance" 223). He wrote *King Priam* "principally in order to repudiate Marxism–to show that the 'inevitability' of the communist utopia will always be subverted by (non-economic) factors beyond the control of man's best instincts" (Kemp, *Tippett: The Composer and His Music* 326).[5] Tippett's producer, Peter Brook, recognized his ideological

---

4   Eliot's verse drama "had the apple" in influencing his work ("Birth" 49), and Tippett's favorite drama was *The Family Reunion*, "the most Greek and least Christian of [Eliot's] plays" (*Those Twentieth-Century Blues* 272). Eliot objected to his earlier play for obscuring the importance of drama with poetic passages. Tippett, however, ignored the linguistic effect of verse and concentrated on the ideology which it expressed; although Eliot's later plays are inferior for their "almost over-cool language," this "language" corresponds to Eliot's gradual incorporation of Christian concerns within his drama. Eliot's prose began to lose its "sharpness and clarity" because of "the continual use of traditional Christian concepts and phraseology" (*Those Twentieth-Century Blues* 272).

5   Kemp further argues that the opera "is a ruthlessly analytic account of what happens when the psychological balance symbolized by marriage is knocked awry by responsibilities,

aim, and suggested that Tippett choose a familiar myth as his source, "otherwise his audiences would not follow him" (Kemp, *Tippett* 356). Apparently to appease Tippett's concerns for intellectual respectability, "Brook also pointed out that the use of traditional epic material was a long-standing theatrical practice" (Kemp, *Tippett* 356). For Tippett, the articulation of intellectual thought should be the primary concern of what can only very loosely be termed an operatic adaptation.

Nonetheless, Tippett was not indifferent to criticisms of his intellectual aesthetic. Brook's observation of the potential for the audience not to "follow" Tippett was doubtless based upon the initial reception of *The Midsummer Marriage*. Tippett's previous attempt at libretto writing had resulted in disastrous reviews; the *Times* had asserted that "the force behind the conception of the opera had been too much for [Tippett's] control," the *Daily Express* had declared the libretto "one of the worst in the 350 year old history of opera," and the *Daily Telegraph* had termed it "an extraordinary jumble of verbal images and stage mumbo-jumbo" (qtd. in Bowen, *Michael Tippett* [1997] 33). Such "mumbo-jumbo" was generally agreed to have resulted from Tippett's attempt to articulate various intellectual ideas through his libretto; the work is concerned with Jungian philosophy, pacifist politics, and atheism, all the while presenting an ostensibly simple love story. This criticism of *The Midsummer Marriage* may have inspired Tippett to turn to a pre-existent source in a defensive attempt to isolate a dramatic context through which better to express his ideas.

Intriguingly, Tippett's defensiveness about the ideology and narrative of *The Midsummer Marriage* manifests itself as a reaction against the increasing credence given to literary figures writing libretti. He notes that "all the other operas receiving premieres at Covent Garden in the 1950s had libretti by well-known playwrights or writers," and argues that "this was no guarantee of the operatic viability of their texts" (*Those Twentieth-Century Blues* 219). Instead of defending his own libretto, Tippett places himself in the role of musician (rather than literary intellectual) to imply that libretti are no longer being valued in terms of their accessibility to music, thus contradicting his own assessments of his role: "No matter how often I have said that my texts are for singing and not to be read as literature, this is how they tend to be assessed" (*Those Twentieth-Century Blues* 219).[6] In the face of dramatic and literary criticism, Tippett argues that the composer, rather than the renowned literary

---

war and fate" (*Tippett* 323). Whittall isolates a greater emphasis on war, reading the opera as almost "like a pacifist's calculated response to the decade of Korea, Hungary and Suez" (*The Music of Britten and Tippett* 185), whereas Richard Elfyn Jones identifies in the opera a predominant concern for the implications of freedom of choice (*The Early Operas of Michael Tippett* 103–8). White's discussion of the work is similarly entitled "Freedom of Choice" (*Tippett*). Clements sees the opera as "a profound demonstration of the utter folly of war from a composer who had been prepared to go to prison for his pacifist beliefs" ("Tippett at 80" 21).

6   It was only many years later that Tippett admitted to potential flaws in his first libretto: "I think I would go so far as to say that with the success of *A Child of Our Time*, which has a simple libretto, I was led to believe that I could do more along this line than I was ready for; and in composing the libretto for *The Midsummer Marriage* I took perhaps too many liberties" (Bowen, "Tippett in Interview" 156–7).

figure, has a greater understanding of musico-dramatic concerns, and is therefore best able to write a libretto. Despite attempting to claim his status as an intellectual independent from his role as composer, Tippett returns defensively to the role of musician to argue the worth of his libretto. When considered in the context of his writings, however, such assertions do not enforce Tippett's aesthetic principles. Instead, they reveal Tippett's need to affirm the importance of the musician in the face of what he perceived to be an undue critical interest in the literary qualifications of the British opera librettist.

Tippett's literary defensiveness is evident in *King Priam*, which concertedly calls attention to its literary qualities. The libretto is replete with literary references; Hermes' aria concludes with Yeats's line, "mirror upon mirror, mirror is all the show," the chorus sings in the second interlude of Dylan Thomas's "force that through the green fuse drives the flower," and the concept of the "loop in time" at the end of the opera is borrowed from Eliot's *The Family Reunion* (Kemp, *Tippett* 363). Referring to the Thomas allusion, Tippett notes that "very few people know that quotation is there in *King Priam*. If you're not a literary person and you write your own text, you have to be willing to take things from a variety of sources whenever the underlying concept is traditional and everlasting" (Bowen, "Tippett in Interview" 158). This declared indebtedness and subservience to the writings of recognized literary figures is uncharacteristic of Tippett. Tippett has argued that a musician is rarely accorded intellectual (hence literary) respect. In order to obtain this respect, Tippett attempts to validate his opera not by paying conscientious attention to his literary source or by collaborating with a known librettist, but by demonstrating his own literary awareness and knowledge in the text of the libretto.

The overall effect of these allusions, potentially elliptical to the average listener, is to encourage a literary appreciation of the libretto independent of the drama and music. Only a reading of the libretto will reveal the inserted quotation marks that draw attention to the opera's specific literary allusions. By placing himself simultaneously within musical and literary tradition, Tippett implies his independent intellectual, literary, and musical mastery of the opera. Indeed, as if in recognition of Tippett's ambition, the composer's critics frequently articulate a similar competitive literary spirit in their analyses. Bowen notes that Tippett's later opera, *The Knot Garden*, is "steeped" in "back-references to Shakespeare's *The Tempest*," and "sports one of the most successful, indeed virtuoso pieces of libretto-writing to be found in any contemporary opera" (*Michael Tippett* [1997] 43–4). At the same time as he attempts to validate the worth of the libretto by praising it in literary terms, however, he echoes Tippett in his suggestion of the superiority of the composer to the literary dramatist: "The themes and preoccupations of Tippett's four operas are widely encountered in plays and films by his contemporaries ... Tippett's music, of course, places him at an advantage. It could well be used, for instance, to breathe life into the characters in R. D. Laing's play *Knots*" (*Michael Tippett* [1981] 87). Reinforcing Tippett's self-identification as a dramatist in a literary tradition, Bowen further asserts that in *The Knot Garden*, "Tippett manipulates his characters in the manner of Shaw in *Heartbreak House* or Edward Albee in *Who's Afraid of Virginia Woolf?*" (*Michael Tippett* [1997] 115).

Both Tippett and his biographer want the best of two apparently separate worlds; recognizing the greater intellectual reputation to be achieved in literary, rather than musical endeavor, they place his works in a literary dramatic tradition. At the same time, they elevate Tippett's operas within this tradition by invoking the poetic beauty of music. These claims react against the increasing creative authority of British writers in operatic composition. Nonetheless, that authority is enabled by people such as Tippett himself, who isolate opera's primary worth in its text and ideology. Although he invokes the authority of a composer to do so, Tippett ultimately reacts against "outside encroachment" upon what he defines as the most important element of opera—its libretto. Tippett discussed with Eliot "whether Auden had not bemused Stravinsky with a poetic *tour de passepasse*, in their collaboration on *The Rake's Progress*" ("Birth" 64). He is unable to perceive, however, that he discursively creates a similar capability for the composer-librettist towards his own musical score.

King Priam can be read as an attempt to respond to, counteract, or supersede the libretti of famous British writers which were receiving significant attention from critics and composers alike. Ironically, this response implicitly accepts the redefinition of opera created by these collaborations, and underlines the increasing importance of words and text to opera's aesthetic effect. Tippett writes of agreeing with Eliot that "since opera is an art in which music must finally eat up action and setting ... on the creator of the music is put a greater burden of judgment than on the creator of the words or the scenery" ("Birth" 64). Indeed, "unless the composer has gained some degree of awareness of his real needs, perhaps even of his music, he is in danger of accepting stage actions offered him by the librettist, which would be rejected by a more fully awakened judgment" ("Birth" 64). He does not argue that music is the primary dramatic element in opera, but that the musician must be central in determining the entire structure and thematic interest of the work. The critical and popular definitions of opera, score, and libretto must be questioned when both librettists and composers imply a greater "profundity" to words in opera than to the expressive, dramatic, and intellectual potential of music.

Throughout his writings, Tippett equates his achievement with that of verse drama. Tippett was not the only figure to make this connection: his assertions mirror the claims of verse dramatists such as Fry, Eliot, and Duncan about the essential musicality of their dramas. These claims come close to disregarding essential differences between spoken drama and opera, and between musical and literary creativity. A brief consideration of these assumptions gives some support to Tippett's defensiveness about the composer's authoritative role, and demonstrates the extent to which the involvement of these librettists could redefine the aesthetic assumptions of modern British opera.

William B. Wahl recounts a frustrated interview towards the end of Auden's life. Intrigued by Auden's verse dramas, Wahl recounts: "I began the questions, asking first what he thought of his own plays. They were done in his earlier years; he had for a very long time left off with plays; he wrote libretti now." Asking what Auden "saw as the future of poetic drama in the world of today, especially in England," Wahl could only elicit the response that Auden "had some time ago perceived little future for it, which was why he had changed to writing libretti" (103). Wahl's interview with Auden points to an intriguing connection between the waning of verse drama in the 1950s and the increasing involvement of literary figures in the writing of opera libretti.

In 1956, the critical reception of the Royal Court premiere of John Osborne's *Look Back in Anger* almost single-handedly rendered verse drama instantly regressive. "Modern drama" in Britain became defined by a vernacular emphasis on the reality of working-class life, and the vaguely defined anger of the young post-war generation. The association of "verse with tradition and high-church culture" in the dramas of Ronald Duncan and T. S. Eliot in particular ensured that these works were relegated "to period pieces the moment the first post-war generation of playwrights stormed the theatre" (Innes 462). Furthermore, such verse dramatists as Duncan, Auden, Christopher Isherwood, and Christopher Hassall "shared with [Cocteau, Anouilh, Giraudoux, and Obey] a fantasised, non-naturalistic playfulness which set great store by speculation and paradox" (Rebellato 151). These tendencies did not sit well with those in the English Stage Company, who were bent on naturalistic evocations of the concerns and conditions of contemporary British life. Despite the fact that Duncan, Christopher Fry, and Eliot were among its early supporters, the Company never commissioned a play from Eliot, and Duncan complained vocally about the Company's transgression of its declared aim to foster new and experimental dramas.

Significantly, though, much of what characterizes verse drama is also present in many British operas of the second renaissance: speculation and paradox, an emphatic interest in the allegorical potential and contemporary relevance of myth, and a conscious manipulation of various verse forms and verbal images. Auden's arguments for a "secondary world" of artistic achievement beyond the "primary world" of everyday experience were at considerable odds with the naturalistic approach of successful drama after 1956. Nonetheless, they were very sympathetic to the approach taken by a number of successful operas: *King Priam* is a strong example. *The Rake's Progress* ostensibly details the picaresque adventures of the rake of Hogarth's engravings, but its musical and textual structure juxtapose eighteenth- and twentieth-century artistic expression to invite an allegorical, rather than merely historical, interpretation. Similarly, despite its specific setting and linear narrative, *Peter Grimes* discourages a purely naturalistic interpretation. Both Tippett and Eliot were concerned with integrating modern concerns within a mythical or classical context.[7] Ronald Duncan's adaptation of André Obey's play into the libretto for *The Rape of Lucretia* further exploits verse forms, mythological reference, and traditional dramatic structures. These operas all reinforce Duncan's aesthetic for verse drama:

---

7   According to Eliot, verse plays "should either take their subject matter from some mythology, or else should be about some remote historical period, far enough away from the present for the characters not to need to be recognizable as human beings, and therefore for them to be licensed to talk in verse" (*Poetry and Drama* 22–3). Tippett's interest in classical sources was more thematic: "There is nothing in Homer which makes Priam the central figure of the story as the opera does. One does not go to a past work of art for the past, but for the present. It becomes one's own work, to live or die on its own merits" (Tippett, "Resonance" 232).

"all of us live at various levels at one and the same time … it is not the dramatists [sic] job to reproduce life naturalistically, but to give it depth" (Introduction viii).

These apparent sympathies between verse drama and opera give extra weight to Tippett's claims, and to Duncan's extensive complaint against the English Stage Company. Objecting to what he saw as the artistic close-mindedness and political regressiveness of the Royal Court, Duncan phrased his ambitions for the modern theater with an operatic example: "It is too much to hope that we can find the equivalent of a Diaghilev," a person who was able to "put a Cocteau in touch with a Stravinsky. But it is not too much [to] hope that we could find somebody who is aware of contemporary trends in art" ("Artistic Policy of the English Stage Company" 114). That the composition of opera libretti allowed verse dramatists to translate their aesthetic into an alternative dramatic form is suggested by the fact that Duncan, Fry, Stephen Spender, J. B. Priestley, Hassall, and Auden not only wrote enthusiastically of music in relation to literary endeavor, but also collaborated with composers in operatic creations. Duncan's most well-known drama, *This Way to the Tomb*, was inspired by an interest in Ben Jonson's masques; Duncan had been reading them because he was "interested in dramatic forms which had music integrated within them" (Introduction vii). He wrote the libretto to *The Rape of the Lucretia* in the same year in which he wrote *This Way to the Tomb*, perhaps seeing in the libretto a logical extension of his interest in experimenting with the ways in which music might be integrated into drama.

The aesthetic aims of verse dramatists suggest an essential sympathy with the musical instincts celebrated by opera. According to Christopher Fry, "Poetry in the theatre is the action of listening … pure sound, has logic, as we know in music, and what does that logic accord to if not the universal discipline felt along the heart?" (137). At the same time, however, "the truth of poetry deepens under your eye. It is never absolute. There is no moment when we can trumpet it abroad as finally understood" (137). Fry emphasizes the potential mutability of meaning to be achieved through a poetry which he claims must aspire towards musical effect. In contrast, T. S. Eliot criticizes two passages of his own drama *The Family Reunion* for being so "remote from the necessity of the action" that the passages become "too much like operatic arias. The member of the audience, if he enjoys this sort of thing, is putting up with a suspension of the action in order to enjoy a poetic fantasia" (28). The play and the language of the play should never be enjoyed "as two separate things," for "verse is not merely a formalization, or an added decoration" (13, 19). Both dramatists (apparently unknowingly) articulate two sides of an operatic debate: one advocates musical beauty transcending text, and the other argues for the ultimate subservience of musical effect to drama.

Despite the applicability of both sides of this debate to operatic aesthetics, the aims of verse dramatists embody an inherent animosity towards traditional opera. Both Eliot and Fry identify musicality as existing within verse. If he were to translate verse drama into opera, Eliot would have to ensure that his text allow a perfect synthesis with music itself, rather than the musicality of verse. Fry, on the other hand, would have to allow music to fulfill the idealized function to which his verse aspires. A perfect operatic translation of this aesthetic would therefore require that both dramatists deny the artistic function of their verse. The creative involvement of prominent verse dramatists as librettists suggests that the tradition of verse drama evolved into that of the opera libretto. Nonetheless, the nature of the interaction between music and text in verse drama is very similar to that between music and text in opera. This similarity ensures that verse drama can never be fully translated into opera as a whole without the abdication of the consciously musical versifier. It is highly unlikely that verse dramatists would part with such artistic authority, nor indeed that they would acknowledge the necessity of musical collaboration.

The involvement of verse dramatists in the writing of libretti therefore gave the libretto a greater artistic prominence. Moreover, it challenged the essential meaning of "musicality" and musical composition. Such redefinitions necessarily query the ultimate authority of the composer as musical dramaturge. Ironically, Tippett in many ways reinforces these assumptions. He asserts his own creative role by attributing the primary dramaturgical worth of his opera to the libretto and its literary "cleverness." Indeed, he goes even further to reveal an apparent indifference about music as an innovative, vital, and dramatic participant in opera. These claims are of course counteracted by the operas themselves, which, despite their imposing libretti, are nonetheless constructed within a self-conscious modernist musical idiom. That Tippett would not acknowledge this in his writings, however, reveals the extent to which "musicality" had become rhetorically redefined by the role of the contemporary librettist.

The Bassarids

The Bassarids offers an opportunity to investigate the extent to which Tippett's defensiveness was in fact justified by the involvement of literary figures in operatic collaboration. All of these librettists—Tippett, Auden, Kallman—recognized an artistic value to the libretto. Their approach towards that art, however, was quite different. Tippett generally associated literary achievement with ideology, and defined opera by its themes. As a poet and dramatist, however, Auden had very different ideas of the role and function of literary, "musical," and dramatic aesthetics within the opera libretto.[8] Furthermore, he and Kallman approached the original

---

8   If Auden seems to be given more attention as a creative force than Kallman, this is because he was much more forthcoming about the opera and its "meaning" in his writings about the work and opera in general. The libretto itself is unquestionably a work of collaboration, however; as Henze noted, "In writing their librettos, they would discuss everything as intellectual equals, a discussion that lasted all day, in the course of which they would jot down odd words and phrases" (*Bohemian Fifths* 163). When Auden and Kallman collaborated on *Elegy for Young Lovers* (1961), they worked as if they were in "some playful competition: which of the two was the wittier, which was better at striking the note they were aiming for? Who could offer a quicker or better solution to the question of how the story should continue? Who would find the most suitable rhyme?" (*Bohemian Fifths* 164). Stravinsky's amanuensis has asserted that "the older poet could never have written librettos without his younger colleague. What is more, in everything that Auden wrote, he relied on Kallman's critical judgment" (154). Kallman wrote one libretto independently of Auden (*The Tuscan Players*, 1953, for Carlos Chàvez), translated nine by himself, and reviewed music for *The Michigan Daily* in 1942 and opera for *Commonweal* magazine from 1945 to 1946. Aside from his operatic projects, Kallman collaborated with Auden and Noah Greenberg on

source with an assumption of interpretative authority apparently sanctioned by their literary credentials. This interpretation, we shall see, was not always acknowledged or appreciated by the composer.

Like Eliot, Auden recognized the apparent necessity of keeping poetry in verse drama "drab" so as to avoid drawing attention to verse "as Poetry with a capital P." This task is far from rewarding, as the poet is obliged to pretend not to "[make] a scene" ("World" 116). Auden's identification of opera as the "last refuge of the High style" and the "only art to which a poet with a nostalgia for those times past when poets could write in the grand manner all by themselves can still contribute" implies that he saw in opera an opportunity for self-emancipation from the necessity of writing in a "drab" style ("World" 116). Identifying a crisis in Auden's later literary career as originating from an inability to express emotion in poetry, Alan Jacobs asserts that Auden was liberated from traditional poetic constraints in his operatic projects: since "emotional extravagance is virtually [opera's] *raison d'être*," it became "Auden's unequivocal duty to *unleash*, rather than restrain, the emotional resources of poetic language" (*What Became of Wystan* 92).

At the same time, however, Auden asserts that the poet must "take the pains to learn the metier" ("World" 116). The verses of a libretto "are not addressed to the public but are really a private letter to the composer." Their moment of glory exists in "the moment in which they suggest [to the composer] a certain melody"; once that is over, "they must efface themselves and cease to care what happens to them" ("Notes on Music and Opera" 473). Auden relegates poetry to a secondary role not dissimilar to the function of verse in Eliot's verse plays. Indeed, his songs for *The Rake's Progress* are much "thinner and more open" in texture compared to those he wrote independent of musical setting (Spears, *The Poetry of W. H. Auden* 288–9). His poetry, "like that of Eliot's later plays," is "a deflated balloon until the music blows it up ... the words will not call attention to themselves as words, but [are] absorbed into the music" (Spears, *The Poetry of W. H. Auden* 288–9). The apparent glory for Auden in the writing of a libretto comes not from his ability to write in a High style, but from his participation in an artistic form that ultimately achieves this stylistic grandeur through music.

Unlike some of his contemporaries, Auden explicitly argues against attempting to subsume musical effect into literature. The poet should never hope to say that "Poetry should be as much like music as possible": "the people who are most likely to say this are the tone-deaf. The more one loves another art, the less likely it is that one will wish to trespass upon its domain" ("Making, Knowing, and Judging" 52). One of his requests to Stravinsky during their work on *The Rake's Progress* was that the composer "change the soprano's final note to a high C," and take "fewer pains in the future in making every word audible" (Craft, "The Poet and the Rake" 152). Auden was so concerned with musical effect that, without any demands from

---

An Elizabethan Song Book (1955), and produced three books of poems. I am not concerned with attempting to separate Kallman's contribution to the libretto from that of Auden. In the words of Auden and Kallman: "In a literary collaboration, if it is to be successful, the partners to it must surrender the selves they would be if they were writing separately and become one new author" ("Translating Opera Libretti" 483).

the composer, he willingly rewrote sections of his libretto to better accommodate musical effect. Unlike Tippett, whose proficiency in his chosen "second art" is limited to an ideological appreciation for literary works, Auden recognizes and respects a difference between music and literature in language, technique, and aesthetic aim.

This respect might derive from Auden's own musical ability and knowledge. Stephen Spender equates Auden's period of libretto writing with that of his interest in theology,[9] but Auden's interest in music was more than spiritual. Auden played the piano, was able to be "very impressed" at the music to Henze's *König Hirsch* upon reading the score, could discourse knowingly about musical forms and various compositional schools, and attended concerts and operas regularly (H. Carpenter, *W. H. Auden* 398).[10] Furthermore, many of his poems address the subject of music or musicians, and others are constructed in musical forms (e.g. *A Christmas Oratorio*). These works resist attempting to encapsulate musical form in poetry, and the majority were intended for musical setting. Auden's understanding of the different tools and methods needed to construct musical language and form (rather than any vague appreciation for musical effect) informed his respect for the complexities of music.

Despite asserting that words are ultimately subservient to music in opera and disapproving of poetic attempts to emulate other arts in text, Auden frequently found composers unwilling to collaborate with him on operatic projects. The rift that developed between Auden and Britten following their collaboration on *Paul Bunyan* (1941) is often thought to have established Auden's reputation as a difficult collaborator. Furthermore, Tippett (and undoubtedly others) perceived Auden as having performed a "poetic tour de passepasse" with *The Rake's Progress*; when Auden asked him to collaborate upon an operatic project, Tippett became "uneasy at the prospect of working with such a domineering librettist" (H. Carpenter, *W. H. Auden* 428). Auden met Harrison Birtwistle with a similar hope, but allegedly lectured the composer on opera and libretto to such an extent that nothing came of the project (428).

Despite his belief that a composer ultimately defines dramatic tone through music, Auden was equally certain that a librettist could envision an appropriate musical style. When he insisted that Stravinsky familiarize himself with *The Beggar's Opera* while working on *The Rake's Progress*, Auden was attempting to define a musical

---

9   "He now had two main intellectual interests: one, theology; the other, Italian opera" (*World Within World* 271). Craft notes that theology "was a frequent topic in Auden's conversation with Stravinsky" while working on *The Rake's Progress* (150). In an early poem, Auden equates music with divine absolution: "You alone, alone, imaginary song,/Are unable to say an existence is wrong,/And pour out your forgiveness like a wine" ("The Composer" 12–14). According to Oliver Sacks, "[The] elemental musical sense—musical literally and musical figuratively, musical in the sense of Mozart or Bach, and equally in the sense of Pythagoras or Leibniz—was absolutely fundamental in Wystan's thought and sensibility, as in his technical virtuosity. He was lyrical, he sang, because the world was lyrical and nature was a song" ("Dear Mr. A...." 190).

10   Furthermore, "Wystan was passionately fond of hymns, of which he knew an inordinate number ... one of his last reviews was on a new English hymnary, as one of his last poems (in conjunction with [Pablo] Casals) was the composition of a glorious Anthem. Hymnody and psalmody to him were as basic as prosody, as basic as melody" (Sacks 190).

style for the work. Furthermore, Craft notes that talk frequently "turned to the Wagner and Strauss operas that [Auden] most admired but that were far from Stravinsky's present interest" (150). Later, when Stravinsky mentioned that he wished to write a one-act opera (*Delia*), Auden decided, "I see that what he wants is a Jonsonian Masque, (I have lent him the Masques to read)." He roots the project in a literary tradition and thereby assumes the role of both musical and literary mentor towards the composer. He further asserts his musical taste by satirizing specific compositional schools: "the comic antimasque will, of course, present some of our bugaboos like Twelve-Toners, Sociologists etc." (letter to Kallman, qtd. in Auden and Kallman, *Libretti* 630). Stravinsky seems immediately to have accepted Auden's vision for his work, writing to his publishers: "the theme is ... a celebration of Wisdom in a manner comparable to Ben Jonson's Masques" (qtd. in Auden and Kallman, *Libretti* 630). When he was away from Auden, and perhaps more able to recognize that the libretto was dictating a neoclassical idiom from which he had intended to distance himself, Stravinsky refused to set the work.

Auden's attempt to define the musical aesthetic of an opera was not restricted to his collaboration with Stravinsky. Henze acknowledges a quotation from J. S. Bach's *St. Matthew Passion* at the end of the intermezzo to *The Bassarids*: "this is something Auden wanted. He was never very keen on explaining what he wanted, but I think the reference is completely clear" (Interview 832). Although Henze places the aria musically in the opera, he is ultimately left, like the audience, to interpret the meaning of that quotation.

Auden's attempts to determine musical effect demonstrate his ambition that the composer fulfill the librettist's musical and dramatic vision. Auden notes that he and Kallman "found it helpful to let [their] choice of words and style be guided by a platonic idea of a suitable melody." Although they were "not such fools as to breathe a word about this" to their composers, to their "utmost astonishment and delight, every time, both Stravinsky and Henze composed actual music that corresponded to [their] platonic ideas" ("World" 93). No matter the "astonishment" of the librettists, a slight glance at any of Auden's libretti reveals that he perceived in the libretto an opportunity to determine musical effect through dramatic structure. In *Paul Bunyan*,[11] Auden specifies musical style; one section is entitled "blues" while another is entitled "lullaby" (*Paul Bunyan* 15, 29).[12] Auden's next opera, *The Rake's Progress*, goes further by stipulating which lines in specified duets, trios, and quartets should be sung with those of other characters, and which should be sung individually. The libretto dictates musical texture by specifying "recitative secco" and "orchestral recitative," and simultaneously determines musical style, form, and

---

11   All quotations from the Auden-Kallman libretti and Auden's libretto to *Paul Bunyan* are taken from the complete libretti as they appear in *W. H. Auden and Chester Kallman: Libretti and Other Dramatic Writings by W. H. Auden, 1939-1973*. Unless otherwise indicated, I have focussed my discussion on the original libretto, rather than the revised version produced by Henze in 1974, as neither Auden nor Kallman had any hand in the revisions. All references refer to page numbers.

12   Textual evidence suggests that these indications were made before the text was set to music.

tempo when it indicates that a duet should be sung "prestissimo" with "voices in canon" (63).

Perhaps out of a desire to move away from the strictly dictated forms of the neoclassical *The Rake's Progress*, Auden's next libretto to be set to music (*Elegy for Young Lovers*) abdicates musical control. Sections that had been given musical indicators in earlier operas (e.g., "trio," "finale") were now given thematic headings (e.g., "farewells," "scheduled departures," "the flower"). The subject of *Elegy*, with its multi-charactered, pseudo-allegorical examination of the role of the poet in society, is close to that of Auden's verse dramas. This return to the traditional subject matter and themes of Auden's verse drama might be attributed to the fact that, for the first time, Auden and Kallman were writing an entirely original scenario. They were working with a composer (Henze) who was less inclined to respect the artistic control demanded by the libretto of *The Rake's Progress*.[13] This clear reminder of Auden's literary accomplishments may have more easily convinced Henze of the artistic authority of his librettists. The unfavorable reception of *Elegy*, however, seems to have encouraged them to return to the successful idiom of *The Rake's Progress*, and thus to a more controlling compositional role in *The Bassarids*.[14]

Although *The Bassarids* contains fewer sections in which arias, trios, and duets are specified in the libretto, this is no indication of the librettists' structural leniency, but of a change in style; *The Rake's Progress* is neoclassical, and thus generically indebted to structural conventions. In comparison, the dramatic structure of *The Bassarids* allows for few formal ensemble pieces. The libretto nonetheless contains numerous directions that dictate orchestration, tempo, dynamics, and musical style. The scene following the intermezzo is to start "at a restrained Allegro and [get] faster and faster, returning to its first tempo only towards the end" (293). In describing what they specify to be the Hymn of the Bassarids, the librettists write that the music is to grow "ever more solemn, exultant, sustained, deliberate and slow, in marked contrast to the nervous banter and obsessive questioning fear being played stage front" (257). Later, the sisters "punctuate all their remaining conversation with light cultivated laughter," the Captain enters "with a hint of fanfares in the music," and as Pentheus descends from the tomb of Semele, "the sound of a guitar being tuned" is to be heard offstage (259–63). Throughout the confrontation between Pentheus and the

---

13   The printed libretto of *Elegy for Young Lovers* is dedicated "to the memory of Hugo von Hofmannsthal, Austrian, European and Master Librettist," by "its three makers." By dedicating the work to Hofmannsthal, Auden and Kallman (Henze had little to do with the published version of the libretto) subtly assert the importance of the role of the librettist over that of the composer. Hofmannsthal's collaborator, Strauss, is not mentioned, and by ascribing the dedication to Henze as well as to themselves, the librettists suggest that composer and librettists alike have recognized that the true worth of an opera lies in the libretto.

14   Auden reported that the English premiere at Glyndebourne "could not have been worse"; according to H. Carpenter, when Auden explained to John Christie (the founder of Glyndebourne) that he had written the libretto, Christie remarked: "You shouldn't have" (*W. H. Auden* 401). Andrew Porter deemed the libretto "a concoction whose only merit is that it provides a framework for the music": "one feels no interest in the characters or their fate; one is constantly interested in the development of the musical complexes associated with them" (qtd. in H. Carpenter, *W. H. Auden* 402).

Stranger, the voices of the Bassarids "extend the final vowels of [the Stranger's] last words, these 'echoes' becoming increasingly prolonged" (281). The Maenads later sing "each line louder than the one before" until their first full stanza, which is "at first fortissimo, then rapidly [dies] away into distance" (302). When they specify that the Stranger's answers are to be like "his remarks to Tiresias earlier," the librettists demand the recurrence of music that the composer may not have intended to repeat in the confrontation scene. These answers are to be "soft, even-toned, with a slight pause between each word, sometimes even between each syllable" (279).

The librettists go so far as to delineate how the dramatic motivation of a character should be embodied in music: "it is as though [the guitar sounds] were spurring Agave on to an exaltation beyond her actual words" (263). Such detailed instruction regarding tempo, rhythm, dynamics, style, and musical structure leaves little room for the dramatic creativity of the composer. Furthermore, the librettists demand that the opera refer recurringly to the music of another composer. The libretto specifies, "tune: Chorale in the Intermezzo." The Chorale in the intermezzo had been marked with "The tune—Matthäuspassion?—or a variant of it, we shall hear again when Pentheus' body is brought in" (292). Auden and Kallman place the work within a particular tradition with the subtitle, "Opera Seria with Intermezzo in One Act." Opera seria is characterized not only by its classical sources, but also by specific musical and dramatic forms. That Auden did not merely use the musical term to offer his libretto an archaic respectability is evident in his defense of the intermezzo: "In the early days of opera it was the custom to sandwich a one-act opera buffa between the two acts of an opera seria. Such a convention provided a musical and verbal contrast which both we and Henze felt would be desirable if it could be made an integral part to [*The Bassarids*]" ("World" 113–14).

It is no wonder that Auden should perceive a potential "glory" in the writing of a libretto when he expects and demands that the composer conform his music to the dramatic plan and musical aesthetics specified in the libretto. Such demands elevate the role of the librettists by allowing them a greater musical authorship. They also ensure that the unique musical authorship of the composer is qualified into a constant musical acknowledgment of earlier creations.

A composer, of course, need not choose to recognize the demands of his librettists. Auden claims that Henze endorsed the inclusion of the intermezzo, yet Henze states, "my two authors called the piece an *opera seria*, which seemed to me to point the work in an entirely different direction, although even this suggestion I followed to only a limited extent and up to a certain point" (*Bohemian Fifths* 207). Despite claiming not to have endorsed the intermezzo, Henze nonetheless set the text, and apparently failed to indicate his dissent to his librettists. He waited until after the death of Auden and Kallman to claim never to have "believed in the dramaturgical need for the Intermezzo" and remove it from his work, "thereby ... considerably increasing the dramatic tension" (434, 433). Henze suggests that he was coerced into musically endorsing an appreciation of opera seria that inhibited his drama. Noting the success of the opera without the intermezzo, he defensively argues that his "somewhat disrespectful attitude towards [his] two librettists was proved to have been correct" (433). This expression of both respect and defensiveness demonstrates the potential complexities involved in a collaboration between artists simultaneously deferential towards each other and their particular "arts," and assertive in their musico-dramatic vision.

Henze had previously collaborated with Auden and Kallman only three years before the composition of *The Bassarids* on *Elegy for Young Lovers*. Because *The Bassarids* was not based upon original material, the librettists' autonomous mastery of the subject was rendered less explicit than it had been in the earlier project. Furthermore, Henze was warily aware of Auden's tendency to be assertive with collaborating composers: "Just as Auden, that experienced old pedagogue, had led Stravinsky to the peak of classicism with the libretto for *The Rake's Progress*, so too he wanted to squeeze things out of me that he had already detected in other pieces of mine" (*"The Bassarids*: Tradition and Cultural Heritage"143–4). This wariness defines much of Henze's approach towards the libretto. Indeed, his reservations were justified: Auden only agreed to write the libretto after Henze promised to attend a production of *Götterdämmerung*. Auden sent Kallman along "to make sure [he] really sat through it right to the end"; Henze complied, and "sat through *Götterdämmerung*—quite joylessly" (Henze, "Tradition and Cultural Heritage" 143–4).

The librettists seem from the outset to have conceived of *The Bassarids* as ideally complementing or continuing Wagner's musical and dramatic legacy. Despite his claim to have allowed himself to be treated like "a pupil [who] passively bends to the will of his mentor" ("Tradition and Cultural Heritage" 144), however, Henze argues that "in the structure of *Bassarids* there is nothing Wagnerian at all" (Interview 831). To avoid further questions of Wagner's influence, he asserts the importance of Mahler: "The important composer to this score is Mahler. When I wrote the score he was my daily life, my bread, my creed—and still is" (Interview 831). These influences need not be mutually exclusive, of course. Indeed, Henze himself half-acknowledges Wagner's potential influence on the opera. His receipt of the libretto from Auden and Kallman "came at a time when [he] was beginning to discover the great forms of nineteenth-century symphonic music (and *Götterdämmerung*, of course, had made its impact, too)" ("Tradition and Cultural Heritage" 144). He concedes, "Of course I am well aware what Wagner signifies, wherein his greatness lies; *Tristan*, which I have never seen, although I have studied the score in detail, has subsequently become a kind of bible for me" ("Tradition and Cultural Heritage" 144). Henze goes so far as to trace a direct route from Wagner to Mahler, stating that "the road from Wagner's *Tristan* to Mahler and Schoenberg is far from finished, and with *The Bassarids* I have tried to go further along it" ("Tradition and Cultural Heritage" 145). Ultimately, Henze's objection to Wagner is political: "I think Mahler is the composer who has helped music to get away from this Wagnerian aloofness: one could almost say he was a proletarian composer" (Interview 831). Wagner's music is flawed by the "sense of an imperialist threat, of something militantly nationalistic, something disagreeably heterosexual and Aryan in all these rampant horn calls, this pseudo-Germanic *Stabreim*, these incessant chords of a seventh and all the insecure heroes and villains that people Wagner's librettos" (*Bohemian Fifths* 206–7).[15]

---

15 Interestingly, Drummond suggests that Nietzsche's theory of Apollo and Dionysus is embodied in the subject matter and music of *Tristan und Isolde*, which emphasize the

Henze attributes Auden's attempts at musical mentorship to a perception of musical sympathies between his work and that of Wagner. He does not seem to recognize that it is also the dramatization of "insecure heroes and villains" that inspired the enthusiasm of his librettists. *The Bassarids* was written by two librettists very much aware of operatic tradition and the way in which "their" opera could fit within that tradition. Auden specifically demanded that Henze attend an opera that deals with the fall of a people and a race of gods due to their failure to heed portent. While *Götterdämmerung* may have been the only Wagner opera playing at the time, the libretto to *The Bassarids* indicates that Auden and Kallman had more than symphonic composition in mind when they forced Henze to attend.

Both operas detail the destruction of a civilization and remind the audience of the greatness of the powers involved in this destruction. In Wagner's opera, the annihilation of the gods and the return of the Rheingold to the Rhine Maidens is ensured by the failure of the gods to heed the curse of Alberich (who notably has forsworn love). In *The Bassarids*, the failure of Pentheus and his mother to acknowledge the power of the sensual god Dionysus results in their destruction and the triumph of the forces which they sought to ignore and suppress. Euripides' tragedy ends with the banishment by Dionysus of Cadmus and Agave after the death of Pentheus. In the libretto to *The Bassarids*, however, Dionysus further orders the Captain of the Guard to set fire to the palace: "The scrim descends and flames rise, completely hiding the stage. From behind the scrim Dionysus is heard summoning his mother, Semele from the grave to be apotheosized on Olympus as the Goddess Thyone" ("World" 114–15). This description resembles the end of *Götterdämmerung*, in which the fire of the pyre for the fallen hero, Siegfried, ignites the stage:

> From the ruins of the fallen hall, the men and women, in great agitation, watch the growing firelight in the heavens. When this reaches its greatest brightness, the hall of Walhall is seen, in which gods and heroes sit assembled … Bright flames seize on the hall of the gods. When the gods are entirely hidden by the flames, the curtain falls. (*The Ring* 360–62)

Both operas end with some assertion of cyclic regeneration: Semele will rise again just as the Rheingold is returned to its proper place. Unlike the *Bacchae*, *The Bassarids* does not end with the destruction of the palace; when the scrim rises, all gods are gone and the palace is but a "jagged blackened wall." The audience is left to contemplate the destruction, until a little girl who had earlier been tortured "runs forward with a doll, which she smashes against the base of the tomb and then stamps on" ("World" 115). The girl's existence despite her torture at the hands of Pentheus might suggest the complete triumph of Dionysus. At the same time, the doll represents the Dionysian idolatry for which Pentheus had punished his people. By smashing this doll, the girl denies the complete triumph of Dionysus. The doll

---

opposition and merging of "an immediate perception of the truth by means of the innate expressiveness of music (Dionysos), and the necessary veiling of this power by images and musical shapes (Apollo)." He further suggests that *The Bassarids* continues this tradition by bringing the confrontation between the gods directly onto the stage ("Apollo and Dionysos" iv).

repeatedly cries "mamma," echoing the maternal themes expounded in the opera and in the play. The smashing of the doll cyclically re-enacts the maternal destruction performed by Agave, and draws attention to the death of Pentheus and the potential continuity of such mother-son conflicts. This conclusion therefore denies the absolute triumph of the Dionysian influence and mirrors the potential ambivalence of *Götterdämmerung*'s final dramatization of the destruction of Valhalla and the restoration of the Rheingold.

The librettists explicitly align their creation with the narrative and themes of a pre-existing, seminal opera. Henze's reaction to Auden and Kallman's enthusiasm for *Götterdämmerung*, however, suggests that he did not recognize this declared affiliation in the libretto. He perceived that his librettists were attempting to influence his musical style, but not the overall dramaturgy and operatic affiliation of the work. Indeed, despite his declared wariness, Henze seems often to have been quite unaware of the musical and dramatic "plan" of his librettists. Unlike Tippett, however, he did not possess the cultural instinct to look for that musical plan in the libretto, or to acknowledge any dramatic supremacy to the libretto's artistic vision.

The often conflicting readings that result produce an essentially incomplete opera whose constituent parts regularly contradict the interpretative approaches of individual collaborators. No matter his claims about the relative importance of words in opera, Auden creates a musical role for himself and Kallman by asserting musical and operatic tastes in the libretto. The libretto implicitly asks the composer to acknowledge these tastes, and thus to limit his own creative and interpretative freedom. It also offers a strongly engaged interpretation of the original source, which conflicts fundamentally with Henze's reading. The results deserve close consideration, particularly because the composer was neither linguistically nor culturally accustomed to acknowledging the textual intricacies or musical authority of the opera libretto. Henze had his own reading of the source, and his own musical ideas for the opera. All three collaborators shared a respect for classical drama, operatic tradition, and their artistic right to borrow from those traditions. It remains to be seen, however, how those artistic visions complemented each other, and the nature of the opera that resulted.

Auden and Kallman were fundamentally concerned with the musico-dramatic viability of their adaptation. Not only is drama much slower when sung than spoken, but certain dramatic techniques cannot be easily sustained or translated into a musico-dramatic form. The librettists therefore edited many of the *Bacchae*'s conventional lengthy monologues and secondhand narratives from messengers and choral figures. Auden notes in a letter to A. E. Dodds that the large role of the chorus "is a snare because, if one isn't careful, the thing turns into an oratorio which is boring as a stage-work" (qtd. in Auden and Kallman, *Libretti* 680). In the opera, the role of the chorus is diminished and Beroe and the Captain are added to underline the importance of character. The libretto postpones the conversion of Agave and Autonoe, allowing for a greater exposition and exploration of individual conflicts, characters, and themes.

The librettists also perceived a creative, interpretation function to their role, which transcended any "straightforward adaptation." Instead of attempting merely to translate the *Bacchae* successfully into opera, they sought to render its concerns dramatically relevant to a twentieth-century audience. Wanting to avoid "any species of that Gluck-y Greekiness," they turned to the Strauss-Hofmannsthal *Elektra* (1909) and the Stravinsky-Cocteau *Oedipus Rex* (1927) for inspiration; those works had "allowed no irrelevant reverence for mere duplication to interfere with the making of a new work in a new medium" ("Why Rewrite a Masterpiece?" 705, 707). Kallman[16] writes:

> Why not merely 'adapt' Euripides' play—fill in some of the missing bits, prune the rest to the composer's requirements—didn't the conventions of Greek Drama found the conventions on which opera has developed? It might work. Frankly, though, it would have been a task for other librettists preparing a text for quite another composer. (Auden and Kallman, "Why Rewrite a Masterpiece?" 705)

In their attempt to lessen cultural differences between their audience and that of Euripides, Auden and Kallman avoid visual realism and specify costumes that denote various historical eras and attitudes. The citizens wear "with a certain stiffness the traditional white draperies of a generalized classical antiquity;" Agave dresses in the style of the French Second Empire, Tiresias as an Anglican Archdeacon, the Captain as a fourteenth-century Frankish Knight, and Pentheus as an athletic and scholarly medieval king. Dionysus appears as a languid Byron, an effeminate youth, and a Beau Brummel dandy, while his followers variously appear in "some elements" of the traditional Bacchic costume, barefoot in dirty dungarees, in sports-shirts (in a fawn-skin pattern), and in red wool stockings and ballet slippers with "hair à la Brigitte Bardot." These costumes suggest that the libretto is both emphasizing and enhancing the literary and social implications of its source. By distancing characters from their original cultural and religious context, Auden and Kallman hope to "escape" the creation of "Neo-Classical plaster-casts" ("Why Rewrite a Masterpiece" 706). They demand that the work be considered for its themes, characters, and ideas, and not merely as a musical translation of a historical artefact.

The libretto forcefully asserts this modern perspective, and thus the creative interventions of the librettists, in its allusions to Christianity. As directed by Auden, Henze quotes from Bach's *St. Matthew Passion* twice: at the end of the intermezzo, and at the entry of Pentheus' body. The music emphasizes the connection between Adonis and Pentheus, and thus the repetitive nature of their sacrifice. By quoting from a Christian source, it suggests the potential continuation of similar sacrifices, or destructive group rituals, in a Christian world. The libretto supports these allusions: Pentheus' anguished search for "the One, the Good" before his seduction by Dionysus evokes Christ's torment in the Garden of Gethsemane (281); Dionysus' statement: "I was torn that I be gathered,/I fell who have arisen,/Died I. I live" (277) clearly alludes to Christian belief; and the description of the Bassarids who sing while they are tortured (278) resembles descriptions of the early Christians. Pentheus is dressed in "monastic and soldierly garb," and Tiresias in his Archdeacon attire resembles a

---

16   The original draft to this article is to be found in one of Kallman's notebooks now at the University of Texas (Auden and Kallman, *Libretti* 704). It is probable that he was the primary author of the article.

Vicar of Bray figure. Pentheus' differentiation between Cadmus' gods who punish and "the Gods" who do not (267) thus acquires a Christian theological relevance distinct from the play's original Greek context.

Auden and Kallman ensure that the significance of these allusions remains consistently ambiguous. While *The Bassarids* might be read "as evoking a god of love by emphasizing its absence from the Euripidean text on which the libretto is based" (Alan Jacobs 94), its Christian references equally suggest the absence of such a god from modern society. Although Dionysus is potentially Christ-like when he overcomes violence, recruits peaceful followers, and refers to his own resurrection, he is at other times associated with the night, pagan idolatry, the Old Testament, and pre-Reformation superstition. The sympathetic characterization of Pentheus when he is punished by a vengeful and spiteful god lends credence to his objections to the worship of Dionysus, and further denies the god any absolute moral or righteous authority. Furthermore, Pentheus ultimately re-enacts the fate of Dionysus at the hands of the Titans. By emphasizing a connection between Pentheus and Dionysus, the librettists diminish the divine status of Dionysus to that of a resurrected mirror-opposite of Pentheus. In so doing, they invite the audience to consider the potential for Pentheus (or the ideals he represents) to share a similar resurrection to that of Dionysus.

The overall effect is to deny an absolute moral authority or Christ-like function to any of the characters. Rather than imposing a Christian moral upon the narrative, the libretto merely evokes a Christian context through which to consider the events of the drama. Indeed, the historical allegory and military costuming ensure that the evocation of ritual acquires a political, as well as religious, significance. The libretto is just as much about inward conflict, repression, political intolerance, and familial relations as it is about the psychological implications of mass adoration, religious tolerance, or divine justice.

Throughout the libretto, Auden and Kallman clearly aspire to maintain such thematic and cultural ambiguity. Henze, however, consistently takes a more conclusive interpretative stance. The libretto ends both with the apotheosis of Semele and with the actions of the child who "smashes her doll at the foot of the tomb and jumps up and down with joy." Henze makes no musical acknowledgment of this last event; the scene finishes with a slowly pronounced chordal reiteration that begins with the adoration of Dionysus, and the opera ends forcefully upon this chord. This less ambiguous interpretation allows for a more definite musical statement: it does not demand the simultaneous presence of the convergent musical themes that Henze uses to represent Dionysus and Pentheus. Henze argues that "even at a first hearing, the listener will surely perceive the opposition between the Pentheus and Dionysus themes, and the gradual dominance of the latter, until the end, when it has eliminated everything else" (Henze, "*The Bassarids*: Psychology in Music" 150). Furthermore, the opera is structured according to a symphonic pattern, and conforms to traditional notions of cadential and thematic musical resolution.[17] This structure

---

17　The one-act opera consists of a sonata movement "followed by a scherzo—a series of bacchanalian dances with a calm vocal ensemble as trio. The third movement is an adagio with fugue, interrupted by an intermezzo—the satyr play, an opera within the opera; the fourth,

allows a less ambiguous thematic ending, and ensures that Henze precludes the modernist ambiguity to which the libretto aspires. Auden seems to have recognized the contrasting intentions of the composer; in apparent acknowledgment of the change in meaning effected by the score, he refrains from discussing the conclusion to the published libretto in his program-notes.

Henze's treatment of the conclusion indicates a significant disregard for (or ignorance of) the thematic concerns of the libretto. Furthermore, he frequently discusses his musical vision in terms of a resistance to that of his librettists. Aware that Auden "wanted an opera seria, with arias and all that," Henze boasts of his defiance: "but I wrote a symphony" (qtd. in Robert S. Clark 113).[18] Henze's musical treatment and comments about the opera consistently reveal differences between his interpretation and that of Auden and Kallman. Nowhere is this difference more manifest than in the opera's treatment of what the librettists clearly considered to be the two central concerns of the original source: the injustice of the gods, and the role of Pentheus and Dionysus as representations of essentially opposed elemental forces.

Auden perceived the *Bacchae* as interrogating the justifiability of Dionysus' behavior. In a letter to E. R. Dodds, he notes that Euripides resembles Aeschylus and Sophocles in "insisting that the gods are great powers who must be worshipped," but differs from them in raising "the ethical question: 'Are they righteous?'" (qtd. in Auden and Kallman, *Libretti* 681). In the *Bacchae*,[19] Pentheus opposes Dionysus because he is not convinced of his divinity. As the play makes clear, such concerns are irrelevant; if others worship, one must also worship: "The law tradition makes/ is the law of nature" (895–6). Pentheus, however, objects to what he considers to be the "impostures" of the stranger and the unruliness which he inspires (247–8). He identifies this unruliness in Dionysus' usurpation of his own kingly authority, and in his demand for worship in erotic rituals. Recognizing Pentheus' hubris, Teiresias warns him not to be certain that "power is what matters in the life of man" (310–11), and Dionysus "shuns the thoughts/of proud, uncommon men and all/their god-encroaching dreams" (427–9).[20] Teiresias attempts to secure the humility (and thus the life) of Pentheus by assuring him that such moral questions are irrelevant

---

with its Ash Wednesday mood, is a passacaglia" (Henze, "Tradition and Cultural Heritage" 145).

18   Wagner is often credited with introducing symphonic elements to opera. In an apparent recognition of the potential similarities between his own approach and that of Wagner, Henze contradicts this common assumption: "Wagner is very unsymphonic really; it's the technique of the leitmotif, of continuous melody. In my work there is the symphonic form instead" (Interview 831). Ironically, Helm has isolated such elements of the leitmotif in *The Bassarids*: "Through all of [his] forms and subforms, Henze weaves a number of what are to all practical purpose leitmotifs, which are varied and transformed almost à la Wagner in keeping with the psychological developments" (411).

19   All quotations from the *Bacchae* are taken from the translation by William Arrowsmith in *Euripides V*. References are to line numbers.

20   Unlike the weakly hypocritical Teiresias in *The Bassarids*, Euripides' Teiresias is wise: "three times in Cadmus' opening speech he is called *sophos* ... Thus even before the King can voice his suspicions, an association between Dionysianism and wisdom is established and

when it comes to worshipping gods. Nonetheless, he recognizes the need to assure him that Dionysus' demands are not morally objectionable: "even in the rites of Dionysus,/the chaste woman will not be corrupted" (317–18). While he recognizes the potential justification to Pentheus' conflict, Teiresias is further aware that it is only by worshipping the gods according to their will that one can prevent social and moral chaos.

Interestingly, while the play contains such warning statements from Teiresias, Cadmus, and the chorus, it also gives considerable credence to Pentheus' objections by emphasizing parallels between the nature of Pentheus and that of Dionysus. Pentheus is warned against being "pleased when men stand outside [his] doors" and glorify his name; his ambition resembles that of "the god: he too delights in glory" (319–21). Pentheus imprisons the followers of Dionysus in an attempt to enforce the supremacy of his rule; he orders the stranger to be chained for presuming to mock him and declares, "I am the stronger here" (504). Similarly, Dionysus vows to punish Pentheus for "[presuming] to wage a war with god" (637). While Pentheus' "disregard for the gods" indicates that he is "infatuate of soul/and hardened in his pride" (884–5), Dionysus is similarly hardened by pride in his pursuit of vengeance. Euripides emphasizes this similarity in the final exchange between the god and Cadmus, who had earlier demeaned himself to make "an ancient foolish pair" with Teiresias to appease the god (323). Objecting to his punishment, Cadmus states, "we have learned. But your sentence is too harsh" (1346). Dionysus, however, is less concerned with the enlightenment of Cadmus and Agave than he is with their punishment: "I am a god. I was blasphemed by you" (1347). Declaring that "gods should be exempt from human passions" (1348), Cadmus expresses what the audience has been made to feel by Dionsysus' gleeful reaction to the destruction of Pentheus: "this exultation in disaster—it is not right" (1040).

While Dionysus ultimately succeeds in punishing his opponents (and those of his mother), he loses the unquestioning allegiance of an audience accustomed to the rightful destruction of hubristic characters. Furthermore, while his followers repeatedly worship him in a static avowal of humility and reverence, his opponents experience a new solidarity through their victimization. Expressing compassion for each other, Agave and Cadmus are able to declare "their humanity and a moral dignity which heaven, lacking those limits which make men suffer *into* dignity and compassion, can never understand or equal." This compassion ensures that man is made "human, not mere god" (Arrowsmith 159).

Auden and Kallman clearly attempt to address this question of the righteousness of the gods in their libretto. The *Bacchae* begins with Dionysus introducing himself and his vengeful intent. He then exits the stage, introducing the devoted chorus of his followers. Auden and Kallman, however, begin the opera with a chorus of citizens as yet untouched by the effect of Dionysus, praising their new king, Pentheus. Soon, however, they respond to the cry of "the Voice," Dionysus, and run off to welcome the god. This decision to follow Dionysus is presented as sudden and irrational; there is no god for the audience to see as justly inspiring such devotion, nor is there any

---

this is rendered the more explicit by Teiresias' own warning" (Conacher, *Euripidean Drama* 61).

wise figure present to sanction such worship. Cadmus, Beroe, Agave, and Teiresias ("Tiresias" in the libretto) soon enter; Agave is not yet affected by Dionysus, and scornfully rejects suggestions that she join in his worship. Instead of being placed at the centre of the stage as specified in the *Bacchae*, the tomb of Semele is placed at the left, subtly suggesting a greater importance to those characters who appear in the centre of the stage, and the relative absence of the divine from the concerns of those in the drama.

In *The Bassarids*, Pentheus is not the only character to be seen resisting the power of the god. Furthermore, Tiresias is no longer a figure of authority; he is possessed of a "hurried and portentous self-importance" belied by his "androgynous corpulence" (253). He is ineffective as an orator and as a sexual being; Agave dismisses him as "the blindest of all women/Thrust upon by Eros, and limpest man" (256). (Auden had originally intended that the role be sung by a mezzo-soprano [Auden and Kallman, *Libretti* 680]). In the published program-notes to the opera, Tiresias is a "vain, stupid, impotent old man ... enthusiastic about the cult of Dionysus simply because it is new, the latest thing in religious fashion" (Auden and Kallman, *Libretti* 699). Auden claims that the prophetic powers of Tiresias are not in evidence in Euripides' tragedy (Auden and Kallman, *Libretti* 698). Given the many warnings that Tiresias gives Pentheus in the *Bacchae*, this claim is misleading, and suggests that Auden is attempting to validate the considerable change effected in the libretto. By eliminating Teiresias' prophetic authority, Auden and Kallman diminish the credibility of his assertions.

Cadmus is similarly changed in the libretto; he does not recognize the initial cry of the god until Tiresias informs him of Dionysus' presence. Because Cadmus is "the embodiment of legendary age" and visually more respectable than Tiresias, his inability to recognize Dionysus implies a rashness to the immediate devotion of the citizens and Tiresias. Indeed, Cadmus constantly expresses doubt as to the presence of divinity; because the gods do not reveal themselves in divine, but in human form, he is unable to recognize their status. He even asks himself, "Could a new young god be my grandson?/They are the ageless forebears of ageing/Man and were never children of man. No./Never. And can they change, can the Gods change?" (258). No matter his uncertainty as to the immediate presence of the gods (he asks Tiresias, "Are you certain of this God you follow?" [254]), Cadmus responds in fear to the name of Dionysus, recognizing his power. Equally fearful of the potential revenge of Hera if he were to worship Dionysus, however, Cadmus appeals in vain to Tiresias for guidance.

Cadmus is worried at being caught between the pique of one god and that of another; the appointed prophet is unable to help. He later tells Pentheus that Dionysus understands that he should stay in Thebes rather than worship at Kithairon (267), but the conclusion of the opera indicates the error of that belief. Unlike the *Bacchae*, in which Cadmus is promised that his suffering will be rewarded when he is brought to live among the blest with his wife (1339), *The Bassarids* does not differentiate between the fate of Agave, who had refused to recognize Semele or Dionysus, and that of Cadmus, who had presumed an understanding nature to the god he feared. Auden and Kallman emphasize the ultimate ineffectiveness of Cadmus' attempt to moderate between the force of Dionysus, the force of Hera, and the concerns of his city. These changes underline themes the librettists perceive in the original source. They stress the unfairness of the gods' demands for devotion, and their lack of understanding and compassion for their worshippers.

To further accentuate the injustice of the gods, Auden and Kallman endow Pentheus with an alternate belief that emphasizes morality and justice. In a letter to A. E. Dodds, Auden writes that Pentheus is "secretly, a believer in To Theon," or in a 'True Good' uninhibited by human passions. Pentheus "knows that the people must have their myths and cults, but is determined to suppress those which represent the Olympians as immoral" (qtd. in Auden and Kallman, *Libretti* 680). Discussing whether or not Semele had been impregnated by Zeus, the libretto's Pentheus therefore demands angrily of Cadmus, "would they, the Serenely Pure,/Ravish our blue-eyed children? Can you be awed/To have sired an Olympian slut?" (267). Furthermore, "Cadmus's Gods may punish, the Gods do not./Chance rules u̲s̲ when we know them not:/Light unsullied, they beckon us/To perfect brief lives in Immortal Truth" (267). Pentheus confides to Beroe his conviction that "the best in Thebes/Do but worship shadows/Of the True Good." Noting that truth and righteousness "glimmer through/ The ancient rites," Pentheus vows that his people shall not be allowed to worship "the Ungood":

> They honor Its excellence
> Under many a name
> Of God and Goddess:
> But the Good is One,
> Not male or female,
> They acknowledge Its glory
> With statues and temples
> Fair to behold:
> But the Good is invisible
> And dwells nowhere. (269)

Echoing convictions resonant with Christian belief, Pentheus invites his Western audience to identify with his concerns. The libretto demands a greater sympathy for Pentheus from the audience at the beginning of the opera, and further diminishes the credibility of the ideals articulated by Tiresias, Cadmus, and the followers of Dionysus.

Auden and Kallman further emphasize their critical approach by representing the final solidarity of Agave and Cadmus not as mutual compassion, but as a mutual resistance to the harsh justice of the god. Echoing Euripides' text, Cadmus states, "An Immortal/God ought to forgive, not be angry/Forever like ignorant men" (310). His belief is contradicted by Dionysus' harsh declaration:

> I came to Thebes
> To take vengeance;
> Vengeance taken,
> Now I go.
> Down slaves,
> Kneel and adore. (311)

Not only has Dionysus taken vengeance, but he has reduced mortals to slaves abandoned by their master. The librettists have Agave (to whom they have given a greater dramatic weight) reinforce Cadmus' objections, recognize the destructive power of Dionysus, and defy his omnipotence:

> You have done your worst, Dionysus:
> Now I need fear you no more.
> In this hour of your triumph, I say this,
> Say it not only to you
> But to Zeus and all on Olympus:
> Think of the altarless Fates.
> Where is gelded Uranus? Or Chronos,
> Once an invincible God?
> Rape, torture and kill while you can: one
> Tartarus waits for you all. (311)

Agave and Cadmus are united in their punishments and in their voiced objections to Dionysus. The libretto suggests that the only consolation to divine injustice is not mutual compassion, but a mutual recognition that the gods might yet be destroyed by a fate over which they have no control.

Despite the libretto's clear focus on the injustice of the gods, Henze does not provide an equal musical emphasis. He eliminates the first five lines of Agave's final speech and has Agave sing the remaining five simultaneously with the Bassarids' cry of "go, go." The effect is ultimately to ignore Agave's final prophecy and defiance in favor of emphasizing the collective power of the Bassarids. Furthermore, Henze eliminates both Cadmus' objection to the anger of immortal gods and Dionysus' most explicit expression of personal pique and vengefulness: "They insulted my mother, they mocked me./The result you can see with your own eyes" (309). When Cadmus urges Agave to look at the head of her son, he sings, "If the Gods listened/ To mortal prayers, your mind would remain/Forever dark" (304). Significantly, however, Henze omits Cadmus' explanation that "the Gods are without/Pity" (304). Indeed, Henze only gives pronounced musical treatment to one line that expresses an objection to Dionysus, Agave's "the strong Gods are not good" (309). This line occurs in Agave's arioso to her son, however; as a result, the thematic emphasis of the line is assimilated into the context of Agave's grief.

Henze's different approach is most evident in his omissions: he excises Pentheus' explanation about why he objects to Dionysian worship (269), Cadmus' assertion of faith that Dionysus will allow him to remain in Thebes, and Pentheus' questioning of gods who would "ravish our blue-eyed children" (267). The librettists claimed that Euripides' audience would have immediately understood Pentheus' violence and arrogance towards Dionysus as a tragic manifestation of hubris. In contrast, "as authors in the 20th century, writing for a public of the 20th century," they felt it necessary that Pentheus should have "a nobler motive than mere arrogance" and "made him into a platonic idealist" (Auden and Kallman, "Euripides for Today" 834). Henze, however, eliminates the "nobler motive" of Pentheus, and considerably weakens the thematic intentions of his librettists.

Henze recounts that when asked at a press conference how he perceived the characters in *The Bassarids*, Auden "got to his feet and, in a loud, firm voice, declared ...'Dionysos ist ein Schwein'." The composer notes that the journalists and opera lovers present "were all as dumbstruck as I—I who had spent the last few years grappling with the god of pleasure and drugs and delving ever deeper into his musical world. And again the poet was right" (*Bohemian Fifths* 215). Henze's apparent ignorance of his librettists' interpretation evidently influenced his treatment of the libretto. Indeed, he states that where Euripides ends with the expulsion of Agave and Cadmus, Auden and Kallman include "the apotheosis of Dionysus" who rises up with his mother "into the sky, from where he will henceforth rule the world with her. A clear and unmistakable analogy with Christ" ("*The Bassarids*: Symphony in One Act" 156). He ends the opera by equating the Dionysian musical theme with a Christian hymn in order to link Dionysus unambiguously with Christ. Any resurrection scene (particularly when composed in a style evocative of baroque church music) invites Christian analogies. Nonetheless, Henze's assumption that Auden and Kallman intended an ultimate equation of Dionysus with Christ shows a clear disregard for (or ignorance of) his librettists' intentions.

These contradictions between libretto and score are further exacerbated by the fact that while Henze takes a single interpretative approach towards his source, Auden and Kallman maintain two emphases. Henze claims that his "sympathies could lie neither only with Pentheus, nor only with Dionysus"; both ultimately represent two psychological forces "which are let loose on one another and finally become one" ("*The Bassarids*: Psychology in Music" 147). The libretto, however, attempts to both characterize Pentheus and Dionysus individually, and to acknowledge this more archetypal function. Thus, despite having declared Dionysus an unequivocal "Schwein," Auden claims that Dionysus is less a physical enemy to Pentheus than he is an opposing psychological force:

> Our Pentheus experiences his fall not so much because of his arrogant behaviour towards others, but much more through ignorance of his own nature, an ignorance that results from a philosophical error. His refusal to understand the Dionysian elements in himself and to reconcile himself to them makes him an easy victim as soon as Dionysus exercises his hypnotic magic. ("Euripides for Today" 834)

On one level it is not Dionysus so much as the psychological force he represents that destroys Pentheus. Pentheus attempts forcefully to suppress the sensuality represented by Dionysus and to adhere to an eighteenth-century belief "that, in the conflict between the Rational and the Irrational," the Rational will prevail ("Euripides for Today" 833). As Pentheus' attempts to suppress the Dionysian influence increase, so too does the power of that influence; ultimately, Pentheus' own "emotional nature ... overwhelms him" (Auden, letter to A. E. Dodds, qtd. in Auden and Kallman, *Libretti* 680).

This interpretation is invited by the original source, and is closely detailed by E. R. Dodds. Auden's extensive communication during the composition of the libretto with Dodds, whom Auden referred to as "the Master," helped to ensure an interpretation remarkably consistent with that articulated in *The Greeks and the*

Irrational and Dodds's introduction to the *Bacchae*. Dodds notes that the worship of Dionysus in the *Bacchae* is for the most part "hysteria subdued to the service of religion." To resist Dionysus is "to repress the elemental in one's own nature; the punishment is the sudden complete collapse of the inward dykes when the elemental breaks through perforce and civilisation vanishes" (Dodds, *The Greeks and the Irrational* 272–3). Dionysus is "the principle of animal life," the "unrestrained potency which man envies in the beasts and seeks to assimilate" (Dodds, Introduction xx). The destruction of Pentheus is an ultimate enactment of the consequences of this unrestrained potency and attempted assimilation, and is brought about when Dionysian elements are threatened with suppression. While Dionysus is at times "beyond good and evil" by being "what we make of him" (Dodds, Introduction xliv), he is throughout the play both a traditional "'Olympian' deity" and "the amoral and daemonic personification of the force he represents" (Arrowsmith 155).

Euripides simultaneously questions the justice of the gods and explores the psychological implications of repressing Dionysian elements. It is thus that Auden was able both to declare Dionysus "ein Schwein" and to contemplate the necessary consequences of Pentheus' rejection of the god. As Dodds notes, if Euripides' intention had been simply to condemn the gods or Dionysiac psychological forces, he would have made Pentheus a more immediately sympathetic character.

While acknowledging these themes in the *Bacchae*, the libretto does not offer a thoroughly faithful translation of the original play. The *Bacchae* emphasizes Pentheus' inability to recognize the importance of inward Dionysian forces when the Stranger tells him, "you do not know who you are" (507). In the libretto, Pentheus achieves a certain self-recognition at the end of the opera when he declares, "No! No! This flesh is me!" (301). Auden and Kallman's Pentheus is more self-aware than that of Euripides: he recognizes and consciously suppresses the potential Dionysian influence within himself (and engages in a sexual fantasy an intermezzo-length long). Euripides' Pentheus is young, slightly obtuse, and ignorant: he is unable to consider the relevance of the recounted violence of the Maenads, he does not hear the repeated warnings of Dionysus himself, and his curiosity to see the revels on the mountain comes across as innocent, rather than voyeuristic. Indeed, Euripides' Pentheus never seems to make the connection between Dionysus as a god whom others worship, and Dionysus as a daemonic force within himself. He is to a certain extent unknowingly destroyed by the powers he has been too stupid to recognize and acknowledge. In contrast, the operatic Pentheus goes half-knowingly to his fate after having violently disavowed the very forces which he pursues to the mountain.

By emphasizing the self-repression of Pentheus rather than his ignorance, the librettists render him more responsible for his fate. Furthermore, they define this self-repression as sexual and thereby explicitly define the Dionysian force in a way in which Euripides does not. Pentheus' vow of chastity to Beroe, for example, comes immediately after his declaration against Dionysus. Auden and Kallman emphasize the thematic importance of sexual repression by significantly expanding upon the mother-son theme present in the *Bacchae*. In the Euripides play, Dionysus is concerned with ensuring appropriate devotion for his mother. Pentheus is destroyed by his mother who boasts in her madness of having "raised [her] sight" from the shuttle at the loom to such "higher things" as "hunting animals with [her] bare hands"

(1237–8). She thus abandons her socially defined maternal, female occupations to become more destructive than man and hope only that her son can equal her success (1253). By the end of the play, she abandons the thyrsus and its destructive powers to wander alone in exile.

This mother-son theme is considerably expanded in the opera. Auden and Kallman dramatize a difficulty to the Agave-Pentheus relationship that is not inspired by Pentheus' refusal to worship Dionysus, but by Agave's apparent refusal to assume a maternal role. Agave flirts with the captain, appears more like a coquettish single woman than a mother, and mocks Pentheus' nurse, Beroe. Furthermore, she harbors an apparent jealousy towards Beroe; when Cadmus asks where Pentheus is, Agave points to Beroe, stating, "She/sees him. Ask her" (255). This jealousy could be either sexual or maternal; Beroe herself sings of Pentheus as the "child of [her] breast" (261), her "dear Lord" (271), and "the King [she] loved" (310). In so doing, she subtly creates for herself the role of lover and mother, a role that Agave can only reclaim in the destruction of her son.

Auden and Kallman devote themselves to this mother-son theme in the intermezzo. Pentheus is driven to his death by a need to witness the promised erotic rituals of his mother who is "obviously more a woman than a mother" (252–3). He does this despite the warnings of Beroe, to whom alone Pentheus feels he can open his heart and declare a vow of chastity (269). Pentheus fantasizes about the flirtations of his mother and her role as Venus "the fertile" who, as Queen of Love, temporarily abandons her child only to reclaim him as a lover just before he is torn apart. Agave then returns to her sexualized role, claiming of the Captain, "when once I have my hands on him,/They'll never tear us limb from limb" (292). The end of the opera reinforces the importance of the sexual relationship between Pentheus and Agave. The powerful statement of the unity of mother and son through Dionysus and Semele is mirrored by the union that Agave feels with Pentheus:

> At your bier-side, my dead son,
> I will not speak of a mother's care
> Or a son's love that were not there.
> Without choice we are made one:
> A bond binds us for all time,
> For your death is my crime. (308)

The song is constructed as an aria, and gains a musical and dramatic importance in the opera: even though Henze does not set the last three lines of the stanza, the piece emphasizes both the individual grief of Agave and the importance of this mother-son-lover theme as it appears throughout the opera. Auden and Kallman essentially define their exploration of sexual Dionysian liberation within a dramatization of the potential sexual relationship between mothers and sons. While the relationship is emotionally powerful, it is incestuous and destructive, continuing a claustrophobic cyclic pattern in which mothers beget son-lovers in an apparent inability to break free of this familial pattern.

The libretto therefore suggests that the Dionysian liberation achieved at the end of the opera is less liberating than it might initially appear. Like Euripides, Auden and Kallman imply that moderated Dionysian release is necessary to avoid the violence that characterizes the end of the drama. They ensure that the drama signals a "universal" and thus contemporary relevance by emphasizing the continuity of mythic pattern. As Tiresias states in the intermezzo:

> It would never do
> To divulge what's true
> Of kin and kith
> Too nakedly
> In Arcady:
> We must find a Myth
> To drape it with. (286)

By "draping" the "myth" of the original drama in Christian and cultural allusions, the librettists signal their attempt to explore the themes of the source and make them relevant to a contemporary audience. At the same time, they particularly underline Euripides' questioning of the righteousness of the gods, expand upon the sexual undertones to the mother-son relationships, and reinforce an essential opposition between Dionysian and Apollonian forces.

Unlike his librettists, who attempt to dramatize and "modernize" complex themes and tensions in the original source, Henze isolates a basic conflict in the source. This essential conflict is "between social repression and sexual liberation: the liberation of the individual. It shows people as individuals breaking out of a social context, as a road to freedom" (*"The Bassarids*: Symphony in One Act" 156). In the *Bacchae*, however, Dionysus claims to have "stung" the women of Thebes "with frenzy, hounded them from home/up to the mountains where they wander, crazed of mind" (33–4). Because the women's "liberation" has been forced upon them, Henze's claim that the individuals involved in this mass frenzy have been enabled independently to "discover themselves" and "release the Dionysus within themselves" is difficult to accept (*"The Bassarids*: Symphony in One Act" 156). The libretto problematizes any realization of Henze's political interpretation with its ambivalent attitude towards Dionysian liberation. As in the play, the Bassarids are entranced by Dionysus: under the influence of this apparent Dionysian liberation, Agave destroys her son. No social repression is evident in the opera until after the citizens become Bassarids. Henze's assertion that the people have somehow broken free of an oppressive social context therefore presumes that any adherence to social order necessitates unhealthy self-repression.

Henze's isolation of an essential, unambiguous conflict is nonetheless made strikingly clear in the performed opera. Henze attributes particular musical motifs to each "force" in the opera, and ends with the final triumph of the Dionysian theme. To a limited extent, Henze equates Dionysus, apparent god of sexual and moral disorder, with melody, and Pentheus, apparent representative of repression, with a more modernist, experimental musical style. At the end of the opera, Henze quotes from Bach and Mahler to emphasize the triumph of Dionysus. As Drummond notes, "when the composer wishes to portray Dionysos, he uses Apollonian means of which we are aware. When the composer wishes to portray Apollo, his Apollonian shapes are less perceptible than the Dionysiac sound-effects" (257).[21]

Henze's musical opposition between Pentheus and Dionysus belies the more complex treatment in the libretto, and glosses over the objections raised by Agave and Cadmus to the righteousness of the god. Neither Pentheus nor Dionysus specifically embodies clearly defined forces of repression or liberation in the libretto; Pentheus grows towards a self-acknowledgment, and Dionysus evolves from being calmly in control to being as unjustly tyrannical and violent as Pentheus may have first appeared. Both the Dionysus and the Pentheus of the libretto therefore require a greater complexity of musical language and thematic interaction than the deliberately polarized treatment they are accorded in the score.

In order to ensure the dramatization of this central conflict, Henze demanded cuts to the libretto. Auden objected: "It is, I think, our extensive treatment of the story that distinguishes it; and cuts could (I don't say must) weaken the impact of the complete work by narrowing its vision" (qtd. in Auden and Kallman, *Libretti* 681). When Henze persisted, Auden wrote, "C[hester] and I are vain enough to believe that our text is worth reading an-und-für-sich," and requested that the text be printed in its entirety with an indication of "which bits have not been set" (qtd. in Auden and Kallman, *Libretti* 682). Although the librettists did not insist upon this inclusion of uncut text in the score, they clearly recognized that the thoroughness with which they had treated the themes and narrative references in the *Bacchae* would be considerably lessened, and the drama significantly altered.

Despite having demanded cuts to the libretto to ensure the realization of his own dramatic interpretation, Henze speaks in glowing terms of the complexity to the original libretto:

> The libretto teems with cultural and historical ideas, with parallels and discoveries, of which only a fraction can be caught and grasped by the listener at any one time. It is one of those librettos that it is advisable to read and study in detail, even if only on account of the beauty of the language and the magnificence of the vision that unfolds on stage. (*Bohemian Fifths* 215)

Henze recognizes an inherent independence to the libretto. Indeed, his appreciation of its structure and language responds to the libretto as a competitive, rather than complementary, composition. In offering a rationale for his later omission of the intermezzo, Henze suggests that his admiration for the intellectual and poetic abilities of his librettists allowed him to be intimidated into setting text that he did not feel to be dramatically effective. Considering the intermezzo "a literary, rather than a theatrical device" which stands out "from the measured Euripidean directness of the main plot through its volubility and campness," Henze removed it to "considerably [increase] the dramatic tension and [allow] listeners a clearer insight into the form and nature of the great central Adagio that is the seduction scene between Dionysus and Pentheus" (Henze, *Bohemian Fifths* 433–4). Henze defines his motives as dramatic, but emphasizes the importance of appreciating the musical form of his

---

21 Ironically, Henze uses a musical idiom defined by conventional harmonic resolution to celebrate the triumph of Dionysus over a strict, imposing, and repressive authority.

Adagio. Furthermore, he defines the intermezzo as literary despite the form's origins in operatic tradition: perhaps he objected less to the literary origins of the intermezzo than to the intermezzo's invocation of older operatic practices. Given the literary complexity and wordiness of the libretto, Henze may well have attempted to right the balance by omitting the intermezzo and emphasizing his musical constructions. Underlining the importance of the libretto as a text to be read that might conflict with musical forms, Henze distances himself from the libretto. In so doing, he implicitly separates himself and his score from the "cultural and historical ideas, with parallels and discoveries."

Despite their objections to Henze's cuts, Auden and Kallman similarly recognize the necessity to separate the original libretto from the score in order for it to be truly appreciated. They emphasize the importance of reading, rather than merely hearing, the libretto. In the published libretto, they append a quotation from Gottfried Benn, encouraging the reader to find philosophical precedent for their work in other writings, and further expanding upon themes they are unable to make explicit in their libretto. Auden notes that "for a reader, certain mythological and genealogical information is a help to understanding the work" (letter to Henze, qtd. in Auden and Kallman, *Libretti* 682). Similarly recognizing the potential confusion to an audience unfamiliar with the "mythological and genealogical information," Kallman has Dionysus state in a later prologue to the opera, "But you know what's going to happen. You've all no doubt read the libretto" (qtd. in Auden and Kallman, *Libretti* 715).

The final opera, then, is the product of a compromise between two creative and interpretative camps, both of which aspire to explore particular themes and realize a specific musical plan. Auden declares that "since music is in essence immediate, it follows that the words of a song cannot be poetry," and that in song "the words must be able to do what they are told" ("Notes" 472–3). The libretto, however, contains many poetic and descriptive passages written in a tight metrical form; if they were set in a musical setting faithful to the meter, they would severely limit the expansion of musical rhythm and structure. In apparent ignorance of the libretto's complexity, Auden wrote to E. R. Dodds: "As you can see, the 'poetry' has to be pretty bare in order to be able to be set to music" (qtd. in Auden and Kallman, *Libretti* 681). Nonetheless, he acknowledged the impossibility of his strict meter existing alongside Henze's own symphonic structure, asking that the text be published as written to do justice to the metrical complexity not apparent in the musical setting: "In listening to your opera, the ear cannot, of course, detect this," but when lines are "also omitted from the printed text, the reader's ear will be vexed" (letter to Henze, qtd. in Auden and Kallman, *Libretti* 682).[22] Despite his articulated respect for the supremacy of music and subservience of the poet, Auden does not always conform his language to a style that would allow for such subservience. The meaning of the verse in the libretto is frequently obscure, and would become even more so if sung. Furthermore,

---

22   Interestingly, Dodds makes specific mention of the linguistic style of the original play; in diction and style the play "reverts to an older manner" so that "the play's tremendous power arises in part from the tension between the classical formality of its style and structure and the strange religious experiences which it depicts" (Introduction xxxvii, xxxviii).

the words demand an attention to text-setting that might ignore the overall dramatic plan of the music:

> Hunter and hunted on those high hills
> Whirled as one in a wild daedal,
> Renewing life. Ichneumon's children
> Fed on the paralysed flesh of Arachne,
> So fell before to flies. (276)

Despite Auden's acknowledgment of the supremacy of the composer in operatic collaboration, the libretto contains musical constructions and literary complexities that defy thorough musical setting. These complexities demand an acknowledgment of the published libretto as an autonomous operatic authority.

Henze himself admitted that he did not always understand the text of the libretto and that he was somewhat in awe of his librettists and their interpretation. Perhaps because of this combined deference and confusion, the cuts he does make do not consistently clarify his own thematic interests. Furthermore, his music at times conforms to the directions specified in the libretto, even if it was not composed to underline the interpretative intentions of the librettists. In part as a result of this confusion between music and text, and in part as a result of the discursiveness and metrical complexity of the libretto, the opera demands an advance reading of the libretto in order to be understood as *performed*. As one reader and audience-member objected:

> To follow the story, one has either to be a connoisseur of Greek mythology or to spend a good bit of time boning up and studying the four-folio-pages-long introduction in the piano and vocal score ... My own considerable homework proved to be insufficient at the dress rehearsal. But at the second performance I had things well worked out and felt pretty smug after the show when I was able to explain matters to unprepared (but by no means illiterate) friends, who were utterly baffled by the goings on. (Helm 409)

The libretto to *The Bassarids* is so controlling in its attempt to determine musical style and structure as to limit the creative independence of the composer. At the same time, the composer's conflicting interpretation of the source and his resistance to what he perceives as excessive literary devices and references limit the full realization of the librettists' hopes. Neither the score nor the libretto as performed manifest the intentions of any of the collaborators. They are left to plead for the potential of their work as it might exist if independent of (necessary) collaboration.

No matter his assertion of the importance of music in opera, Auden considers his adaptation to have surpassed the dramatic possibilities of opera, and therefore to be worth the independent perusal against which he had objected in *Secondary Worlds*: "The verbal text of an opera is to be judged, not by the literary quality or lack of it which it may have when read, but by its success or failure in exciting the musical imagination of the composer" ("World" 90). Unlike Tippett, who valued such "literary" constructions in the libretto, Henze adopted a much more traditional, authoritative stance as musical dramaturge. Nonetheless, although he resisted and excised much of what he did not understand or appreciate, he recognized an independent value to the libretto as a whole. All three collaborators return the essence of the libretto to the realm of the "musical" poet or verse dramatist. In so doing, they grant the libretto an ultimate autonomy that questions the relevance of musical contribution to "operatic" composition.

Because *The Bassarids* and *King Priam* are based upon literary sources appreciated for their presentation of "universal" human concerns and characters, it is fitting that the creators of the operas should have attempted to emphasize the universality of those concerns by distancing their creations from their specific literary origins. Auden and Kallman attempt to translate the concerns of their source into a modern dramatic context by emphasizing operatic tradition and musical effect. In contrast, the libretto to *King Priam* aspires towards an intellectual self-consciousness that proclaims the work's indebtedness to spoken drama. The interpretative license taken by both operas towards their original source is to some extent invited by the antiquity and numerous cultural associations of that source. What happens, however, when the source of an opera is an acclaimed exemplar of a national literary tradition?

Chapter 2

Nation, Modernity, and the Operatic Stage

In comparison to the sources of *King Priam* and *The Bassarids*, the Gawain poet's *Sir Gawain and the Green Knight* (c.1370) and Chaucer's *Troilus and Criseyde* (c.1385) tend to be associated quite consistently with literary and scholarly tradition. There is no international culture of artistic appropriation of these two narratives as there is for classical Greek and Roman narratives, nor have they been widely adapted, even in Britain. Instead, the choice of these sources for operatic adaptation seems to respond to scholarly and literary trends.

The first half of the twentieth century had witnessed considerable interest in Old and Middle English narratives. The studies of W. P. Ker, E. V. Gordon, I. Gollancz, Eugène Vinaver, R. S. Loomis, J. R. R. Tolkien, Charles Williams, and C. S. Lewis signaled a concerted critical effort to establish a scholarly appreciation of the Anglo-Saxon and medieval tradition, based upon models established in classical studies. These appreciations contributed to a certain celebration in academia and literature of the depth and history of the "culture of the nation," and its potential to express "universal" themes within a slightly overlooked, national literary idiom.

This awareness was further ensured by the engagement of many poets and novelists with Anglo-Saxon and medieval narratives. Just as Robert Graves had popularized the study of classics in his *I, Claudius* series of novels, Tolkien applied his awareness of medieval conventions and language to the epic *Lord of the Rings* trilogy. Auden and Ezra Pound demonstrated their fascination with the poetic possibilities of the construction and imagery of Old English verse in their translations of "The Wanderer" and "The Seafarer."[1] Auden's further interest in Middle English narrative reflects the influence of T. S. Eliot, who distanced modernist concerns from the perceived nostalgic approach of the Victorians towards Arthurian myth, and embodied medieval images of the Quest, the Fisher King, and the Grail in poems dealing with political, social, and cultural concerns.

The close relationship between these modernist artists and academics often meant that writers signaled their scholarly research in their works. Auden and Kallman's consultation with E. R. Dodds and their writings about the libretto to *The Bassarids* mirror the scholarly conscientiousness with which modernist intellectuals tended to approach sources of literary inspiration or adaptation. Eliot's notes to *The Waste Land* state unequivocally that "not only the title, but the plan and a good deal of

---

1   Auden's interest in Old English and Old Norse was particularly acute; his *Letters from Iceland* and translation of the *Elder Edda* demonstrate the enthusiasm with which he studied and attempted to convey the complexities of earlier linguistic practice and custom.

the incidental symbolism of the poem were suggested by Miss Jessie L. Weston's book on the Grail legend: *From Ritual to Romance* (Cambridge)" (68). Similarly, in *In Parenthesis*, whose central themes centre around medieval ritual and romance, David Jones emphasizes his appreciation of medieval tradition: in one footnote, for example, he supplies the original medieval French verses from the *Chanson de Roland* along with information indicating the translation from which he has taken the text (225).

The libretti to both *Gawain* (1991) and *Troilus and Cressida* (1954) similarly acknowledge the cultural and critical status of their sources. In his introduction to the libretto of *Troilus and Cressida*, Christopher Hassall cites the criticism of C. S. Lewis and claims that the "chapter on Chaucer in *The Allegory of Love*, a study of medieval tradition, by C. S. Lewis, provided the first hint for the subject of [the] Opera" (3). When Walton discussed with him the kind of heroine he wished to portray, Hassall "happened to recall" a "description of a woman's character that [he] had read some years before in a work of literary criticism" ("And Now—Walton's First Opera" 12). The book was *The Allegory of Love*, and the heroine was Chaucer's Criseyde. Hassall also offers a history of the origins of Chaucer's narrative, and notes Troilus' first appearance in a Latin text in the fourth century A.D., his evolution in Benoît de Sainte Maure's contribution to the *Chansons de geste*, and his appearance in Boccaccio's *Il filostrato*. He asserts that the opera owes its greatest debt to Chaucer, whose Criseyde is "so different from Shakespeare's heroine" (*Troilus and Cressida* 3). Emphasizing the informed nature of his appreciation, he reinforces in his dismissal of Shakespeare's play a scholarly valuation of the earlier, arguably more esoteric, narrative text.

Hassall's appreciations reflect a critical era that placed particular value on the perceived intent of an author. By the time of *Gawain*, the scholarly discussion of such sources was well established, as was a tendency to challenge the authoritative status of the author and academic. David Harsent claims in his introduction to the libretto that he has "retained little of the original save the essential narrative drift" (6). He speaks of the language and meter of the original as being "of limited use" to him, and of his bending moments of direct speech "to [his] story's purpose" (6). He resembles Tippett in his efforts to emphasize the originality of his creation, claiming that the original poem "doesn't provide much for a dramatic version": "I was glad to be freed into my own composition and, so far as the investigation of character and motive go, my own discoveries and inventions" (6). Nonetheless, Harsent emphasizes his appreciation and knowledge of the cultural context of his narrative, and demands a similarly educated appreciation from his audience. He ensures his published libretto a scholarly status by asserting the cultural and historical knowledge that has informed his contribution. One section, for example, includes the full Latin text for the Marian antiphons quoted in the opera. Harsent does not articulate a fealty to the literary intricacies of the original source, but expects that his libretto be appreciated as a poetic, culturally informed, and creative retelling.

The extent to which the composers of these operas similarly acknowledged the scholarly status of their sources remains to be seen. Overall, both operas respond to their sources within the literary aesthetic of modern British opera, but manifest that response in different ways. *Troilus and Cressida* was the first British opera conceived by a major composer (other than Britten) after *Peter Grimes*, and can be seen in part as a reaction to Britten's work.[2] As such, it deserves particular consideration for the way in which it acknowledges and reinforces an emerging operatic aesthetic. According to Walton, "Ben had written *Peter Grimes* ... and I thought it was not a good thing for British opera to have only one opera by one composer. I thought it my duty to try and write an opera" (qtd. in S. Walton 133). Walton's choice of *Troilus and Criseyde* as a source through which to attempt to equal, if not better, the literary, dramatic, and musical achievement of Britten's operas points to an acknowledgment of the work's national status and the literary aims of modern British opera.

Decades later, of course, composers such as Britten, Walton, and Tippett had more firmly established a "new tradition" of British opera. *Gawain*'s consequently less self-conscious engagement with its source differs considerably from that of *Troilus and Cressida*. Nonetheless, it too manifests the interpretative conflicts between libretto, score, and source that characterize the earlier operas. The work emphasizes the extent to which these conflicts have become an integral part of modern British opera, and suggests the impossibility of their ultimate resolution in a form whose collaborators insist upon their own, often very particular, literary and interpretative integrity.

Gawain

David Harsent consciously responded to the operatic project as a poet, rather than as a collaborator or dramaturge. He was "delighted" when Birtwistle asked him to write the libretto: "the magnitude of the task ... that *benchmark for any English poet!*" (Vianu). He speaks of "having to square up to the Gawain poet" in writing the libretto. For Harsent, the task of adaptation affiliates him with the English literary tradition of which the Gawain poet is a "benchmark." This affiliation allows him to "prove" his own poetic credentials, and enforce his position within that tradition.

Harsent is clear to differentiate between the art of a poet and that of the verse dramatist. For Harsent, successful verse drama requires an acknowledgment of broad gesture that conflicts with the tight construction and focused interiority of his own poetry. Eliot's plays are "dead on the page, let alone on the stage" because they lack such gesture: "dramatic verse has built-in emphases; perhaps its mannerisms need to be matched by broad expression, broad narrative movement and equally broad responses in the audience" (Vianu). Such broad expression and narrative movement are characteristically celebrated by music and staging in opera. In accepting the task of collaboration, Harsent acknowledges inherent differences between opera and verse drama, and between the function of the libretto and that of music. The libretto demonstrates no interest in manifesting "broad gesture" and "broad expression" in the verse, nor in determining musical style.

---

2   Although the opera was not performed until 1954, it was commissioned in 1947, only two years after the first performance of *Peter Grimes*.

Like Auden, however, Harsent recognizes an essential difference between his constructed libretto and its realization in opera. He protests that "in a sense, it's pointless to write libretti in verse because the music has its own way with the words." Nonetheless, he perseveres: "it's necessary for the librettist to have his own compositional strategy." According to Harsent, a reading of the libretto to *Gawain* reveals that it is "poetry on the page; in the opera house, I'm not so sure" (Vianu). In divorcing his aesthetic from that of verse drama, Harsent allows a greater musical role for the score. Nonetheless, by promoting his own role as that of the interpretative poet, no matter the eventual manifestation of that role in the score, Harsent defines his primary project as poetic rather than dramatic. Indeed, he objects to dramatic composition because it demands a collaboration which does not interest him: "drama is, quite properly, a joint venture; poetry is not. Drama is democratic; poetry is not" (Vianu). Such statements enforce a separation between his own poetic endeavor and that of the composer, justifying his comment that he was "prepared to wage war" in the collaboration.

Harsent approaches the task of writing the libretto as an essentially poetic, "undemocratic" project. He recognizes that his creation might become corrupted in its eventual collaboration with the score, and maintains the libretto's primary identity as a published text. Birtwistle's approach is not entirely different, and assumes a certain creative and interpretative autonomy. Birtwistle generally attempts to translate (or represent) the themes and narrative structure of the original source. The libretto's primary function, it would seem, is to provide some narrative reference for Birtwistle's musical engagement with the source and his own dramatic plan. A brief examination of these two approaches will reveal the extent to which Harsent's anticipated "war" is in fact manifested in the final creation.

Gawain marks one of Birtwistle's few attempts to adapt a narrative source into opera. The earlier *The Mask of Orpheus* (prod. 1986) is ostensibly about Orpheus, but the "problems of non-linearity" are so central "to the whole concept and richness" of the opera (Clements, "Gawain" 874) that Orpheus as a character becomes relatively unimportant: Birtwistle "could have just as easily chosen Faust for his libretto (and almost did)" (Samuel 163). Birtwistle is typically drawn to sources or characters that allow for the imposition of his own thematic and structural occupations with time and ritual. These occupations rarely allow for conventional narrative patterns, and his works are famous for their musical experimentation and deliberate disruption of dramatic structure. Indeed, his dramatic experimentation has been such as to invite comparisons with the ritualistic explorations and dramatic unconventionality of Peter Brook, T. S. Eliot, W. B. Yeats, and Antonin Artaud. Birtwistle's decision to adapt a renowned literary source seems initially to conflict with his tendency to subvert traditional expectations in order to declare the originality of his dramatic, ritualistic aesthetic.

Sir Gawain and the Green Knight, however, contains much that corresponds with Birtwistle's characteristic concerns with time, ritual, and pattern. The poem is written in alliterative verse, an Old English form of versification revived in the fourteenth century. The verse is therefore both "old" and "new"; although the poem is unique in its narrative and psychological complexity, the form in which it is related harks back to an earlier literary tradition. Furthermore, the sound repetition in alliterative verse evokes a simultaneous regression and progression. This pattern is also suggested in the poem's overall organization: a group of long lines is followed by a word or phrase of two syllables, followed by a quatrain that rhymes with that word or phrase. The number of lines that precedes this pattern tends to vary, allowing for structural variance within a repetitive pattern. This structural evocation of cyclic variation corresponds with Birtwistle's thematic and musical interests. Samuel isolates "a fundamental melodic line" in *Gawain* that is generated by musical repetition, rather than thematic development (167). When he structures his score with large, slightly varying musical patterns that suggest an overriding structural unity, Birtwistle (consciously or unconsciously) mirrors the poem's overall effect.

Furthermore, the poem supports the implications of its formal structure with a thematic exploration of the past, regeneration, and progress in a restrictive society. The Green Knight enters immediately after Arthur has bewailed the absence of opportunities for heroic trial. His entry suggests a fateful inevitability, reinforced by the fact that Gawain must mirror the Knight's action exactly a year later. This idea of fated, cyclic patterning is emphasized by the narrative's many descriptions of physical landscape and changing seasons. Also, Gawain is both tempted by the host's wife and submitted to the axe three times. His temptation is evenly juxtaposed with descriptions of Bercilak at the hunt: when combined with the final three-part trial of Gawain at the chapel of the Green Knight, these actions reinforce the thematic importance of repetition and pattern. The poet uses this motif of development and repetition to compare the civilized court of Arthur with crude nature, represented by the Green Knight. The tale suggests that man and nature are inextricably linked in a process of regeneration and decay. Only man's potential to grow into self-awareness can challenge this cyclic degeneration.

This evocation of ritual, repetition, and potential stasis through multiple cyclic and associative patterns reflects Birtwistle's characteristic thematic and musical interests. Birtwistle recognizes this apparent cohesion most overtly in the "Seasons sequence" and "the extensive intercutting of the Hunt and Seduction." He claimed that this section of the opera, which dramatizes Gawain undergoing a ritualistic preparation for his re-encounter with the Green Knight, was his "own creation" (Samuel 166–7). This claim to authorship must apply to the dramatization of the scene, rather than the text itself, which was provided by Harsent. The libretto is quite sparse, however: it is the music that signals the section's importance. Indeed, it originally took 30 minutes to perform.[3] The scene simultaneously presents the passage of five days and the events of a year as Gawain is stripped, washed, and armed for his confrontation. Baldwin alternates between singing Marian motets and excerpts from the *Dies Irae*, enforcing the relationship in the opera between death

---

3   The opera was revised in 1994, its most notable alteration being the reduction of this scene. At the time of the opera's revision, in an unconventionally conventional acknowledgment of audience expectations, Birtwistle stated in an interview with Mark Pappenheim: "Gawain is about story telling"; the revised version "is better, that's all—simpler, clearer, tells the story" (21).

and regeneration. These themes underline those of the source, and Birtwistle sets them with extended musical patterns and repetitions.

Although Birtwistle's "own creation" underlines key themes of the source, however, it also enforces a significant narrative interruption that goes against the rhythm of the original poem. *Sir Gawain* is distinguished by its narrative voice, which is alternately comic, suspenseful, and ominous. This voice is constantly present to elicit particular reactions or interpretations from the reader. As a result, the poet is able to ensure the constant integration of thematic concerns with narrative progression. No matter its repetition and patterning of actions and themes, the poem is characterized by the force of its narrative propulsion. The music, however, effectively halts the narrative action to emphasize structural and thematic concerns. In so doing, it hints at a fundamental incompatibility between the narrative priorities of source and music.

Birtwistle's approach does not disregard dramatic context entirely. Instead, the score vacillates between acknowledging dramatic moments and character, and highlighting its own thematic focus. These two approaches never fully reconcile within the setting. Thus, the evocation of the Knight's knocking at the door is a strictly dramatic effect that encourages the audience to appreciate a narrative context. This effect contrasts significantly with the setting of the Hunt and the Seduction, which comments upon the implications of action, but does not dramatize that action. Similarly, the music generally refrains from individuating characters: their melodies tend to allude to musical material previously introduced by other characters. The score makes an exception with the character of Morgan, whose lullaby constitutes one of the few moments of self-expression by a single character. Her musical patterns echo earlier musical material, particularly the "AEIYA" cry that both Morgan and Lady de Hautdesert had sung at the end of the earlier Seasons passage. Unlike the other characters, Morgan remains consistent in the expression which she gives to this cry. Her ability to retain her musical line creates a constancy and strength to her character that overrides that of any other. This music startles the audience into a recognition of dramatic context and a narrative emphasis on character not always prominent in the opera.

The score seems to vacillate between its project to dramatize the themes of the source, and its interest in individual characters and narrative events. This apparent inconsistency calls attention to the music's attempt to engage with its source. Ironically, in so doing, it implicitly acknowledges the narrative, structural, and thematic self-referentiality of the original source. In the poem, the narrator manipulates the reader to expect the moral collapse of Gawain into sin with the host's wife: he describes Gawain's weakness, evokes the wife's manipulative ability, and uses the familiar medieval narrative motif of The Temptation to Adultery. The poem only half-fulfills those invited expectations, however. Gawain does not fully succumb to the wife. Instead, he falls into a different moral shame; he accepts the gift of a green sash, which the wife tells him will protect him, and out of cowardice, lack of faith, and embarrassment, does not reveal its existence. The poet subverts the expectations of the reader by qualifying the causes and consequences of seduction and moral weakness. He encourages the reader to recognize and appreciate the means through which narrative unconventionality can reveal greater, implicitly more profound truths about social and moral behavior. The music's inconsistent approach towards narrative, theme, and character to some extent mirrors this subtle disruption of traditional expectations.

Nonetheless, the overall effect is quite different. The poem's narrative unconventionality serves to reinforce themes that pertain directly to a specific narrative and characters. Birtwistle's musical formalizations, however, "[chafe] with the contrary, narrativisitic impulse to observe 'the sanctity of the context'" (Adlington, *The Music of Harrison Birtwistle* 29). Unlike his source, Birtwistle minimizes the psychology of his hero in favor of emphasizing a vaguely defined importance to the ritualistic process. Thus, the temptation scene in the opera can be associated musically and dramatically with the similarly extended ritual scene in which Gawain is armed. This parallel disregards the narrative events which have occasioned Gawain's particular situation. [4] These different emphases suggest an ultimate incompatibility between Birtwistle's aesthetic approach and the structure, narrative, and themes of his source.

Unlike the score, however, the libretto is much more focused on narrative linearity and character. At the same time, it recognizes and attempts to translate the thematic role of narrative unconventionality in the source. Both the libretto and *Sir Gawain* play with the idea of finality. The poem invokes and ultimately confuses any sense of definitive moral message. The libretto translates this effect by signaling and ultimately thwarting its apparent intention to detail narrative progressing to a conclusive resolution. *Sir Gawain* ends with a final "moral" taken from the Order of the Garter, which condemns the man with evil in mind: "Hony Soyt Qui Mal Y Pense." The finality and certainty of this moral comes across as ironic, given the poem's attention to moral confusion, particularly in the seduction scenes. The libretto begins by suggesting that it, too, will lead the audience into some higher understanding. Ultimately, however, it subverts that expectation by emphasizing that all journey is infinite. Seeking a brave knight, Arthur asks:

> who'll make the journey
> over the badlands of sleep,
> trekking through clods and brine,
> through mists and swarming shadows,
> to meet himself there
> waiting for the worst dream to begin? (18)[5]

He associates his need to witness heroic action with his own need to define himself, and repeatedly asks, "tell me my bloodline." This desire is never appeased. Similarly, Gawain recognizes that all his "heroic" journey has revealed to him has been "a mirror-image retreating before [his] face" (82). At the end of the opera, Morgan encourages an undefined audience to "think only of dreams and promises," for "then/with a single step/your journey starts" (86). The libretto invokes this idea

---

4   He uses the scene as an "occasion for an extended musical verse scheme, whose static, cyclical qualities seem wholly appropriate to the 'timelessness' of ritual" (*The Music of Harrison Birtwistle* 28).

5   References are to page numbers.

of a journey in relation to its characters and its audience, only to emphasize the impossibility of narrative resolution.

At the same time as the libretto establishes an affiliation with the narrative and thematic focus of its source, it complements Birtwistle's interest in ritual and repetition. Indeed, like Birtwistle, Harsent valued the idea of structural repetition in his work. He claims that his poems "almost always begin with an image that, as often as not, arrives with a phrase or two attached and continues to accrue language as [he] start[s] to work it" (Vianu). This process of patterning mirrors Birtwistle's use of leitmotifs and melodic lines constantly generated from other melodic lines. The libretto manifests this interest in repetition, however, by translating it into a narrative, rather than stylistic, context. It is replete with references to dreams, journeys, and meetings of "oneself" in the lines of various characters. Morgan inspires Gawain's dream journey, and sings of her own dreams. In their final encounter, the Green Knight tells Gawain that "dreams of death" shall "journey" with him "like something [he's] hoarded,/like something [he needs] to own" (71). This promise mirrors Morgan's constant dream of "the year's dead end" with "old wounds opening." Gawain arrives at a similar state of repeated reflection; he sings, "Moment by moment, we overhaul yesterday/falsehood and vanity ... so the world turns" (83).

This idea of cyclic, potentially fated repetition is further emphasized in the libretto's extensive development of mirror imagery. The libretto demands the staging of a "world outside" and a "world inside," and often brings these worlds into unknowing contact with each other. As Gawain makes his journey to Bertilak's house, "we will become aware of Bertilak and Lady de Hautdesert occupying the 'world inside'." These two worlds are represented by two doors that "represent either side of the same door" (46). When Gawain arrives at the house, "the 'other' Gawain" knocks at the door three times. Both doors open and "both" Gawains enter. Furthermore, characters unconsciously (or subconsciously) mirror the actions of others. When the "other" Gawain knocks at the door of Bertilak's house, he mirrors the knocking of the Green Knight at Arthur's court. His knocking three times further parallels his own three-part temptation at the hands of Lady de Hautdesert and his final encounter with the Green Knight.

All of these repetitions and associative patterns emphasize the libretto's central suggestion that Gawain's journey and the worlds and characters he encounters are to some extent elements of a single self which has yet, if ever, to thoroughly cohere. The libretto emphasizes that the metaphorical journey (and the mirror-imagery with which it is associated) is not cathartic, and necessitates continuous repetition. This "message" reflects Birtwistle's idea of constantly changing patterns and ritual, opposed to distinct structural change. At the same time, it engages directly with central themes articulated in both the narrative and structure of the original source.

Unlike the score, then, the libretto integrates its structure and thematic focus within the drama's narrative context. When Gawain repeats "Cross of Christ," for instance, he is not merely articulating a thematic concern, but acting within a specific narrative situation. At the end of the opera, Morgan invites the commencement of a journey in the words with which she began the opera; she is inviting the audience to undergo an expedition similar to that of Gawain. The audience has already undergone this journey, however, in the very act of watching the opera. Any commencement of an expedition on the part of the audience would constitute a repetition, rather than renewal, of experience. The implications of this dramatic structure ensure that Harsent involves the audience in the very process of ritual that so dictates Birtwistle's musical structures.

Despite their appreciation of the source and their similar interests in structural repetition, Harsent and Birtwistle are unable to ensure a coherence between libretto and score in the opera. This seems in part to be the result of two adapters perceiving their own response to the source as inherently complete, rather than collaborative. Thus, the narrative structure of the libretto often contradicts the abstract musical patterning in the score. The libretto is committed to exploring themes within a narrative context, while Birtwistle tends to define his primary focus as inspired by, rather than dependent upon, narrative events and characters. Birtwistle generally associates repeated musical patterns with lines as they occur rhythmically; these patterns do not always correspond to the repeated textual phrases in the libretto. Morgan's "Night after night, the same dream" and Gawain's "Cross of Christ," for example, are repeated frequently throughout the libretto in various narrative contexts. The music does not acknowledge this repetition, and sets the lines to conform to Birtwistle's formal structures. The ultimate effect is to undermine the structural and thematic importance of those lines in the libretto.

In *Gawain*, both collaborators seem to assume the inherent independence of their particular contribution. For Harsent, the libretto allows him the relative independence to engage with and position himself in relation to poetic tradition. Birtwistle asserts an almost autonomous musical explication of the perceived themes of the source. Nonetheless, both contributors are apparently inhibited by the necessary "democracy" of the project. Harsent recognizes that the music inevitably "has its own way with the words," and Birtwistle's structural argument is implicitly challenged by the narrative and textual demands of the libretto. In *Gawain* at least, opera has evolved to assert the independent strength of its collaborative components, and thus to hint at the ultimate limitations of the form itself.

At the same time, however, the operatic components of score and libretto are defined by the increasing intermediality of the arts. Indeed, the literary, intellectual aesthetic of British opera has been promoted by composers and writers alike, who emphasize the importance of an informed, literate, and structured response to the original source. Tippett assumes that this response must be articulated in the libretto text alone. In the score of *Gawain*, Birtwistle asserts the ability of music to articulate the literary and intellectual interpretations initially attributed to the literary adapter alone. Neither libretto nor score is fully independent of each other: their very claims of autonomy underline their existence within a collaborative aesthetic.

Ironically, the resulting tensions in *Gawain* between libretto and score underline the appropriateness of *Sir Gawain and the Green Knight* as a source. The subtle inconsistencies within the original poem are mirrored in the opera's narrative, thematic, and structural inconsistency. Neither traditional drama nor innovative music ritual, the opera inhabits an undefined generic territory that emphasizes the journey "through mists and swarming shadows" which the libretto recognizes in the source. This journey has yet, if ever, to terminate in certainty.

Troilus and Cressida

Both *Gawain* and *Troilus and Cressida* are characterized by the concerted efforts of their librettist and composer to faithfully represent, if not literally adapt, the themes and narrative of their literary source. These attempts are defined by very different aesthetic approaches: *Gawain*'s narrative is used by both collaborators to emphasize their own stylistic, structural, and thematic interests. These interests never fully reconcile into a close collaboration, and offer two essentially discursive commentaries on literature, culture, and the universal psyche. In *Troilus and Cressida*, the collaborators signal their intention to place the work within a modern operatic idiom. At the same time, they work to redefine that modern idiom by making it conform to more conservative dramatic conventions and the social philosophies implicit in those conventions.

As we shall see, despite these very different intentions, both operas achieve a similar effect in relation to their source. This has much to do with the nature of the source itself, which resists traditionalist assumptions about narrative and character. This resistance allows for the apparently inevitable tensions that result from the nature of the collaboration that has come to define modern British opera.

Troilus and Cressida was written at a time when the "new" idiom of modern British opera was still establishing itself. Its collaborators therefore had to work more concertedly to both define and position their work within this new tradition. The reception and manifestation of their effort underlines some of the assumptions that informed the formulation and identification of this new form.

In January of 1947, Dylan Thomas wrote to his parents that he had been asked to write "a full-length grand opera for William Walton" (qtd. in Ferris 615). Although Thomas soon lost interest in the project, his letter indicates that Walton had considered writing an opera even before he was commissioned to do so by the BBC in February 1947. This interest may have been partially awakened by the reopening of the Royal Opera House (1946), an act which established a full-time opera company largely dedicated to the promotion of British opera. As a member of the Covent Garden Opera Trust, Walton would have been concerned with the increasing developments in British opera. Furthermore, not only had *Peter Grimes* achieved unprecedented national and international success, but it had also helped to define opera as the source of British musical creativity. As a prominent British composer, Walton would have felt considerable artistic pressure to assert himself musically within the genre.

Walton's project must also be seen as having been motivated by artistic rivalry. Although Walton wrote congratulatory letters to Britten, encouraged him early in his compositional career, and spoke on his behalf at a judicial hearing for conscientious objectors, he felt unduly neglected by the critical establishment as a result of Britten's popularity. Walton discouraged the British Council from recording *Peter Grimes* in 1946, and opposed the idea that Britten should become music director of Covent Garden. Most evidence supports the idea that Britten and Walton "had a relationship based largely on a sincere, warm-hearted respect, rather than upon any real bond of affection" (Tierney 155). Walton's wife has asserted that "while it is true that William considered Ben his great rival, they respected each other" (S. Walton 124).

This artistic respect doubtless encouraged Walton to attempt to match, if not better, the critical and popular success of Britten.

By the time that *Troilus and Cressida* was performed, Britten had achieved success not only with *Peter Grimes*, but also with *The Rape of Lucretia* (1946), *Albert Herring* (1947), *The Little Sweep* (1949), *Billy Budd* (1951), and *Gloriana* (1953). Commissioned by Covent Garden to celebrate the coronation of Queen Elizabeth II, *Gloriana* was hyped as the first "royal" commission since Handel's Water Music. A year later, when Walton's Pandarus sang, "Nothing but royal patronage can save us now," the audience erupted in laughter in implicit acknowledgment of the rivalry between the two composers (White, *A History of English Opera* 421). Walton's later opera, *The Bear* (1967), performed at Aldeburgh, begins by mocking Britten's musical style. Such references underscore Walton's awareness of the extent to which his compositional reputation had suffered at the expense of Britten's fame.

Indeed, before Britten's emergence, Walton had been seen as the composer who would herald a new, more legitimate music for Britain. In 1935, a BBC announcer described Walton as "England's White Hope" (Kennedy 134). Such hopes were based primarily on one work, which had gained instant notoriety and earned Walton the reputation of musical "enfant terrible." In 1922, Walton composed *Façade*, a "drawing-room entertainment" comprised of a series of brief poems by Edith Sitwell with musical accompaniments. The work was conceived of by Walton and the Sitwells, who had "adopted" Walton into their literary circle and home. *Façade* was considered scandalous at its debut (Osbert Sitwell gives a thorough account of its reception, 168–98). Aside from its outlandish "staging" (in a drawing room, with poems declaimed to music through a megaphone hidden behind a curtain), *Façade* was the first major musical work to declare a definitive reaction against the movement epitomized by Ralph Vaughan Williams.

The work is characterized by nonsensical, deliberately anti-traditional verse, and frequently abrasive, deliberately parodic music. Its reference to Continental influences and its failure to recognize the importance of a folk idiom were not enough to ensure its revolutionary status. *Façade* is most important for having implicitly adhered to a British musical tradition by offering a clear text-setting of verses by an English poet. In its own facetious way, the work articulates a contempt and disregard for the self-conscious literary folk aesthetic developed by composers of the first renaissance, particularly with its settings of poems entitled "Hornpipe," "Mariner Man," "Scotch Rhapsody," and "Fox-Trot 'Old Sir Faulk'." More than any other previous work, *Façade* brings together the musical and the contemporary literary by deliberately acknowledging and parodying established traditions. In this work, Walton redefined the relationship between text and music, and rendered his own music more relevant by associating it with a perceived avant-garde literature. Furthermore, he created for the literary artist (or allowed the literary artist to create for him or herself) a much greater potential for involvement in the musical creative process.

The "newness" of *Façade* is therefore located primarily in its unabashed musical celebration of avant-garde verse. When critics lamented the conservatism of Walton's works after *Façade*, they failed to recognize that the majority of experimentation in the work had been parodic. Walton's next major works, the orchestral overture *Portsmouth Point* (1925), the Viola Concerto (1929), and the oratorio *Belshazzar's*

Feast (1931, lyrics by Osbert Sitwell), helped to define a personal musical style that was more traditional, that appeased early critics, and that eased Walton into a more accepting, relatively conservative musical idiom. The "seriousness, scope, and traditionalism" of the Viola Concerto "erased Walton's earlier reputation as an *enfant terrible* and established him as the leading English symphonic composer of his generation" (Morgan 271). To have gained the reputation of "enfant terrible" and "England's White Hope" in one's early twenties renders future composition difficult; by 1945 prominent critics such as Blom were already discussing the style of the "later Walton." After *Façade*, Walton tended to be stylistically consistent within his own musical idiom, a consistency that subjected him to criticism from those hoping for innovative parallels with the development in style of such composers as Stravinsky or Schoenberg. Deeming Walton "fundamentally conservative," one critic concluded that "on the strength of *Façade* and the artistic environment it implied, Walton had been "too hastily classed with an *avant garde* that was, if not wholly mythical, altogether alien" to his own nature (P. Evans, "Sir William Walton's Manner and Mannerism" 297). Walton's initial reputation had been established by his association with a collaborative project whose modernity was signaled as much by its subject and verse as by its music. This musico-literary statement enabled composers such as Britten to explore other literary sources, to enlist the collaboration of self-professedly modern writers, and to redefine British operatic endeavor in terms of its self-conscious literary and dramatic interests.

Ironically, the increasingly consistent characterization of Walton's style as conservative, backward, undeveloped, or at the very least, no longer promising, can be traced to the emergence of Britten as the perceived great hope for British opera and British musical composition generally. Britten's success was to take the literary and musical principles established in *Façade*, and to translate them into a more democratic, narrative-based dramatic form. No matter the reputation of opera as elitist, it is a considerably less elitist form than "drawing-room entertainment." Furthermore, the traditionalism of Britten's dramatic and musical structures invited a certain amount of trust from British audiences more open to restagings of Verdi and Puccini than to the innovations of Schoenberg or Stravinsky.

Walton's subsequent efforts were almost always assessed in terms of their perceived progressiveness. Although *Troilus and Cressida* "is a significant addition to the repertory," it is of limited artistic value as the "musical theatre of the twentieth century has gained no fresh impetus from it" (Müller 92). Although the opera "contains beautiful and moving music," it "is no landmark in the history of opera" (Boyden 241). Compared to *King Priam*, "*Troilus and Cressida* is a Hollywood B movie" written in a "1940s British film-music-style" (T. Sutcliffe, "British Journal" [1995] 38). The opera's critics almost universally deplore the work's apparent indebtedness to previous composers, equating this indebtedness with a determined lack of progressiveness on Walton's part. Britten's musical executor, for example, found it "a curious revolution of the historical wheel that one of the foremost leaders of our musical renaissance should have written an opera" which owes "so much to the Wagnerian and post-Wagnerian music drama" (D. Mitchell, Rev. of *Troilus and Cressida* 36). Arguing that a work "which does not employ a valid contemporary style cannot hope to communicate anything valid to its audience" (D. Mitchell,

"Troilus and Cressida" 90), critics have dismissed the work for being so strongly "reminiscent of the later Verdi" and so "frankly Romantic in tone" (Boyden 239) that Walton comes across as deploying "second-hand mastery" (Müller 91).

Nonetheless, this reassessment of Walton as essentially conservative and musically unambitious says much about the unspoken assumptions that defined ideas of musical modernity. Despite the assertions about the derivativeness of *Troilus and Cressida*, no critic has offered a close reading of the opera in the light of these claims. Where Britten's setting of Claggart's aria in *Billy Budd*, "Oh beauty, handsomeness, goodness," has been frequently compared to the "Credo" of Verdi's Iago, Walton's music has not been subjected to any such explicit comparison. Indeed, some critics have objected in the same breath to the opera's derivativeness and to its failure to evoke sufficient comparison with its Romantic models: "Child of the wine-dark wave" fails for not providing "the first big solo-lyrical moment, the 'Celeste Aida' of the opera" (Arthur Jacobs 420). Furthermore, while Britten's style is undoubtedly modern, it exhibits many characteristics of Walton's apparent conservatism in its general adherence to tonal structures, its interest in recurring musical themes, its concern for dramatic continuity, and its musical emphasis on moments of emotional self-revelation. Although critics discuss *Troilus and Cressida* in terms of the allusiveness of its music, their objections are directed less at the work's musical formalism (which is just as characteristic of *Peter Grimes* as it is of *Troilus and Cressida*) than they are at its approach towards its narrative subject.

Donald Mitchell claims that the fault of *Troilus and Cressida* lies not in "the antique character of [the] opera's plot" ("Troilus" 88) but in the music: the music that surrounds the lovers "largely rehearses familiar romantic gestures which belong to another century, to other composers, to another operatic world" (Rev. of *Troilus and Cressida* 36). Mitchell seems to equate Walton's choice for musical evocation with his musical style; a romantic relationship such as that between Troilus and Cressida belongs to a past century, and therefore cannot be translated into a contemporary musical idiom. Similarly, any attempt to write an opera "which in its plot combines a formal crisis of statecraft with a formal crisis of sex" in "an unquestioning, non-ironic, romantic musical idiom is almost bound to fail today" (Arthur Jacobs 420). Despite articulating their criticism in terms of musical analysis, the chief detractors of the opera ultimately find fault in the work's formal musical endorsement of the dramatic legitimacy of the narrative conflict and relationships it presents.

This approach to the opera is similarly taken by those who appreciate the work; Walton proves an exception to the rule that "most English operatic composers fumble shyly when required to write love music" (qtd. in Foreman, "Walton's Words" 248). *Troilus and Cressida* was deemed "a musical landmark" for returning British opera to a "healthy course"; "it was not composed for a small band of intellectuals. It is an opera *everyone* can understand and enjoy. It will advance the love of opera at home and enhance the fame of Britain abroad" (qtd. in Foreman, "Walton's Words" 248). Just as the detractors of *Troilus and Cressida* criticize the work for its musical endorsement of a traditional romantic plot, its enthusiasts praise it for the clarity and strength with which it presents its emotional subject.

Such a strong emphasis on the emotional center of the opera stems from the critical climate encouraged by the operas of Britten, Tippett, and their literary collaborators. Britten's operas frequently present sexually ambiguous relationships which might have been considered "untoward" had it not been for the subtlety of their treatment in libretto and music. For those aware of the sexual orientation of Britten and many of his librettists (Auden, Forster, Plomer), this subtlety merely underscores the potential articulation of homosexual themes. Indeed, the very narrative ambiguity of a number of Britten's chosen subjects (*Billy Budd, Turn of the Screw,* "Owen Wingrave," *Death in Venice*) mirrors the lack of clarity with which such homosexual composers as Britten, Tippett, and Henze were able to present their own concerns on the public stage. Britten "modernized" British opera less through musical experimentation than by choosing subjects that challenged popular conceptions of opera as a dramatization of heterosexual romantic passion. Britten's choice of literary subjects was (and continues to be) seen by many as a manifestation of his own preoccupation with the impossibility of direct articulation. No matter its formal similarity to many musical techniques employed by Britten, *Troilus and Cressida* differs most strongly from the modern British operatic idiom defined by Britten in its choice and treatment of subject. The opera's reception was unquestionably informed by these changing intellectual approaches towards art and traditionalism, and the frequently blurred line between "modern" innovation in art and "new" ways of thinking about society and culture.

Troilus and Cressida conforms sufficiently with trends in British operatic tradition to be considered as a critical (or populist) response to the inherently philosophical and social differences that divided Walton from some of his operatic contemporaries. Hassall's emphasis on his scholarly appreciation of *Troilus and Criseyde* ensures that the work be considered in terms of the literary emphasis which similarly characterized the majority of "modern" British operas. Walton's first choice of Dylan Thomas can be seen as a recognition of the increasing expectation that a librettist possess some independent literary status, and perhaps as an attempt to evoke comparison with his earlier collaborative success with the Sitwells. Nonetheless, Walton's initial concern was that the source of his opera provide appropriate material for a grand opera—and thus celebrate the musical and narrative conventions of nineteenth-century Italian opera: lengthy arias, doomed heroes and heroines, and heightened explorations of passion. This emphasis signals Walton's musical and dramatic "traditionalism," and his endorsement of ideas of romantic love no longer celebrated in contemporary artistic movements.

Walton initially considered four possible subjects: *Volpone* (based on Ben Jonson's play), *Antony and Cleopatra*, *Byron*, and *Duke Melveric*. These choices could easily have provided narratives for nineteenth-century operas. Unlike the sources of Britten's operas, these subjects, with the exception of *Volpone*, evoke larger-than-life characters famous for their passion and ambition. *Volpone* is a slightly more contemporary choice due to the play's moral vacillations, although it invokes a long tradition of adapting Renaissance dramas (particularly those of Shakespeare). Later, Walton discussed choices with Hassall—these subjects differ significantly from the earlier considerations: *Troilus and Criseyde*, *Queen Jocasta* (based on Jean Cocteau's *The Infernal Machine*), *The Woman of Andros* (based on Thornton Wilder's novel), and *Hassan* (based on a play by James Elroy Flecker). The second choices formed with Hassall are less traditional in their concern with social and psychological portrayal rather than narrative clarity or grandiose passion. *Troilus and Criseyde* possessed some intellectual and poetic currency in the critical and artistic climate of the 1940s. The other three sources were written in the twenties or thirties, and signal an attempt on the part of the collaborators to render their choice more contemporary. Hassall's collaboration seems to have ensured that the subject of Walton's grand opera sympathized with contemporary literary and critical interests, and helped to validate the potentially regressive musical form in which the subject was to be set.

Nonetheless, Hassall was not himself a "typical" librettist of modern British opera. He did not explicitly identify with a single literary role, and described himself variously as a playwright, biographer (Rupert Brooke, Edward Marsh), lyricist, and poet. His works often revealed a strong resistance to modernist aesthetics. In "To a Contemporary Poet: An Epistle," for example, Hassall compares his ideal contemporary poet

> whose pen
> Provokes no discord on the ears of men,
> But speaks of beauty, past, and yet to be,
> The depth of love, or height of reverie

to those who write

> in syncopated prose,
> Parade their still-born *opera* in rows,
> Scribble in fits, and in a seizure die,
> Then gnash their teeth at all posterity:
> Young men and old, fired by a common passion
> To weave conundrums at the call of fashion (55–8, 131–6).

This conservatism no doubt helped to ensure the almost instantaneous disappearance of Hassall's critical and artistic reputation after his death. Furthermore, it queries the extent to which he could be affiliated with the essentially modernist literary origins of modern British opera.

Hassall's correspondence suggests that he perceived the role of the librettist to be ultimately subservient in his "craft" to the dramatic and musical instincts of the composer. While he claims, for example, to have "made a careful study of the technique in Matthew Arnold's *The Strayed Reveller*" in order to write Cressida's free-verse monologues, he emphasizes the importance of close collaboration: "A librettist is his composer's literary limb: and it is not to disclaim any detail of the libretto, but rather to acknowledge the great benefit of a close collaboration, when I say that in the last analysis a composer of opera is his own dramatist" ("And Now—Walton's First Opera" 12). This emphasis on craft is uncharacteristic of the claims of other librettists such as Auden and Harsent, who asserted their literary creativity and interpretative authority. It seems to derive from the fact that Hassall had an equally distinguished career writing lyrics for Ivor Novello's musicals. (Works included *Glamorous Night* [1935], *The Dancing Years* [1939], *Arc de Triomphe* [1943], and *King's Rhapsody* [1949].) Where many "serious" poets may have felt demeaned by writing for musicals, Hassall apparently embraced the task as not incongruous with his artistic and literary interests.

In many ways, of course, the social and artistic aims of these musicals ran directly contrary to those of modern British opera. Their populism demanded a celebration of nation that was more reminiscent of the works of the first renaissance than of the self-consciously modernist efforts of Britten and his contemporaries:

> Rose of England, thou shalt fade not here,
> Proud and bright from rolling year to year.
> Red shall thy petals be as rich wine untold
> Shed by thy warriors who served thee of old.
> Rose of England, breathing England's air,
> Flower of Chivalry beyond compare;
> While hand and heart endure to cherish thy prime,
> Thou shalt blossom to the end of Time. (*Crest of the Wave*, 1937)

Such sentiments were implicitly opposed to those in the "serious" drama of the 1930s and 1940s, the "realist" drawing-room dramas of Graham Greene and Somerset Maugham, and the allegorical verse dramas of Eliot and Auden which inspired and influenced modern British opera. In his eulogy for Novello, Hassall argues an inherent philosophical contest between these dramatic traditions:

> In an age of cynicism he maintained unspoiled his faith in the simple and tender affections; when our spirits were oppressed with dullness he came to our rescue with Romance; when we were jarred by the crude realities of our time he visited us with the balm of make-believe; not the humdrum of modern life he brought colour, colour ever new and more resplendent, and the continual surprise of refreshing laughter; for with him, whatever might happen in the newspapers, gay was always the word.

Such philosophical and literary conservatism was at odds with the prevailing philosophies of British opera after 1945. Nonetheless, Hassall's work in a theatre that aimed to elicit emotional reactions through music and plot was not entirely dissimilar to Walton's interest in grand opera. This potential sympathy between librettist and composer was problematic for Walton, however. No matter his own formal interest in nineteenth-century Romantic opera, he needed to establish himself and his opera within an aesthetic defined by self-conscious literary modernity. This, he seemed to feel, was not sufficiently evident in the achievements and interests of his librettist.

Much of Walton's correspondence is characterized by a latent literary snobbishness towards Hassall. He blames his own inability to write satisfactory love-music on the language of the libretto, claiming, "It evokes the worst type of music from me, real neo-Novelloismo" (qtd. in S. Price 194). These frequently disparaging assessments signal that Walton associated himself with a more advanced literary aesthetic than that of his librettist. His association with the Sitwells and his general involvement in literary circles seems to have contributed to these assumptions. At one point, frustrated by the opera's conclusion, Walton sought the advice of Auden, by then known for his early collaborations with Britten. When Auden offered a completed sextet, Walton used it to manipulate his librettist into acknowledging some literary rivalry in the project. He apologized to the offended Hassall, but later gleefully wrote to his publisher: "The Auden intervention seems to have put [Hassall] on his mettle & he has produced something better than either A's solution or the previous version" (qtd. in S. Price 201).[6] Walton, like Tippett, positions himself in a simultaneously deferential and superior role towards his literary contemporaries, and manifests a greater literary elitism than that expressed by the very writers with whom he associated.

Despite the relatively conservative narrative interests of the collaborators, the opera can be expected to manifest similar tensions between libretto and text, primarily because of the composer's implicit awareness of the necessity of their presence. A closer examination of the opera itself reveals two collaborators aware of their reputations as artistic conservatives, equally aware of their project to produce a major British opera to equal the modern achievement of *Peter Grimes*. Their approach simultaneously manifests their traditionalist aesthetic (and social) philosophies, and their interest in asserting the modern relevance of their work. It remains to be seen, however, how closely the opera manages to translate its source material, position itself in relation to contemporary operatic achievements, and conform that source to the grand opera project envisioned by the composer.

At first glance, the source seems extremely difficult to adapt. The work is written in Middle English and in verse, thus preventing any direct translation of either language or literary style. Hassall and Walton adapt *Troilus and Criseyde* by translating that stylistic and linguistic distance into the opera. They write traditional set-pieces, inviting comparison with pre-Wagnerian opera and thus with traditional, if not antiquated, musical and textual structures. This distance from modern aesthetic expectations is further encouraged by the opera's largely Romantic musical style. Furthermore, the opera enforces a cultural distance with its constant reference to Greek deities, omens, and customs. Although *Troilus and Criseyde* is purportedly set in Greece, it does little to exploit this setting. Hassall, however, emphasizes the distance of the opera from its literary source by evoking not medieval England, but ancient Troy. As Hassall himself has noted, "the world of Chaucer's poem is medieval England with its conception of 'courtly love'." Deeming this code of manners "too remote from present-day custom for its followers easily to engage the sympathy and understanding of a modern audience" (*Troilus and Cressida* 3–4), Hassall emphasizes the ancient setting. In so doing, he aligns the Chaucer narrative with the settings of many eighteenth and nineteenth-century operas. This allows him to translate the aesthetic and cultural distance with which he was faced in the adaptation into a recognizable operatic context.

The language in the libretto further acknowledges the difference between the linguistic and cultural understandings of a contemporary audience and those of the

---

6   It is tempting to read in the Auden consultation the potential imposition of a second librettist or, at the very least, to consider Hassall's later ensemble as a response to Auden's contribution. A close comparison of the suggested sextet and the final ensemble in the opera, however, reveals a compromise between the original goals of the collaborators, the structure (rather than content) of Auden's sextet, and the final text.

readers of the original source. The libretto is written primarily in verse and often uses antiquated terms (e.g., "thee," "thou," "parly") and stylistically affected lines: "A sea-wind, coldly veering,/carries the taste of dreams/from labyrinths of coral/where lie the sleeping Streams" (37).[7] Although these are not Middle English words and phrases, they nonetheless evoke a bygone linguistic tradition. The libretto links this linguistic tradition specifically to literature by alluding to previous literary works, reinforcing its indebtedness to a written source. Troilus sings of Cressida as a "child of the wine-dark wave" (17), evoking the "wine-dark sea" of Homer's *Odyssey* (1.420). Later, he encourages Cressida to accept his love as "life that withers like a rose" (19); this statement echoes the Apocrypha, Spenser, and Herrick to suggest both the universality of the lovers' situation and the constant articulation of that universality in literary sources.[8] After her first staged encounter with Troilus, Cressida sings; "Two solitudes/have hail'd each other and gone by./Life offers nothing more save what is bought/with anguish" (19). Her statement offers an ironic echo of Rilke's "love that consists in this, that two solitudes protect and border and salute each other" (59). In alluding to works both ancient and modern, Hassall emphasizes the contemporary relevance of the opera's narrative and the foundation of that relevance in literary tradition. He thus offers in his libretto a defense of the score's much-criticized moments of musical regressiveness, and a literary justification for the thematic and stylistic relevance of Chaucer's narrative as operatic subject.

At the same time as the source allows Hassall to assert its contemporary thematic relevance, it also allows for Walton's plan of grand opera. The narrator of *Troilus and Criseyde* claims at the outset of the tale to be serving the God of Love (1.15) and declares his narrative intention to be to show "Swich peyne and wo as Loves folk endure" (1.34). The tale contains a pining hero of noble birth and military prowess, a vacillating heroine, feuding national families, and tragically separated young lovers. All of these characteristics would immediately appeal to any composer in search of a subject for a grand opera. Furthermore, the presence of two principal characters and one essential conflict allows for a direct dramatic translation not afforded by narratives with a greater social, historical, or thematic canvas.

Romantic opera traditionally contains static moments of passionate musical self-expression; these moments occur as arias, duets, and ensembles. *Troilus and Criseyde* allows for these moments by having the narrator support his narrative details with lengthy speeches from his protagonists.[9] These speeches are often emotional and reflective, and highly reminiscent of operatic expostulation. At one point, for example, Cressida states:

---

7   All references to the *Troilus and Cressida* libretto refer to page numbers.

8   "Let us crown ourselves with rosebuds, before they wither" (Wisd. Sol. 2.8). "Gather therefore the Rose, whilest yet is prime,/For soone comes age, that will her pride deflowre:/ Gather the Rose of love, whilest yet is time,/Whilest loving thou mayst loved be with equall crime"(Spenser 2.12.75.6–9). "Gather ye Rose-buds while ye may,/Old Time is still a flying:/ And this same flower that smiles to day,/To morrow will be dying" (Herrick 1–4).

9   T. R. Price determined that 64 percent of *Troilus and Criseyde* is composed of dialogue, 18 percent of monologue, 14 percent of group scenes, and 4 percent of scenes involving three speakers.

I, woful wrecche and infortuned wight,
And born in corsed constellacioun,
Moot goon and thus departen fro my knyght!
Wo worth, allas, that ilke dayes light
On which I saugh hym first with eyen tweyne,
That causeth me, and ich hym, al this peyne! (4.744–9)

Cressida repeatedly conveys her anguish at being separated from Troilus. The speech's repetition of a single idea in escalating emotional rhetoric mirrors the effect of the traditional aria, whose focus is less on a complexity of ideas or narrative details than on a character's individual passion. Although not all of these speeches contain text suitable for direct translation, they create a dramatic structure sympathetic to that of traditional opera.

Furthermore, traditional opera demands both musical expression and physical gesture. *Troilus and Criseyde* allows for such gesture by emphasizing the physical and vocal manifestation of the emotional state of characters. Once Criseyde is resigned to follow Pandarus' advice, she enters the room "arm in arm" with him to physically indicate her acquiescence. Furthermore, she "Avysed wel hire wordes and hire cheere," conforming her words and tone of voice to this decision (2.1725–6). When Calkas begs for the release of his daughter to him, he is similarly described in terms of voice quality and physical presence:

Tellyng his tale alwey, this olde greye,
Humble in his speche and in his lokyng eke,
The salte teris from his eyen tweye
Ful faste ronnen down by either cheke. (4.127–30)

This description occurs after Calkas has made his plea. The speech is prefaced with the information that Calkas addressed the Greeks with "a chaunged face" (4.68). By describing the physical appearance and emotional state of Calkas before and after the speech, the narrative allows for an operatic presentation of that transformation through music and gesture. The opera's creators are thus enabled by the narrative simultaneously to trace the emotional development of a character, to maintain dramatic momentum, and to stage that development and momentum both musically and physically.

Chaucer's text also contains descriptions of the physical effect which words and aspect can have upon others. This allows for a continuous musical interaction between characters, and ensures the effective musical and physical dramatization of emotional impact. At the beginning of the tale, Troilus scoffs at concerns of love. When he gazes upon Criseyde, however, he is immediately struck: "And upon cas bifel that thorugh a route/His eye percede, and so depe it wente,/Til on Criseyde it smot, and ther it stente" (1.271–3). As a result of this gaze, Troilus "wax therwith astoned" (1.274). He later gives way to lengthy effusions of love. When the two lovers hear of Criseyde's imminent departure, Criseyde exclaims, "O Jove, I deye, and mercy I beseche!": "And therewithal hire face/Upon his brest she leyde and loste speche" (4.1149–50). This physical and vocal reaction causes Troilus not only to grieve for Criseyde by physically attempting to bring her back to life, but also to sing:

"his song ful ofte is 'weylaway!'" (4.1166). Such description of emotional reaction allows for a musical emphasis of the encounter, and for exaggerated melodramatic gesture characteristic of grand opera.

The source also invites conventional dramatic adaptation in its overall structure. The work is separated into five equal parts, each of which contains an introductory section and a concluding section that sums up preceding action and its moral or narrative importance. This division allows for dramatic adaptation into acts. The third section ends, for example, with a summary of the narrative direction of the tale and the emotional state of its characters. It also contains a concluding image easily translatable into a final tableau before a curtain fall: "My thridde bok now ende ich in this wyse,/And Troilus in lust and in quiete/Is with Criseyde, his owen herte swete" (3.1818–20). The opera takes advantage of this narrative division: the ending of the first act corresponds with the end of the second section of *Troilus and Criseyde*, in which Troilus offers a prayer to Aphrodite. The end of the second act concludes with Troilus, alone after a passionate scene with Cressida. This dramatization of the ultimate solitude of the hero and his desire for Cressida corresponds with the ending of each section of Chaucer's tale.

Each of these sections further invites dramatic adaptation by establishing a narrative pace. The first section ends with, "Now lat us stynte of Troilus a stounde,/ That fareth lik a man that hurt is soore" (1.1086–7). The pace is deliberate, inviting the reader to continue in the narrative and allow events to be revealed. The second section escalates this pace by noting that Troilus is now in a quandary and must pray to the God of love for the first time: "O myghty God, what shel he seye?" (2.1757). The third section ends with a "calm before the storm" soon dispelled in book four, which foregoes any narrative reflection. Instead, it contains a description of Troilus' departure from the room; this is the first time that a book has ended with the absence of its protagonist, and the effect is to create a sense of narrative momentum and emotional urgency: "For whan he saugh that she ne myghte dwelle,/Which that his soule out of his herte rente,/Withouten more out of the chaumbre he wente" (4.1699–1701). This sense of urgency is immediately continued in the next section as the narrator conveys the significance of his forthcoming narrative: "Aprochen gan the fatal destyne/That Joves hath in disposicioun" (5.1–2).

The escalation of narrative pace in the original source allowed Hassall and Walton to translate this urgency into their work. The opera focuses on the relationship between Troilus and Cressida throughout, and signals this focus from the beginning by omitting an overture. The initial pace of the first act is deliberate, allowing for the appearance of Calkas and a lengthy initial exchange between the hero and the heroine. The act escalates in passion and rhetoric as Cressida contemplates Troilus as a match, Troilus reveals Calkas' treachery, Pandarus hands him the token scarf, and Troilus sings an exultant hymn to Aphrodite. The act ends with this hymn, followed by three orchestral swells and a brief percussive pattern halted by a strong chordal statement. In its presentation of immediate passion, its rhythmic suggestion of energy, and its climactically enforced ending, the end to the first act effectively mirrors the dramatic pacing invoked within the source.

The opera does not slavishly follow the structure of *Troilus and Criseyde*, but takes advantage of the inherent translatability of its source into conventional operatic set-pieces. It deviates considerably from Chaucer's narrative, for example, when it grants a climactic importance to the consummation of love between Troilus and Cressida. In Chaucer's narrative, Pandarus concocts a scheme by which to persuade Cressida to sleep with Troilus; Troilus rejects this scheme and unites with Cressida only after much banter between the three. The scene is lengthy and emphasizes the role of the pander and the importance of the eventual consummation between the lovers within the context of medieval conventions of courtly love. The opera recognizes the importance of the scene and the need to grant it a dramatic centrality. It does so not by fully translating Chaucer's extended scene into words, however, but by evoking it in an extended orchestral passage. The passage emphasizes the emotional and dramatic import of the encounter between the two lovers rather than the conventions through which that relationship has evolved, and thus maintains the opera's central focus on the love story.

Chaucer's narrative resumes rather anti-climactically with Troilus returning home to muse on the joy of his experience, and Pandarus entering to discuss the evening with Cressida. In contrast, the opera conflates the climax of this section with news of Cressida's imminent departure with the Greeks. The music immediately contrasts the love/storm music of the night with the military drums of the Greeks at day. In so doing, it not only propels the dramatic movement of the opera, but also articulates the two dramatic concerns of love and military duty that underlie the opera.[10] These changes nonetheless establish a forward dramatic momentum to the end of the act which reflects the increased pace and emotional urgency of the end of Chaucer's fourth section.

Thus, despite the clear affinities between the structure, tone, and emotional rhetoric of the original source and conventions of Romantic opera, these affinities necessitate translation. At times, Hassall's attempts at such translation conflict with those of Walton, and reveal inherent differences in operatic approach. As we shall see, although both establish a similar tone at the beginning of the opera, their approach alters significantly when it comes to establishing the central role of the hero. *Troilus and Criseyde* begins by establishing both a tone and a subject for the ensuing narrative:

> The double sorwe of Troilus to tellen,
> That was the kyng Priamus sone of Troye,
> In lovynge, how his aventures fellen
> Fro wo to wele, and after out of joie,
> My purpos is, er that I parte fro ye.
> Thesiphone, thow help me for t'endite
> Thise woful vers, that wepen as I write. (1.1–7)

The narrator identifies the central theme, character, and narrative focus of his tale. These elements are acknowledged by the score's ominous chords and tolling bell,

---

10   The opera is arguably aided in this presentation by the original source, which presents numerous references to Hector and the Greeks without granting them a narrative centrality. Hassall and Walton translate these references effectively onto the stage not by dramatizing the characters, but by evoking the historical culture to which the original source alludes.

which mark the opening of the opera. The fatalism of the original's prologue is suggested by a constant rhythmic percussion below the prayers of the priests and priestesses in the first scene. The libretto similarly emphasizes this fatalism, having the worshippers and bystanders repeatedly sing, "We are accurs'd/We starve, we thirst." Walton grants these lines a musical prominence by having them underlie and gradually escalate beneath the statements of Calkas.

Hassall further emphasizes the opening tone of the source by granting Calkas a speech at the beginning of the opera (excised by Walton when he revised the opera in 1976). The speech is prophetic rather than self-expository, and, although dense in imagery, maintains a narrative impetus that encourages a fast musical pace: "Now, thro' the smoulder looming, see, in the bowl of a tripod,/Crouch'd like a panther, the Prophetess, naked, wound in her tresses,/Swaying in ecstasy, dazed as a drunkard, fill'd with Apollo" (13). Walton's music complements the libretto to ensure that the speech has only the effect of continuing to upset the chorus; Calkas does not wield the musical or dramatic force of Troilus, who enters to disperse the angry crowd both physically and musically.

When Troilus enters, the crowd's musical mantra changes and fades away, emphasizing the hero's centrality. This centrality is elaborated in the libretto, which implicitly associates Troilus with Christ when he sings: "Are you his judge," and, "This is no place of judgment" (16).[11] The libretto emphasizes that Troilus is not only able to disperse a threatening crowd, but that he is also the only character capable of changing the dramatic emphasis of the scene. After the others leave, Troilus reveals his love for Cressida in the first set-piece of the opera. Juxtaposed as it is with Troilus' initial appearance in the role of a leader, the aria adds a complexity to Troilus' character. It emphasizes his poetic ability for romantic effusion, and his ongoing competence as a leader despite his emotional torment:

> Queen of the wine-dark wave,
> Alone I invoke thee.
> How can the anguish of love
> Fail to awake thee? (18)

The speech is clearly constructed as an aria, contrasting with Troilus' unrhyming introductory statement of his love for Cressida. Hassall repeats images and ideas within the speech to allow for the musical repetition characteristic of traditional arias. Troilus invokes Aphrodite, "child of the wine-dark wave," to bring her "fruitful pleasures." He then beseeches her "in majesty riding" to "come shoreward gliding," only to state definitively, "Queen of the wine-dark wave,/Alone I invoke thee" (18–19). The aria is written in rhythmic rhyming verse rich in descriptive imagery and weak in narrative impetus, allowing for a musical evocation of character and emotion. By granting Troilus the first self-expository set-piece of the opera, Hassall ensures that the initial presentation of Calkas does not override the introduction of

---

11 Jesus stops a crowd of scribes and Pharisees from stoning an adulterous woman by stating, "let anyone among you who is without sin be the first to throw a stone at her" (John 8.7).

his hero. In so doing, he allows the narrative focus of the opera to correspond to that initially articulated by its original source.

Walton, however, does not acknowledge this focus in the opera's score. While the music grants Troilus a heroic function in endorsing his ability to stop the crowd, it does not go so far as to mirror the Romantic heroism attributed to Troilus in the libretto. The music for "Child of the wine-dark wave" is emotionally expressive, but no more so than that of Calkas. Furthermore, it is not sufficiently differentiated in tone, key, or rhythm from the (recitative) text which precedes it as to have the effect of an aria, rather than a minor lyrical song. The setting of the words takes no advantage of the textual repetition for musical embellishment; instead, Walton invests the aria with a generic lyrical tone that neither alters with the text's change from invocation to anguish nor attempts to evoke individual character. By having Troilus sing within a relatively limited range and by restricting that singing to complement the rhythmic and harmonic regularity established by the orchestra, Walton does not allow him the melodic distinction characteristic of the Romantic hero. Furthermore, by using lush strings and harp arpeggios indiscriminately to define the tone of the piece, Walton conforms the style of the music less to that of Romantic opera than to that of popular musicals. In so doing, he not only negates the centrality of Troilus' dilemma, but effectively diminishes any interest which the audience might have in the hero's character. Troilus comes across not as a hero in the throes of love, but as a man capable of singing a lyrical song.

Indeed, despite the condemnation of the opera as Romantic in style and theme, much of *Troilus and Cressida* ultimately resists such classification. Traditional grand opera consists of strong, heroic characters distinguished by their ability to transcend generic musical and social expectations. The grand opera tenor can sing in a higher range and more loudly than his fellow tenors, and this ability is consistent with the overwhelming force of his passion. The arias of the protagonists in Romantic operas are therefore distinct from the music of other characters. Furthermore, their music demands a virtuosity of performance that exceeds any previous motivic introduction of musical material. The passion between the hero and the heroine need not be delineated in order to be credible. As the only characters capable of expressing the heights of romantic passion, the Romantic hero and heroine transcend other characters and situations through the means by which they express that passion; their compatibility (and essential equality) is neither social nor intellectual, but musical.

Because Walton does not grant a musical distinction to his hero, however, Troilus comes across as unsuitable for his beloved. Both Troilus and Cressida have significantly more to sing than other characters, but Troilus' musical material does not elevate him in terms of vocal virtuosity, melodic forcefulness, or emotional power. Furthermore, Troilus is essentially indistinguishable musically from other characters and from the orchestra which defines rather than complements his mode of self-expression. Indeed, Troilus only achieves full musical lyricism and emotional conviction when he sings with Cressida. In "We were alone and then we were together," Troilus sings in unison with Cressida and with the orchestra, indicating the ability of the lovers to subsume all anxieties (be they musical or social) in the power of love. The singing is strongly underscored by the orchestra (rather than undermined or overpowered) to produce one of the more authentically "Romantic" set-pieces of the opera, and a convincing dramatization of the strength of love. Because Troilus only achieves such musical force in these duets, however, he becomes comparatively inconsequential as an individual character. Although Walton evokes the passionate tone of Romantic opera in his orchestra and in his love-duets, he rarely grants that tone a dramatic justification in his solo vocal writing for Troilus. As a result of this lack of musical individualization, Troilus comes across as unworthy of his status as a grand opera tenor, and infinitely unworthy of his heroine.

Troilus' final set-piece, "Sooner would leafless boughs," marks an important exception to this otherwise minimalizing treatment of the hero. As in "Child of the wine-dark wave," Troilus' singing is characterized by lyrical phrasing marked by gently rhythmic orchestral punctuation. Unlike the earlier aria, however, "Sooner" evolves musically. Troilus changes tempo as he sings "thro' the dark I saw you"; this change notably precipitates a change in orchestration as winds enter to reinforce Troilus' rhythmic and melodic line. The orchestration varies according to the experiences of which Troilus sings; when he sings of the flower "becoming" Cressida's cheek, the transformation is marked by a briefly prominent French horn theme. Walton has Troilus sing the word "yearning" twice and echoes each iteration with the orchestra, melodically evoking the separation of the lovers which Troilus feels to be over, but the audience knows only to be prolonged. This musical and textual wistfulness is immediately contrasted with a vocal and orchestral crescendo as Troilus sings emphatically and passionately of the end of his separation from Cressida. Coming as it does after a musical emphasis on yearning, however, the conclusion acquires a tragic resonance which Walton underscores by having Troilus sing his last line, "we did but dream the solitude between," with minimal orchestral accompaniment and in a legato, declamatory style that prefigures Troilus' ultimate solitude.

Despite this musical elevation towards the end of the opera, Walton does not grant his hero a consistently noble status to equal that of his heroine. "Sooner" comes across as stylistically incompatible with the opera's musical characterization of Troilus. Indeed, in the context of the opera, the musical characterization of Troilus' solitude through minimal melody and orchestral accompaniment underlines the hero's essential lack of musical individuality. The aria is sung just before Troilus discovers the betrayal of Cressida. As a result, its ultimate effect is less to reinforce the Romantic nobility of the hero than to suddenly grant him a heroic status in order to elevate the subsequent scene to a credibly tragic level.

Given that Walton conceived of the opera primarily as a love story, the greater musical strength of Troilus and Cressida when together than that of Troilus alone might seem compatible with the overall theme of the work. The opera is problematic, however, in that it grants a greater musical and thematic centrality to the character of Cressida than it does to Troilus. By allowing Cressida a self-aware final aria and implicitly contrasting that final aria with Troilus' blissfully ignorant final set-piece, both Walton and Hassall structurally undermine the heroic status of Troilus and grant a central role to their heroine. Furthermore, Walton's musical writing for Cressida is consistently more sophisticated than it is for Troilus. In Cressida's aria, "Slowly it all comes back," Walton establishes the musical and dramatic status of the heroine. Unlike Troilus' vocal line, Cressida's melody moves through a variety of powerful emotional states, at times complementing, at times conflicting, and at times unifying with a continuously commenting orchestral presence. Coming as it does as the first set-piece to follow "Child of the wine-dark wave," "Slowly" simultaneously enforces the heroic status of Cressida and comparatively demeans that of the hero.

Although Walton failed to do justice to Hassall's clearly intended aria in "Child of the wine-dark wave," Hassall also lessens the stature of his hero in favor of elevating that of Cressida. The words that Hassall provides for Troilus are fitting for a generic Romantic hero in love. In contrast, Hassall's characterization of Cressida is considerably more complex, and allows for Walton's greater musical emphasis. In "Slowly," Cressida sings not only of love, but also of her desertion at the hands of her father, the rejection which she feels from her people, and her conviction that the gods would disapprove of her union with Troilus:

> I'm alone, defenceless.
> What strength have I but love,
> love deep as death, but weak against the world?
> ....
> Forsaken by Troilus, threaten'd by my father,
> tempted by the gods!
> All goad me on one headlong way. (57)

Cressida's text is characterized by a constant fatalism. While Troilus sings a thankful hymn to Aphrodite proclaiming, "in thy name shall I triumph," Cressida sings forebodingly to prefigure the tragedy to come:

> Troilus and Cressida. ...
> The sound of our names together
> is the sound of a rushing wind.
> Unknown is the love, and deeper than the sea,
> that can withstand the gods. (30)

The heroine's ability to foreshadow tragedy grants her a depth of introspection and awareness that distances her from her suitor. Although Troilus' aria similarly deals with individual torment, Troilus expresses only romantic anguish. Cressida, however, has more than one concern. While Troilus is new to love, Cressida has already "tasted" life and love: "Both were bitter" (19). As if to emphasize this difference in experience and knowledge, Troilus sings in rhyming verse that invites Walton's regular musical accompaniment. In contrast, Cressida sings in unrhymed and rhythmically disjunct text so as to allow for a more complex musical treatment. Aside from being more experienced and fatalistic than Troilus, Cressida is also more introspective. She recounts a dream in which she has seen herself abandoned by both her father and Troilus. She sings of Troilus as "blotted out, blurred by disfiguring smoulder" and of her father as a "towering, wavering shade" (24). This visual uncertainty mirrors Cressida's musical and psychological instability in these passages. Unlike Troilus, she comes to a tragic conclusion: "No, you must never, never love me./They would destroy you" (25). Cressida's nebulous fear and fatalism in both libretto and score distance her from her beloved and evoke comparison more with the anxieties of the modernist heroine of Schoenberg's *Erwartung* than those of *Aida*. This stylistic discrepancy immediately weakens the plausibility of the compatibility of the hero and heroine; Cressida is musically, thematically, and stylistically removed from the concerns of romantic love as articulated by Troilus. By making Troilus the musical and psychological unequal of his beloved, Walton and Hassall ensure that Cressida is rendered the dramatic and musical center of the opera.

By granting this greater musical and textual complexity to their heroine, Walton and Hassall deviate from traditional presentations of male protagonists in grand opera. Furthermore, they arguably deviate from the central narrative concern of *Troilus and Criseyde*, identified by the narrator as "the double sorwe of Troilus" (1.1). A closer examination suggests that this discrepancy results from the ultimate resistance of that source to the thematic and narrative conventions of Romantic opera.

Although *Troilus and Criseyde* is essentially about the relationship between Troilus and Criseyde, it develops this relationship in terms that problematize modern translation. As Hassall himself noted, courtly love constitutes "a code of manners between the sexes too remote from present-day custom for its followers easily to engage the sympathy and understanding of a modern audience" (*Troilus and Cressida* 4). The essential discrepancy between this code of manners and modern expectations lies in Chaucer's depiction of Troilus. Like heroes expected of grand opera and high tragedy, Troilus is of a noble family, is accomplished in battle, and is universally recognized for his heroism. Unlike a grand opera hero, however, Troilus never exhibits these qualities in the narrative. Although the narrator recounts Troilus proving himself in battle, he never describes these exploits or their reception; instead, he focuses his account upon Troilus' love for Criseyde. Troilus is thus in a constant state of emotional weakness in the narrative, alternately moaning, weeping, and bewailing a misfortune which is yet to come. His despair is never alleviated by a reinforcement of his military heroism. Indeed, despite his apparent ability in battle, Troilus gives way to despair instead of attempting to rescue his beloved or prevent her departure. This despair is such that, after Cressida's departure, Troilus goes so far as to make his funeral arrangements, claiming, "the sorwe/Which that I drye I may nat longe endure./I trowe I shal nat lyven tyl to-morwe" (5.295–7). As C. S. Lewis, the primary critical authority upon whom Hassall depended, notes, "the drawing of Troilus' character is no principal part of Chaucer's purpose"; Troilus is merely "an embodiment of the medieval ideal of lover and warrior." This medieval concept clearly contrasts with modern expectations of heroic lovers: Troilus' "humility, his easy tears, and his unabashed self-pity in adversity will not be admired in our own age." As a result, "of such a character, so easily made happy and so easily broken, there can be no tragedy in the Greek or in the modern sense" (195).

Ultimately, then, Walton's weak musical treatment of Troilus offers a modern reception of the hero's stature in the original source. Hassall's libretto, however, aspires to translate Troilus' character into a new, modern idiom. Hassall writes conventional speeches for Troilus just as Chaucer ensures Troilus' function as a conventional medieval lover. The speeches of Troilus in the opera are therefore conventional to Romantic drama rather than to medieval courtly romance. Walton, however, does not recognize the translation effected by the libretto. Instead, the opera ultimately presents two conflicting images of Troilus, one as a weak secondary character, and the other as a heroic male protagonist. Walton is simultaneously faithful and unfaithful both to the source and the libretto, failing to differentiate between two different representations of a "conventional" hero.

The essential weakness of Troilus in the opera allows for the domination of Cressida, which is also evident in the original source. Troilus' function in Chaucer's narrative is essentially archetypal, but the vacillation and apparent inconsistency of Criseyde is one of the most memorable aspects of the tale. Criseyde is not a conventional tragic heroine; some have found her to be a victim, some a coquette, and some a passionate lover. That Criseyde appears to be all three at various points in the narrative is indisputable. Unlike Troilus, who constantly confides his innermost thoughts to Pandarus, Criseyde has no such confidant. Indeed, the primary challenge to anyone attempting to depict Criseyde as a conventional romantic heroine is that she is difficult to understand and define.

Chaucer's narrator seems deliberately to emphasize the enigmatic nature of his heroine. When Diomedes first makes his suit, he begins by telling Criseyde that she cannot spare the Trojans (5.912–17). Although Troilus remains fixed in her heart (5.953), Criseyde is practical in her realization that her people might be defeated. She therefore states, "Herafter, when ye wonnen han the town,/Peraventure so it happen may/That whan I se that nevere yit I say/Than wol I werke that I nevere wroughte!" (5.990–93). She promises, "If that I sholde of any Grek han routhe,/It sholde be youreselven, by my trouthe!" (1000–1001). Here, Criseyde exhibits the fear of abandonment and lack of protection which Lewis has defined as her tragic flaw.[12]

This fear is never explicitly defined, however, and no explanation is given as to why Criseyde changes so quickly from her resolution to await the outcome of Troy to decide that night that "she was allone and hadde nede/Of frendes help" (5.1026–7). Indeed, the narrator later contradicts this account by saying, "how longe it was bytwene/That [Criseyde] forsok [Troilus] for this Diomede,/Ther is non auctour telleth it, I wene" (5.1086–8). The narrator tells us that not only does Criseyde succumb to Diomedes the next day, but that she gives him the brooch of Troilus: "and that was litel nede" (5.1040). The narrator thus complicates any simple understanding of Criseyde's motivation by emphasizing the way in which Criseyde surrenders more than necessary. He then juxtaposes this action with Criseyde's lengthy farewell to Troilus in which she remorsefully acknowledges the extent of her treachery and the worthiness of Troilus to predict her future reputation: "Allas, of me, unto the worldes ende,/Shal neyther ben ywriten nor ysonge/No good word, for thise bokes wol me shende" (5.1058–60).

This account of Criseyde's treachery is understandable on one level and elliptical on another. Why, we seem invited to ask, should Criseyde give the brooch to Diomedes if she still loves Troilus? The narrator is apparently at pains to emphasize

---

12 "It is Fear—fear of loneliness, of old age, of death, of love, and of hostility." From this flaw springs "the pitiable longing, more childlike than womanly, for protection, for some strong and stable thing that will hide her away and take the burden from her shoulders" (185).

that he cannot offer any explanation. Referring constantly to other sources for authority ("I fynde ek in stories elleswhere" [5.1044]; "trewely, the storie telleth us" [5.1051]), the narrator concludes that no book can explain or document Criseyde's change of mind: "Take every man now to his bokes heede,/He shal no terme fynden, out of drede" (5.1089–90). He emphasizes his own unclear understanding of the heroine's state of mind: "Criseyde upon a day, for routhe—/I take it so—touchyng al this matere,/Wrot hym ayeyn" (5.1587–9). The narrator's declared uncertainty about Criseyde's actions and motivations ensures that the reader is never entirely aware of whether or not Criseyde has truly abandoned Troilus when she replies to his first letter with "many promises."

Perhaps because he is unable to explain his heroine fully, the narrator only offers incomplete accounts of Criseyde's words. In the letter she writes to Troilus, Criseyde claims that she is restricted by her fear that she might be discovered. She is unable to offer Troilus or the reader any direct statement of her motivations or emotional allegiance. Not only does she write in fear, but she claims not to be able to write well; what she writes cannot be seen as an adequate expression of what she would like to say. Thus, although she concludes, "Th'entente is al, and nat the lettres space" (5.1630), Criseyde reveals very little. Troilus himself initially deems the letter "straunge" (5.1632), but slowly comes to understand the treachery of Criseyde. The enigmatic nature of the letter, however, ensures that Troilus' understanding is less a result of the letter than of Troilus' own willingness to accept his earlier presumption of Criseyde's imminent betrayal. Because Criseyde never offers a complete explanation or makes her treachery absolutely clear in the letter, her character remains ambiguous. The narrative promptly leaves Criseyde after the writing of this letter, to describe the ultimate fate of Troilus. In so doing, it not only suggests the greater importance of Troilus as a protagonist, but also the essential indecipherability of the heroine. All the while, the narrator highlights the evasive nature of his entire narrative.

Such indecipherability is difficult, if not impossible, to translate into traditional opera. The emphasis on direct, passionate expression in Romantic opera thwarts any dramatization of the discursive complexities of a narrator, or of a protagonist incapable of self-expression. Criseyde is necessarily defined musically whenever she sings; such definition demands a certainty of emotional state. Walton and Hassall clearly accepted Lewis's evaluation of the source as "a great poem in praise of love" (197). In order to dramatize the source as a tale of thwarted love, Walton and Hassall had to grant Criseyde a more definitive and sympathetic portrayal. They therefore change the tale's ending: Evadne and Calkas deceive Cressida so as to allow her to die tragic and blameless.

This tendency to "explain" the heroine, however, thwarts the attempted conventionality of the opera's narrative. Hassall claims in his preface that the opera's Criseyde is wholly indebted to her characterization by Chaucer, and cites Lewis's identification of Criseyde's "ruling passion" of fear as "having provided the first hint for the subject of the opera" (3). In the psychological depiction of his heroine, Hassall shifts his dramatic focus away from offering a conventional love story to dramatizing an individual neurosis. Because Cressida is not responsible for her betrayal of Troilus in the opera, this emphasis on her fear distracts from, rather than helps to explain, the heroine's relationship with the hero. The libretto in particular grants a greater narrative importance to Cressida that is independent of her relationship with Troilus. Ironically, this shifting focus to some extent reflects the original's overt vacillations about its heroine.

The opera's fascination with the character of Criseyde can also be seen as a reaction to popular understandings and representations of Chaucer's heroine. Hassall had stated explicitly and emphatically that the opera is not indebted to Shakespeare's representation of the tale. The choice of *Troilus and Criseyde* as a source mediates between two instincts, one towards tradition and the other towards contemporary relevance. By choosing Chaucer's source rather than Shakespeare's play, Walton and Hassall were able to remove themselves from comparison both to (Italian) Romantic Shakespearean opera and to the adaptations of Vaughan Williams and Delius. No matter the critical success of Verdi's *Otello* or *Falstaff*, operatic treatments of Shakespeare have generally been derided for their inability to represent faithfully the psychological and linguistic complexities of the original play. Nonetheless, Walton's decision to write a grand opera invoked the tradition of Romantic opera with its characteristically lavish spectacle and heightened (heterosexual) passion. Perhaps in recognition of such potential criticism, Hassall associated the opera with a more esoteric text. By affiliating himself with a medieval verse narrative rather than a Renaissance drama, Hassall was better able to counter accusations of Walton's stylistic regression as well as to justify changes made to the original for the sake of generic translation. The choice of a literary source that had gained considerable intellectual status with academics and literary figures could only have helped to signal the contemporary relevance of the source and, by implication, that of the opera itself.

Hassall is careful to further emphasize that contemporary relevance by enumerating a number of "necessary" differences between the source and the opera. As he "lifted the story out of the Middle Ages and retold it in a setting of legendary Troy, all that was essentially Chaucerian fell away" (*Troilus and Cressida* 4). Hassall determined to underscore the classical setting of the narrative; in order to do so, he placed a greater emphasis on the Trojan war and on the political implications of the treason of Calkas. The "order of Chaucer's events [was] rearranged, new details [were] introduced, and the whole compressed within much narrower limits of time" so that the latter half of Act III "bears no relation to the medieval poem" (4). Both the text and "some of the action would strike Chaucer as not only unfamiliar but foreign to the spirit of his poem" (4). Recognizing that a lack of emphasis on the rules of courtly love would render Chaucer's Pandarus difficult to comprehend, Hassall determined to give Pandarus "a new justification" (4). In declaring some necessary distance between his source and libretto, Hassall points to the libretto as an interpretative drama, and thus to the scholarly validity of his own role.

Significantly, the changes enumerated by Hassall correspond to differences between Chaucer's work and the Shakespeare play against which Hassall so continuously protests. Hassall's clear awareness of Shakespeare's version necessitates a consideration of the opera as a potential response both to Chaucer and to Shakespeare. Although Shakespeare's play is indebted to a number of sources,[13] Hassall seems to have regarded it as a direct adaptation of Chaucer's narrative with which his own might be compared, and thus as a rival adaptation.

Shakespeare's Cressida is cold, callous, and inexplicably disloyal to Troilus; her treachery comes across as inevitable and consistent with her character. Ulysses notes, "There's a language in her eye, her cheek, her lip;/ Nay, her foot speaks. Her wanton spirits look out/ At every joint and motive of her body" (4.5.64–6). Without any overt encouragement, Cressida strokes Diomedes' cheek, calls him a "sweet honey Greek" (5.2.19), and offers him the sleeve of Troilus. She then appears to vacillate in her action so that even Diomedes states, "I do not like this fooling" (5.2.118). Calling Diomedes back, Cressida invokes a farewell to Troilus which is less of an envoi than a self-incriminating articulation of popular understandings of her character (and possibly of women in general):

> Troilus, farewell. One eye yet looks on thee,
> But with my heart the other eye doth see.
> Ah, poor our sex! This fault in us I find:
> The error of our eye directs our mind.
> What error leads must err. O then, conclude
> Minds sway'd by eyes are full of turpitude. (5.2.126–31)

Apparently ever-mindful of his audience's negative preconception of Cressida, Shakespeare caters to that understanding. Indeed, the play constantly reiterates the potential for Cressida to become an exemplary type. Troilus claims that after poets have exhausted similes and metaphors for truth, "'As true as Troilus' shall crown up the verse" (3.2.172). In contrast, Cressida asserts her faithfulness by dwelling upon her possible immortalization as unfaithful; if she were to be false, "let them say, to stick the heart of falsehood,/'As false as Cressid'" (3.2.186–7). Later, she states, "Make Cressid's name the very crown of falsehood/If ever she leave Troilus!" (4.2.104–5). By having Cressida proclaim the very titles with which she will inevitably be associated, Shakespeare indicates his awareness of and ultimate conformity to popular assumptions about his heroine.

In much the same way as Forster will claim to have "rescued Vere" from Melville in his adaptation of *Billy Budd*, Hassall can be seen to have tried to rescue his heroine from any association with Shakespeare. Although Hassall articulates this rescue in terms of a faithfulness to Chaucer, his response is less to evoke Chaucer's potentially culpable Criseyde than to defend her by granting his heroine an incontestable, unambiguous portrayal. The opera's Cressida is fundamentally different from Shakespeare's fickle heroine in her fear, integrity, and passion. Ironically, however,

---

13 Shakespeare is likely to have been familiar with Chaucer's *Troilus and Criseyde* only as disseminated through Henryson's *The Testament of Cressid*, a poem assumed to have been written by Chaucer that continues the tale to reduce Cressida to a beggar and a leper. The numerous treatments of the story during the sixteenth century (not the least of which was Lydgate's *The Siege of Troy*, from which Shakespeare derived details for the military plot) ensured that "by Shakespeare's time the story had become common property of the people, known undoubtedly to many who had never read Chaucer or Henryson" (Campbell 324).

the very lack of ambiguity with which those characteristics are presented in the opera render Hassall's Cressida comparable more with the heroine of Shakespeare's play than Chaucer's enigmatic Criseyde.

Hassall was the only collaborator to deny the influence of Shakespeare on the opera. Indeed, Thomas Beecham apparently suggested Shakespeare's play as a source for an opera to Walton in the 1930s, and Walton's interest in the subject would have been further encouraged by the enthusiasm of his close friend Constant Lambert for the play (S. Price 184–5).[14] Whereas Hassall claimed that Lewis's chapter on Chaucer provided the first hint for the opera, Walton himself did not read that chapter until 1952, when he described it as "extremely interesting" (qtd. in S. Price 195). Indeed, it is doubtful that Walton read *Troilus and Criseyde* in the original Middle English; he probably came to the source through the scholar Nevill Coghill, whose oral radio translations of the poem were sent to him by Hassall (along with Hassall's program notes) in 1949 (S. Price 204–5). Walton's apparently lesser concern with adapting the original source faithfully is revealed in much of his correspondence with Hassall, who frequently responds to the composer's objections by reminding him of the narrative's origins in medieval literature. When Walton reported Ernest Irving's criticism that the libretto should mirror Greek drama by placing the greatest emphasis on the role of the gods, Hassall had to remind him, "we must not lose sight of the fact that this is a story of medieval origin and character which the author has set in Troy" (qtd. in S. Price 194).

This apparent difference in narrative allegiance is very obvious in the opera's treatment of Pandarus. In Chaucer's narrative, Pandarus acts as the go-between for his niece and his friend, alternately participating empathetically in the sorrows and worries of Troilus, and gently admonishing him to put events in perspective. Pandarus is both a participant and gently ironic commentator upon narrative events. When Pandarus hears that Troilus is grieved, he "neight malt for wo and routhe" (1.582). When he hears of Cressida's fate, he is himself grieved and "Gan wel neigh wood out of his wit to breyde" (4.348). He weeps together with Troilus: "sorwful Pandare, of pitee,/Gan for to wepe as tendreliche as [Troilus]" (4.368–9). At the same time, Pandarus is much more practical and less inclined towards emotional exhortation than Troilus. Calling Troilus a "fol" (1.618) at the outset, he offers his help and admonishes his friend for his excessive reaction:

Lat be thy wepyng and thi drerynesse,
And lat us lissen wo with oother speche;
So may thy woful tyme seme lesse.
Delyte nat in wo thi wo to seche,
As don thise foles that hire sorwes eche
With sorwe, whan thei han mysaventure,
And listen naught to seche hem other cure. (1.701–7)

---

14 S. Price offers a convincing comparison of the action of some scenes in the opera to those in Shakespeare, and suggests that the later denial of Shakespeare's influence was due less to Walton's appreciation of Chaucer's narrative than to his desire to distance himself from comparison to Berlioz's *Les Troyens* or "the decidedly colloquial Shakespearean operas of the pre-war years" (186).

Although Troilus accepts his friend's advice temporarily, he is in such a constant state of grief and apparent weakness throughout the entire tale that Pandarus finally exclaims:

> Artow in Troie, and hast not hardyment
> To take a womman which that loveth the
> And wolde hireselven ben of thyn assent?
> Now is nat this a nyce vanitee?
> Ris up anon, and lat this wepyng be,
> And kith thow art a man; for in this houre
> I wol ben ded, or she shal bleven oure. (4.533–9)

Pandarus bewails what he perceives to be Troilus's unnecessary despair: "Whi, Troilus, what thinkestow to doone?/Hastow swich lust to ben thyn owen fo?/What, parde, yet is nat Criseyde ago!" (4.1088–90). With Pandarus' continued admonitions, the reader is made to appreciate the heroism to which Troilus might have aspired and through which he might have avoided the tragedy of Cressida's apparent treachery. When his character is contrasted with the insight, compassion, practicality, and irony of his friend Troilus becomes even weaker as a credible hero of a grand opera. The complexity of Pandarus and of his relationship with the hero are of significantly greater interest to the modern reader than the relative simplicity of Troilus.

Subsequent adaptations of *Troilus and Criseyde* have attempted to unify the narrative by diminishing the moral importance of Pandarus. If one is to write a conventional love story, one cannot allow the hero to be overwhelmed by his best friend. By defining Chaucer's Pandarus somewhat reductively as a "light-hearted middle-aged schemer" (3), Hassall ensures that his interpretation be affiliated with Chaucer's positive representation. At the same time, he resists acknowledging the potential narrative centrality of Pandarus that a thoroughly faithful interpretation would necessitate.

In the libretto the relationship between Pandarus and Troilus is close, but is not granted the narrative prominence accorded by the original source. Pandarus' text is distinguished by a whimsical tone and chattiness to evoke simultaneously his "light-heartedness" and his inability to aspire to the level of emotional expression of Troilus or Cressida. When Troilus confronts Pandarus in the heat of emotion, Pandarus responds in moderated, sensible tones that mirror the practicality of Chaucer's character:

> Cooler, dear Prince. Calm down. I will explain.
> I've always said
> there's nothing like a sharp misunderstanding
> for bringing young lovers together. (41)

When Troilus and Cressida are united in this scene, Pandarus is simultaneously pleased and distanced from their passion, again resembling Chaucer's well-intentioned, ironizing character:

> Oh, this is going finely,
> if not in all particulars

according to plan. He seems to have reached
the kneeling stage.
I will fetch him a cushion. (41)

Hassall recognized that a direct translation of Pandarus' character into the opera
would have been confusing: Pandarus' function is understandable only in terms of
medieval convention (or in a reinvention of the relationship between Troilus and
Pandarus that would conflict with Walton's social conservatism). Also, the essential
nature of Troilus differs between libretto and source. Hassall translates Pandarus'
good nature and practicality into the opera, but abstains from granting that good
nature the emotional profundity with which it is presented in the original text.

In contrast to Hassall's sensitive approach, Walton treats Pandarus much more
broadly. Pandarus' music is characterized by a recognizably comic pattern. This
recurring music to some extent mirrors Hassall's stylistic differentiation of Pandarus
from the hero and the heroine. Because the music is comic, however, it distances
Pandarus even further from Troilus and Cressida by suggesting the character's
inability to relate to emotional turmoil on any level. When Pandarus sings, "He seems
to have reached/the kneeling stage," he comes across not as Hassall's kind, light-
hearted uncle, but as a comic figure ignorant of the passion which he is observing.
This musical treatment is essentially unfaithful to both the libretto and the original
source. Furthermore, it ensures a musical individuation to Pandarus uncharacteristic
of the musical treatment of any of the other characters. Pandarus gains a prominence
in the opera that occasionally undermines the centrality of Troilus and Cressida, and
the thematic coherence of the opera as a whole.

Ultimately, Walton's comic treatment of Pandarus is indebted less to Chaucer's
source than it is to Shakespeare's play. Shakespeare's Pandarus is a lowly procurer;
he delights in repetitive word games, he takes no emotional part in the services
which he performs, and he demonstrates a constant foolish selfishness:

> A whoreson tisick, a whoreson rascally tisick so
> troubles me, and the foolish fortune of this girl, and what one
> thing, what another, that I shall leave you one o' th's days.
> And I have a rheum in mine eyes too, and such an ache
> in my bones, that unless a man were curst, I cannot tell
> what to think on't. (5.3.112–17)

In contrast to the other characters in the play, Pandarus speaks in prose. This
simultaneous demeaning and differentiation of Pandarus in his language mirrors the
comic musical treatment granted Pandarus in the opera.

Furthermore, although he is not a protagonist of the play, Shakespeare's
Pandarus attracts considerable attention. At the end of the play, Troilus dismisses
him ineffectually by twice saying, "Hence ...! Ignomy and shame/Pursue thy life
and live aye with thy name!" (5.3.125–6, 5.10.34–5). The very fact that a central
character should pay so much attention to Pandarus at the end of the play ensures
him some dramatic prominence. Pandarus is allowed the final words of the drama
as he comically attempts to configure himself as a tragic hero: "Your eyes half out,
weep out at Pandar's fall" (5.10.48). Despite the efforts of Hassall to mirror the

subtlety of his original source, Walton's comic stylistic differentiation of Pandarus attracts attention to the character in much the same way as Shakespeare's treatment affords Pandarus an undue dramatic prominence.

This attention may have been deliberate on Walton's part, and divorced entirely from his dramatic plan. Many have noted Walton's uncharacteristic attention to Pandarus and associated it with his rivalry with Benjamin Britten. Foreman acknowledges the success of "the slightly camp figure of Pandarus" in comparison to other characters ("Walton's Words" 248). Müller claims that whenever Pandarus appears, "the score begins to crackle and sparkle" (92). Dean deems this characterization dramatically compromising: "Pandarus, half comic, half epicene, stands so far apart from the others that he scarcely belongs to the same world, and his habit of repeating his phrases to slightly different notes threatens to become an irritating mannerism" (Rev. of *Troilus and Cressida* 55). Such assessments were based not only on the music granted Pandarus, but also on the original casting of Britten's partner, Peter Pears, in the role. This casting ensured Pandarus a centrality and suggestive complexity not evoked in the libretto. As Milnes notes, the role "speaks volumes about Aldeburgh-Ischia relations (did Pears, whose performance was high camp on a Himalayan scale, know he was being lured into a kind of honey-trap?)" (357).

No matter Walton's motivations for this musical characterization, the opera continues to reflect the effect of Shakespeare's play, particularly in its ending. Shakespeare's primary interest appears to lie in his military setting, specifically the insubordination of Achilles and the attempts of the Greeks to end the war. As much of the play is therefore devoted to scenes between members of the military camps as it is to the encounters between Troilus and Cressida. The play ends with a reinforcement of Troilus' military role at the expense of his romantic endeavors; instead of dwelling on his lost love, Troilus hears of Hector's death and vows to haunt the Greeks "like a wicked conscience still,/That moldeth goblins swift as frenzy's thoughts" (5.10.29–30). By prioritizing the military context, Shakespeare invites his audience to interpret this vow as a military reaction rather than as a manifestation of Troilus' jealousy of Diomedes. The drama does not end with either of the two lovers, but with having Pandarus address all "good traders in the flesh" and "brethren and sisters of the hold-door trade" (5.10.46, 51). By allowing Pandarus to represent the former relationship of the two lovers, Shakespeare ensures that that relationship is seen as peripheral and inferior to the military concerns with which his hero is now occupied. In his prioritization of military concerns, Shakespeare qualifies any narrative primacy to the Troilus-Cressida relationship. No wonder, then, that Hassall should have chosen *Troilus and Criseyde* as his source, with its narrator who claims to serve the servant of the God of Love (1.15).

Nonetheless, the opera in many ways comes closer to achieving the final effect of Shakespeare's play than of Chaucer's narrative. This is a result of the inherent ambiguity of the source, which defies conventional dramatic adaptation. Chaucer's narrator grants his own narrative uncertainty a particular prominence at the end of the tale, undermining any earlier thematic centrality. After receiving Criseyde's final letter, Troilus gives a lengthy speech bewailing his fortune, querying God, and ultimately making a vow: "And certeynly, withouten moore speche,/From hennesforth, as ferforth as I may,/Myn owen deth in armes wol I seche" (5.1716–18).

The narrator then takes over, apparently to offer final narrative details and some personal commentary. He tells of Troilus' exploits, but not in such detail as to grant those exploits a final thematic centrality: "But for that I to writen first bigan/Of his love, I have seyd as I kan—/His worthi dedes, whoso list hem heere,/Rede Dares, he kan telle hem alle ifeere—" (5.1768–71). The narrator then offers a warning to "every lady bright of hewe": "Beth war of men, and herkneth what I seye" (5.1772, 1785). This warning is uncharacteristic of the narrative emphasis on Criseyde's ultimate treachery, and offers a lesson that has not been delineated throughout; it weakens rather than reinforces any central message which the narrator might wish to convey. This final structure therefore creates a series of false endings; the narrator is apparently unable to decide between allowing Troilus to die as a tragic lover, having Troilus conquer his sorrow through military glory, or identifying a didactic function to his tale.

Furthermore, the narrator invites the reader to focus less on the narrative than on the means through which that narrative is conveyed. He calls attention to his role as disseminator of narrated events and attempts to define the literary function of his tale:

> Go, litel bok, go, litel myn tragedye,
> Ther God thi makere yet, er that he dye,
> So sende mygt to make in som comedye!
> But litel book, no makyng thow n'envie,
> But subgit be to alle poesye;
> And kis the steppes where as thow seest pace
> Virgile, Ovide, Omer, Lucan, and Stace. (5.1786–92)

When he later states that he will return to the "purpos" of his "rather speche," the narrator encourages us to identify that central purpose; he is writing both to tell a tale and to give an example of the "diversite/In Englissh and in writyng of oure tonge" (5.1799,1793–94). The tale ends by asserting a Christian didactic function not immediately apparent in the narrative. The reader is thus implicitly invited to appreciate both the plot of the tale and the various literary means through which that tale has been told.

This narrative disruption of any thematic and stylistic cohesion to *Troilus and Criseyde* ensures the significant alterations by Walton and Hassall in their adaptation of the original ending. The opera ends by focusing on the plight of Cressida, rather than Troilus. Instead of being unfaithful, Criseyde is ultimately apotheosized as a wrongly accused Desdemona betrayed by her servants to suffer the wrath of her lover. After Troilus dies at the treacherous hands of Calkas, Diomedes turns in anger to Cressida, telling his followers, "As for that whore, and her comely graces,/she shall remain with *us*. She has her uses" (69). Rather than suffer indignity at the hands of Diomedes, Cressida lifts the scarf of Troilus, reminder of the noble passion in which she once participated. Winding the scarf around Troilus' sword, Cressida transforms herself from hapless victim to heroic decider of her own fate: "never with scorn, nor with hate, shall Death receive me" (70). As she sings, the music evokes both the turning of the scarf and Cressida's natural fatalism in its rhythmic accentuation of Cressida's gently lyrical melodic line. Cressida repeats the final lines of the aria, "you ... may yet forgive me," allowing her voice to trail gently away in an apparent musical evocation of this wistful hope. As the entrance of the soldiers is signaled by harsh, discordant orchestration, Cressida initially shrinks back in fear. Slowly, however, she summons the heroic courage she implicitly gained in the turning of the scarf. The orchestra introduces a rapidly escalating rhythmic pattern. At the height of this pattern, Cressida sings lines reminiscent of Romantic military heroes in a melodically and rhythmically agitated vocal line: "Open the gates./We are riding together into Troy" (71). The next line, "And by this sign I am still your Cressida," is infused with a lush string orchestration and sung with a contrasting melodic and rhythmic certainty to emphasize the romantic strength of Cressida's final passionate act. As she stabs herself, the music gives way to this lyrical orchestration, slowly decreasing in volume. This decrease is marked by a final percussive chordal statement. The opera emphasizes the definitive, almost military strength of Cressida's final act.

The opera therefore ends by decisively dramatizing the heroic courage and determination of its central protagonist. In so doing, it differs significantly from the narrative uncertainty and ambiguous focus of its original source. Indeed, in its presentation of the firm conviction of a transformed character, it comes closest to mirroring the end of Shakespeare's play. In the play, Troilus is no longer weakened by his love for the unfaithful Cressida, and has summoned courage and determination to fight the Greeks. In much the same way, the opera's Cressida allows her love for Troilus to conquer her fear of others and motivate her to perform a final heroic and tragic act. Both characters overcome fear, both overcome the treachery of others, and both demonstrate and articulate a heroism appropriate to the conventions of the dramatic form in which they are presented.

No matter their denial of its influence, Hassall and Walton provoke comparison of their opera to Shakespeare's play in their use of conventions of grand opera. In their evocation of a heroine with easily identifiable characteristics, a nation preoccupied with war, and a comic character oblivious to the conflict with which he is surrounded, they seem to offer a musical rewriting of Shakespeare's adaptation informed by Chaucer's source. By simplifying much of the structural complexity and thematic and narrative idiosyncrasies of the original text, Hassall mirrors the process by which Shakespeare (through his sources) presented a tale of military honor, betrayal, and comic ignorance. The music and text of the operatic *Troilus and Cressida* avoid the direct expression of a clear emotional and narrative centre, a criticism frequently made of the Shakespeare play. The opera further mirrors Shakespeare in its thematic inconsistency and narrative emphasis on individual psychological conflicts and minor characters.

Despite these similarities between the opera and Shakespeare's drama, Hassall in particular clearly attempted a faithful translation of the original source. Both collaborators wanted to make their source accessible to a modern audience, however, and defined this accessibility in terms of offering a clear presentation of character in keeping with the conventions of Romantic opera. Such a presentation necessitated a resolution of the contradictions and ambiguity within much of the original source.

Ironically, it is in their very attempt to resolve these difficulties that Hassall and Walton come closest to successfully translating the concerns of their source. Although

Troilus is changed from conventional medieval warrior and lover to a conventional Romantic hero, his music does not translate that conventionality into grand opera. Troilus becomes the weak, ineffectual character perceived by modern readers of Chaucer's tale. Furthermore, the opera's broad musical characterization of Pandarus disrupts the thematic and structural clarity to which the libretto aspires, and in so doing mirrors the stylistic discrepancies and vacillations within the original source. *Troilus and Criseyde* problematizes direct translation by containing a narrator who is just as interested in drawing the reader's attention to the telling of his tale as he is in presenting a narrative. The contradiction between Troilus' heroism in the score and his status in the libretto ensures that this narrative anxiety and discursiveness become a prominent, if unwitting, feature of the opera.

Troilus and Cressida does not so much faithfully adapt as legitimately translate many of the central characteristics of Chaucer's narrative into the form of grand opera. This translation is facilitated by tensions between a libretto and score that attempt individually to offer a traditionalist response to the source and its perceived cultural position. Ironically, these tensions and inconsistencies not only ensure a relatively faithful translation of that source, but also align the work with the modernist themes and aesthetics which both collaborators sought to resist.

Precisely because of the tensions between libretto, score, and source, both *Gawain* and *Troilus and Cressida*, despite the very different aims and approaches of their collaborators, manifest a distinctly contemporary approach towards the presentation of narrative. This approach—determined by essential interpretative differences between the authoritative voices of libretto and score—ultimately translates some of the defining characteristics of the original source. It remains to be seen whether operatic adaptations of more recent texts offer a similar approach towards their sources, and what new critical areas of investigation might be offered by texts less distanced by convention, language, and time from their operatic translators.

Chapter 3

The Muddying of the Wells

The majority of modern British operas based upon more contemporary sources avoid adapting "major" works in favor of shorter, more obscure, and intensely psychological narratives. These narratives seem to lend themselves by their very compactness to operatic expansion, and deter the more expansive treatments accorded to works such as *Oliver Twist* or *The Lord of the Rings* in the popular musical. Furthermore, many of these works present characters in the context of a larger social or philosophical emphasis. In so doing, they align themselves with key themes in modern British opera. While Conrad's Marlowe (*Heart of Darkness*) and James's governess (*The Turn of the Screw*) are memorably singular characters, for example, the emotional and stylistic distance with which they are presented in the narrative allows them to be interpreted as representative of particular philosophies or as conflicting archetypes.

Although this emphasis conforms to the perceived thematic concerns of modern British opera, such sources as "Owen Wingrave," *The Turn of the Screw*, and *Billy Budd* (all sources for Benjamin Britten's operas) seem initially to resist adaptation: their narratives are inseparable from the literary style in which that narrative is presented. *The Turn of the Screw*, for example, might appear to be a simple ghost story were it not for the narrative voice in which it is told; the tale is as much about the psychology of the narrator as it is about the fate of Miles and Flora. *Billy Budd* contains a narrator who is at times omniscient, at times maddeningly ignorant, and at times self-professedly discerning in his choice of events to narrate. The novella presents a compelling outer shell of narrative events, but its uncertainty, or willing maintenance of ambiguity, prevents the tale from being read as a "simple story," and has ensured the continuance of heated critical debate.[1]

---

1 Some of these ambiguities arise from the debate over the definitive text of the story. Originating from a short story based upon Melville's prose headnote to an early version of his ballad "Billy in the Darbies," *Billy Budd* was left in a semi-final draft when Melville died in 1891, and Melville's wife herself deemed the story unfinished. Raymond Weaver first published the text in 1924, but, as Stafford has noted, the edition in no way attempted "to render all parts of the manuscript" ("The New *Billy Budd* and the Novelistic Fallacy" 4), nor did the revised version of Weaver's text in 1928. In 1946, William Plomer produced an edition for Lehmann in London, making "a few small emendations" to Weaver's text, and in 1948 F. Barron Freeman published what purported to be a definitive text (including the original ballad and short story, as well as drafts and histories of the text), but this draft was filled with so many errors that it was withdrawn by Harvard University Press and rereleased with revisions in 1953. Other minor revisions were made to this text by Sculley Bradley, Richmond Croom Beatty, and E. Hudson Long (1956), Jay Leyda (Viking, 1952), and Milton Stern (Dutton-Everyman, 1958). In 1962, Hayford and Sealts published their "definitive" edition,

Both *Billy Budd* and Robert Louis Stevenson's *The Beach of Falesá* have been transformed into operas by librettists and composers of significant artistic reputation. They share a similar bibliographic and critical history, a proximity in the date of their original composition, and a complexity of narrative voice.[2] Both combine realism with allegory, political and historical statement with moral didacticism, and the presentation of Christian concepts in conflict with imperfect human manifestations of sexual desire.

The extent to which two operas based upon such similar sources can differ so strongly in effect and aesthetic intent reveals the complexity of adaptive approach necessitated by the source and by the redefined roles of librettist and composer in modern British opera. Despite and perhaps because of Alun Hoddinott's nationalist inclinations and Glyn Jones's literary rivalries, the collaborators misread the modernist potential of their source, and tried to offer a conventional presentation of love and vengeance. While Walton and Hassall similarly create a more conventional drama, they did so within the established literary idiom of British opera. Hoddinott and Jones, however, ultimately disregard that prevailing literary aesthetic, and seem to have ensured the relative obscurity of their work as a result.

In contrast, the three creators of *Billy Budd* engage concertedly with the source itself, and aspire individually to manifest their own particular interpretation. The very strength with which these interpretations are articulated in the libretto and score emphasizes the work's distinct literary awareness, and reinforces perceptions about the increasing intermediality of the arts. The result defines *Billy Budd* as one of the most characteristic British operas of the twentieth century. Furthermore, the opera points to the inherent suitability of source texts characterized by narrative ambiguity: these texts both conform to the thematic interests of modern British opera and allow for the apparently inevitable, irresolvable conflicts between librettist, source, and composer.

---

but many continue to contest the reliability of this text, preferring to resort to the manuscript or subsequent editions published with yet more minor revisions.

2   *The Beach of Falesá* was not published in a definitive edition until 1956, in the United States by J. C. Furnas. Jenni Calder's edition (1979), which acknowledges an indebtedness to Furnas, is the first complete publication of the work in Britain. Although the tale was published during Stevenson's lifetime, that edition had been censored by Sidney Colvin (who strongly disliked the tale to begin with) and Stevenson's publishers. Of the censored version of the manuscript there exist several varying editions from Stevenson's own time; the *Illustrated London News* published the tale as *Uma* in 1892 and omitted the marriage certificate entirely, whereas the tale was published under its original title in *Island Nights' Entertainments* in 1893, but with normalized dialogue and a modified marriage certificate. To complicate matters more, there now exist various editions of the unexpurgated text. Barry Menikoff, for example, offers a detailed examination of the manuscript and its evolution (relying on documentary evidence) and prints a version he considers best represents Stevenson's intentions. Vanessa Smith contests Menikoff's approach, and advocates a greater consideration of Colvin and Stevenson's various changes. Any arguments about the narrative structure or thematic emphasis of the tales must be considered in the context of the publication to which they refer. The critical treatment of *The Beach of Falesá* has understandably varied considerably according to the published versions of the tale.

The Beach of Falesá

Hoddinott had originally considered basing his opera on the story of Welsh hero Rawlins White (Fawkes 169). This choice of subject was inspired as much by nationalism as it was by an interest in the operatic adaptability of the source: Hoddinott consistently speaks of the importance of being a Welsh musician ("The Younger Generation" 148), and the work was specifically commissioned by the Welsh National Opera. Although he moved from setting a recognizably nationalist subject to a South Seas tale by a Scotsman, Hoddinott maintained the opera's Welshness. Dylan Thomas had published a screenplay adaptation of the story in 1959; Hoddinott sent the screenplay along with the original narrative to Jones, himself a highly recognized national literary figure, and suggested that he adapt the script (rather than the original source) into a libretto. Hoddinott's nationalist awareness suggests that it was Thomas's adaptation as much as the story itself which inspired his choice.

Furthermore, the thematic focus of Stevenson's narrative to some extent relates to the concerns of a Welsh nationalist audience. The novella tells the story of the crude, ignorant Englishman Wiltshire, who is manipulated by his fellow-trader Case into a false marriage with a native woman (Uma), and a misplaced trust in Case. Wiltshire gradually realizes Case's duplicity and his own natural ability to overcome racial prejudice. Ultimately, the tale condemns English prejudice and articulates a respect for indigenous culture.

Jones himself may have recognized the translatability of Stevenson's thematic focus within his own literary aesthetic, which he also defined as fundamentally Welsh. Although his first language was Welsh, Jones had been submitted to what he termed the "most anglicising influence of [his] life" at school (Norris 2), and consequently adopted English as his creative language. His work is constantly aware of the implications of a Welsh writer writing of Welsh people and culture in English. Jones has adopted in his writings a distinctiveness of style and language to reflect through "linguistic strangeness" his portrayal of a distinct culture: "The familiar is deconstructed, as in modern art, in order to be reconstructed in all its wonderful, unpredictable and gratuitous strangeness" (M. Wynn Thomas 29).

This awareness of the cultural implications of language is similarly developed in Stevenson's narrative. Uma and the natives speak in a language that suggests their cultural difference, and Wiltshire reveals his own distinct social background with mixed metaphors and slang. Stevenson invites the reader to recognize the social (and implicitly moral) differences between the speaker and the natives through his use of language. The tale gradually negates assumed moral differences between cultures and asks the reader, like Wiltshire, to overcome superficial social prejudices. This thematic treatment of language may well have appealed to Jones's keen awareness of the social and cultural implications to the diversity of linguistic interaction.

Aside from sharing an interest in the implications of language with the source, Jones's writing shows a consistent enthusiasm for musical effect and imagery. His poems often contain musical imagery, and in his tale "Robert Jeffreys," he provides an extended description of a character (Dafydd) according to his interest in music. Jones's respect for the task of writing the libretto is indicated by the specific mention he makes of his "verse libretto" in a concise self-profile (Jones and

Rowlands 268). Hoddinott has stated that "the primary conscious aim in writing is the clear presentation of the musical image which forms in my mind. The emotion or feeling expressed in a work is a creative process that is largely unconscious and cannot be forced" ("The Younger Generation" 148). This assertion mirrors Norris's observations about Dylan Thomas and Jones; both writers "seem to have begun with an image, a phrase or two 'given' as it were by some external power, and to have built on that" (57). That Hoddinott and Jones had a comparable artistic "vision" does not necessarily ensure their compatibility as artistic collaborators. Nonetheless, it is possible that with his musical knowledge and interest, Jones perceived in Hoddinott's compositions a musical evocation of his literary process, and was drawn to the project as a result.

Despite Jones's apparent enthusiasm for the project and the thematic sympathies between his work and the source narrative, these sympathies are not translated into the libretto. Instead, the libretto is fundamentally conventional both linguistically and thematically, and resembles more one of Hassall's libretti for Ivor Novello than it does the source text or Jones's poetry. This apparent lack of engagement suggests that the primary "British operatic renaissance" was in fact originated by and generally specific to modernist authors and composers centered in the universities and artistic circles of London, Cambridge, and Oxford. A closer consideration of the libretto also suggests, however, that Jones isolated a different project for himself in the adaptation: to respond to the literary "source" provided by Dylan Thomas.

In sending Jones the script by Dylan Thomas, Hoddinott was indicating an interest in Thomas's work that could challenge Jones's creative potential. Although Jones had been a friend of Thomas, he had also been his literary contemporary, and in the small community of Anglo-Welsh writers, would have felt some professional rivalry. In his profile of Thomas, Jones concludes with a rather qualified assessment: "Pressed to name the finest Anglo-Welsh poet many Welshmen would, one supposes, have to echo and adapt Gide and answer, 'Dylan Thomas, alas'" (Jones and Rowlands 301). Although he also notes that "the word 'finest' of the question would for many far transcend the 'alas' of the answer" (301), Jones is far from excessively complementary. He refused to set Thomas's script, and in so doing asserted an autonomous artistic capacity for himself, no doubt inspired by some literary pride, if not rivalry, towards Thomas. The libretto offers less a direct reading and interpretation of Stevenson's original narrative than a covert response to the pre-existing creative attempt at adaptation by Jones's literary rival and friend.

The Thomas script adapts the source by prioritizing the thematic importance of music and musical imagery. Much of this imagery would lend itself to musical translation. Throughout the screenplay, "the high, gay cries of the children can be heard above explosions of the surf" (16).[3] This musical image takes on the function of a thematic leitmotif, underlining the importance of innocence and deceit. Thomas also uses sound imagery extensively to emphasize the unease between man and nature created by the Englishman Case, and to underscore Case's domination of the inhabitants of the island. Case is able both to produce and to silence sound; a word from Case results in a "hubbub of argument" (66), but he can also effect the

---

3   All references to the Thomas screenplay and Jones libretto refer to page numbers.

demise of "Whistling Jimmie" (12). In contrast, Wiltshire's comparative weakness is signalled by his inadvertent provocation of an "uneasy murmur" amongst the natives, and he unintentionally causes little girls to stop singing (62, 75). At the end of the tale, Wiltshire sees the dead bodies of Case, Randall, and Jack, symbolically impotent before their musical instruments, and recognizes an apparent restoration of natural order (125). Wiltshire himself does not gain a similar musical mastery, however, and the screenplay hints at the lingering influence of Case with musical imagery: "as though from the inside of Case's bungalow, comes the gay music of fiddles and concertina. And beyond the bungalow, the gay music continues to the beach of Falesá" (126).

This extensive use of musical imagery and description to evoke setting, dramatic tension, and thematic concerns mirrors the function of music in opera. It is perhaps for this reason that Jones, unlike Auden and Kallman for example, refrains from any such musical interpolation. Indeed, the only explicitly musical references in the libretto are derived from the original narrative. In Stevenson's tale, Wiltshire is drawn by the music of a church service: "I had turned out for a stroll, and heard the hymn tune up. You know how it is. If you hear folk singing, it seems to draw you ... " (119). Jones translates this recognition of the power of music's attraction into a lengthy aria for Uma; this aria, rather than the appealing glances and mannerisms described in the novel, attracts Wiltshire immediately: "Case and Wiltshire stand listening. Wiltshire is soon entranced" (9). The aria is relatively conventional, however, and relates neither to the original source in particular, nor to the Thomas adaptation.

Jones's apparent resistance to translating Thomas's musical "effect" into the libretto might equally suggest that he chose to ignore the screenplay entirely. Intriguingly, however, the libretto exploits Thomas's delineation of the *thematic* importance of music. With its final invocation of the music emanating from Case's bungalow, Thomas's ending emphasizes the pervasiveness of Case's influence and signals the potential for future conflict. This ending is very different from that of the source. In Stevenson's narrative, Wiltshire finally "[puts] all square with everybody" (168) and no longer dreams of leaving: "I don't like to leave the kids, you see: and—there's no use talking—they're better here than what they would be in a white man's country" (169). Although Wiltshire admits in the final sentence to hating all half-castes with the exception of his daughters, he has nonetheless developed to the extent that he values domestic life above his earlier self-oriented ambitions.[4] The narrative focuses on its central protagonist, and any future development is to take place in his character. Thomas, however, underlines the continuance of a latent evil influence that is not dependent upon Wiltshire's self-realization.

Jones's libretto ultimately conforms to Thomas's revision of the ending. The libretto ends with villagers sadly throwing their flowers over the body of Case and falling to their knees around his body. Like Thomas, Jones emphasizes the presence of Case and the potential continuance of his influence. Case sings a final arioso:

---

4   As Hillier notes, far from being pessimistic, Wiltshire's final statement "represents another aspect of his ignorance and another opportunity for learning from it" (193).

Wiltshire,
You think this is the end, the end
Of all my power on Falesá. Know this—
You cannot conquer me, for me you must
Become. Wiltshire must become Case,
Or perish. This is the only choice. (40)

Both the libretto and the musical setting of the arioso ensure that Case achieves a final prominence at the end of the opera. By distancing itself from the source's central focus on Wiltshire's development, the libretto enforces an unease around Case's demise that echoes the final tone of Thomas's adaptation.

This change in final focus ultimately disregards the central concerns of the original narrative. Stevenson's tale offers a complex portrayal of a protagonist in constant dialogue with himself. Wiltshire is aware that the "truth" he tells is an inevitably subjective construct: he speaks, for example, of "[having] to tell" of how Case came to die (103), and qualifies his descriptions of characters to emphasize the distance between his initial impressions and his current understanding. In one instance, he states, "But of all this on that first morning I knew no more than a fly" (103). Later, he notes, "I forgot even that Uma was no true wife of mine, but just a maid beguiled, and that in a pretty shabby style. But that is to look too far on. I will come back to that part of it next" (127). Wiltshire reveals to the reader the gradual unfolding of narrative events and his own moral progression. As he does so, he also gleans from the narratives of others an opportunity both to piece together the various mysteries of surrounding events, and to reconsider his own perceptions and prejudices.

The narrative therefore emphasizes the importance of interpretation, and the uniqueness of narrative voice. This is further underlined by the tale's consistently realist approach towards its subject and setting. Stevenson himself recognized the "newness" of his approach:

> It is the first realistic South Sea story; I mean with real South Sea character and details of life; everybody else who has tried, that I have seen, got carried away by the romance and ended in a kind of sugar candy sham epic, and the whole effect was lost--there was no etching, no human grin, consequently no conviction ... You will know more about the South Seas after you have read my little tale, than if you had read a library." (*Letters* 161)

Wiltshire's narrative actively discourages any sentimental reading of character, setting, or situation. By the end, he writes: "As for the old lady, you know her as well as I do ... She's turned a powerful big woman now, and could throw a London bobby over her shoulder ... There's no manner of doubt that she's an A-1 Wife" (169). He further counters any romantic response when he idealizes his dream of starting a public-house. Recognizing the absurdity of his utopian vision, he observes: "There was I ... in as handsome a piece of scenery as you could find ... and the whole thing was clean gone from me, and I was dreaming England, which is, after all, a nasty, cold, muddy hole" (115). Significantly, he notes that England does not have "enough light to see to read by" (115). The central theme of the narrative is the importance of reading experience individually, independent of conventional cultural assumptions.

Thomas essentially ignores this aspect of the source, and tends to treat it as a conventional tale of love and vengeance. As Davies notes, Thomas "simplifies Stevenson's complex text into a romantic story" (234). Thomas claims with pride: "I've cut all the introduction-by-the-waterfall cock about Uma. I've cut the Long Randall-&-burial-alive flash back. I've cut Namu, the renegade pastor" (Thomas, *Collected Letters* 687). He cuts "out altogether the *two other traders* and [sticks] to one alone" so that "we talk now about only one person whom we never see; our plot works back only to the *immediate* predecessor of Wiltshire" (*Collected Letters* 687). With these changes, Thomas alters the distinct narrative voice in the source to one of an impersonal narrator. Instead of having Wiltshire guide the reader through his experiences, Thomas has Wiltshire and the reader experience narrative events simultaneously. Stating that "it's an improvement to cut out as many invisible characters as possible" (*Collected Letters* 687), Thomas ignores the fact that these "invisible characters" are in fact vital for the psychological characterization of Wiltshire; their very existence in the narrative depends upon their importance in Wiltshire's consciousness.

To some extent, Thomas seems to ignore the essential narrative focus of the source in order to assert his own authorship. Ackerman has identified in Thomas's script the imposition of his own poetic, Welsh, point of view. Noting the Welsh background of the missionary Jenkins, he isolates instances of Welsh dialogue and images, as well as references to Thomas's own self-characterizations in personal letters (358). These references signal the Welsh origins of the screenplay, and associate Thomas specifically with those origins. They are not, however, expanded beyond particular instances, and do not really cohere to provide an alternative primary focus for the adaptation. Instead, the screenplay isolates essential narrative events, but strips them of the particular tone in which they are related. In so doing, it ignores the distinct characteristics of Stevenson's novella.

Jones responds to Thomas's adaptation not by returning to the original text, but by excising all of Thomas's particular references to Welsh identity and, implicitly, his own authorship. He seems to borrow from Thomas the idea of having a single preacher (rather than the original three), and invokes in his sympathetic and prominent treatment of the priest a comparison more with Thomas's Jenkins than with Stevenson's original "Father Galoshes." Nonetheless, he does not signal the Welshness of that character, nor does he offer any authorial, subjective voice to replace that of Wiltshire.

Instead, Jones assumedly relegates the narrative and thematic complexity evoked by Stevenson to fulfilment by the composer. The opera's first chorus, for example, offers conventional romantic imagery and a simplistic verse structure:

Paddle with joy on the face of the waters,
Over the waters, over the sea;
Fragrance of nut trees and sweet oleanders—
Over the waters, over the sea. (3)

Any irony to this chorus would have to come from the music, as it is not provided in the libretto's verse or overall narrative structure. Throughout the libretto, characters tend to articulate predominant, uncomplicated emotions that characterize them as stock types. Where the pleasant sensations felt by Stevenson's Wiltshire are tempered by a humorous realism, for example—"The land breeze blew in our faces, and smelt strong of wild lime and vanilla ... and the chill of it set me sneezing" (101)—Jones's hero is unfailingly romantic: "[Falesá] is so beautiful, so fresh/Beneath the daystar's diamond and that moon" (1).

Jones also romanticizes the relationship between Wiltshire and Uma in a manner explicitly avoided by Stevenson. Wiltshire falls in love with Uma immediately and declares before the ceremony, "my marriage to her shall be real" (11). The marriage certificate in the opera contains the changes made to Stevenson's original by his publishers; while Jones may have been working from the censored text, this is unlikely, as Thomas's marriage certificate entitles Wiltshire to send Uma "packing to hell whenever he pleases" (35). It is more probable that, like the original publishers, Jones wished to temper the crudity of the illegitimate marriage in order to promote the romantic accessibility of Wiltshire's love for Uma, and to demonstrate the social responsibility and conventionality of his hero and heroine.

Jones's excision of the more complicating elements of the tale extends to his treatment of the natives. At the conclusion to act 2, the villagers take up Black Jack's song about devils which "shall haunt the darkness of its foes" (29) into a full chorus: "To him we turn in time of peril./Ese the king. Ese the king" (30). In Stevenson's tale, Ese is invoked by Uma, who tells Wiltshire of her beliefs in the supernatural. The libretto, however, gives no context for this invocation. As a result, the villager's chorus is rendered inexplicable in the dramatic context of the opera, and distances the audience from the natives. The natives become "others" with incomprehensible beliefs which they seem to invoke at random.

Furthermore, the libretto ignores the definitive language with which the natives are characterized in the source: Jones's enforced distinction between the natives and the white men is only extended to his depiction (rather than explanation) of their beliefs. Linguistic variety is difficult to translate into opera, where the clarity of sung words can be difficult to discern at the best of times.[5] Thus, Jones's native characters are considerably more articulate in the opera than they are in the original tale. Furthermore, what they say aligns them with conventional Western types. Although Jones's work is typically concerned with acknowledging the importance of cultural and social difference through language, this awareness is not translated into the libretto. Indeed, unlike Tippett and Auden, Jones does not see the librettist's project as an artistic extension or continuation of his own literary interests. Instead, he remains defined by his essentially old-fashioned idea of operatic convention, and by his response to Thomas's changes.

Jones appears to be adhering to Auden's maxim that "since music is in essence immediate, it follows that the words of a song cannot be poetry" ("Notes on Music

---

5   Although some librettists have managed to incorporate slang into opera (most notably, Bertolt Brecht in *Aufsteig und Fall der Stadt Mahagonny* and Auden in *Paul Bunyan*), the slang demanded by the original *Beach of Falesá* is dependent upon the representation of a different language and the way in which it is misunderstood and mispronounced. As a result, the librettist's task is rendered significantly more difficult.

and Opera" 472). Unlike Auden, he does not qualify this assumption within the libretto itself by assuming any musical or interpretative authority. Instead, he ensures a simplistic, melodramatic tale that conforms to nineteenth-century populist traditions. This treatment chafes against the very narrative unconventionality of his own nineteenth-century source.

The nature of modern British opera is often such that modernity—be that social or aesthetic—is signalled most clearly in the libretto and in the overall literary focus of the opera. Hoddinott seems to have relied both on the librettist and his potential affiliation with Dylan Thomas to fulfil this function. The score itself only conforms with the libretto's essential sentimentality, and suggests an exotic romance rather than a psychological or realistic exploration.[6] Unlike the other operas examined thus far, the score does not offer an individual interpretative reading. Written primarily in an arioso format with intermittent chorus interjections and the occasional song, the music insists on fundamentally conventional lyrical expression.

Neither the libretto nor the music can be said to observe the common trend in modern British opera towards a concerted engagement with the literary or philosophical intricacies of its source. This might be due in part to the nature of the operatic commission; the opera's premiere was "billed as the most important musical event in Wales for many years" (Fawkes 169). While the operas examined so far conform to an aesthetic of modern British opera, they do not explicitly align that British idiom with a nationalist project, particularly not one that would reinforce rather than question existing notions of national accomplishment. The cultural contribution anticipated by the collaboration of Hoddinott and Jones may have been forced into its traditional idiom by preconceived ideas of "national" opera. Despite being touted in the *Anglo-Welsh Review* as "a tremendous addition to the cultural stock of Wales" (Graham Jones 261), the opera has received virtually no attention from critics outside the country, and has seen little attention in Wales itself since its premiere.

Stevenson himself recognized of the tale: "there is just the possibility it might make a hit; for the yarn is good and melodramatic, and there is quite a love affair—for me ... But there is always the exotic question; and everything, the life, the place the dialects ... are all novel and may be found unwelcome to that great, hulking, bullering whale, the public" (*Letters* 161). Critics seem to have made the interpretative mistake anticipated by Stevenson; they have criticized Hoddinott for choosing the source in the spirit of, "'let's take a story that has all the Puccini-like ingredients of passion, love, hate, and all the rest of them, and turn it into an opera—it can't fail'" (Graham Jones 260). Others have appreciated the source for being what "one would expect from a master story-teller, a splendid travellers' yarn. Its strength lies in its incident and action; it contains neither shading nor development of character" (Deane 57). Ultimately, Hoddinott and Jones seem to have fallen into a similar trap in their approach towards the source.

One could argue that these discrepancies between the original narrative source and the libretto are rendered necessary by the generic change from short prose

---

6   See Deane (56–8) and Boyd (207–9) for a detailed musicological analysis of the opera.

narrative to opera. As Auden has noted, "music is immediate actuality and neither potentiality nor passivity can live in its presence"; opera cannot hope to evoke "people who are potentially good *and* bad, active *and* passive" ("Notes" 470). An examination of the Britten, Forster, and Crozier adaptation of *Billy Budd*, however, reveals a significantly different approach towards a narrative with similar qualities. Despite a complicated source text and strong differences in dramatic intent amongst all three collaborators, the opera's creators produced a work that has simultaneously succeeded as "modern" grand opera and remained in many respects faithful to the original narrative.

Billy Budd

Like Hoddinott, Britten initially contemplated setting a very different subject. His first choice was Richard Cobbold's sentimental and didactic *The History of Margaret Catchpole: A Suffolk Girl*, to which he might initially have been attracted for its setting and evocation of his own sense of Englishness. His earlier choice of *The Borough* as a source for *Peter Grimes* had been inspired just as much by its evocation of the area of England in which he felt roots as by its plot (which was considerably altered by his librettist). Significantly, the choice had been inspired by an article by E. M. Forster in *The Listener* about George Crabbe: "Reading a most perceptive and revealing article ... by E. M. Forster, I suddenly realised where I belonged" (Britten, *On Receiving the First Aspen Award* 21). As a consequence of this reawakening to his roots in East Anglia, Britten declared, "I belong at home—there—in Aldeburgh. I have tried to bring music to it ... and all the music I write comes from it" (*On Receiving the First Aspen Award* 21). Like Hoddinott, apparently, Britten was concerned to provide music for a specific cultural audience rather than to speak directly to musical developments: "I do not write for posterity—in any case, the outlook for that is somewhat uncertain" (*On Receiving the First Aspen Award* 22).

Britten's personal sense of Englishness apparently ensured that his choice of sources was determined both by the cultural setting in which his opera was to be performed, and by what he perceived to be the literary interests and reputation of his librettist. After Forster rejected the suggestion of *Margaret Catchpole*, Britten reportedly proposed a social comedy "perhaps in an English country house setting" (unpublished letter, qtd. in Reed, "From First Thoughts to First Nights" 45). The domestic subject of Forster's celebrated novels, *Room with a View* and *Howards End*, suggests that Britten's proposal was inspired by his perception of Forster's narrative interests. Britten recalled that it was in Forster's *Aspects of the Novel* that he had first heard of his next suggestion, *Billy Budd* (1960 Broadcast, qtd. in Reed, "From First Thoughts" 160). He later contradicted this assertion when he wrote, "Who brought up the idea of *Billy Budd* no one can quite remember; it was probably telepathic and simultaneous" ("Some Notes on Forster and Music" 85). Nonetheless, Forster wrote a letter to Britten at the early stages of collaboration, stating, "I *have* read Billy Budd, and did once broadcast on it" (qtd. in Reed, "From First Thoughts" 45); this suggests that it was Britten who proposed the original source. The increasing influence of the librettist in modern opera seems to have been such that Britten was just as interested in finding a subject suitable to the perceived talents and interests of Forster as in finding one which he deemed operatically adaptable.

Although Eric Crozier also played a significant role in the writing of the libretto, he was only brought into the project at the insistence of Forster, who felt himself inexperienced as a librettist and dramatist, and in need of experienced aid. While both librettists "talked about" the drama, "considered the characters and their motives," and "checked any points of nautical procedure and life aboard ship that [they] did not understand," Crozier was by his own admission "mostly responsible for the technical scenes and the dialogues; Forster undertook 'the big slabs of narrative'" (Crozier, "The Writing of *Billy Budd*" 16). In a letter to Nancy Evans (4 March 1949), Crozier elaborated on the respective roles of both librettists, asserting: "Morgan is the careful, wise mind who will write most of the text and dialogue. I am the technician and will write what is needed in the way of shanties and songs" (qtd. in Crozier, "Writing" 17). In another letter which he speculates to come from the end of the first week of collaboration, Crozier again asserts his role as historical consultant and dramatic technician: "Morgan is in charge of the drama, I am in command of the ship, and we share matters out between us" (qtd. in Crozier, "Writing" 18). Forster both assumed and was accorded the role of primary librettist by Britten and Crozier.

This is not to say that Britten necessarily agreed with all that Forster had to write of *Billy Budd* in *Aspects of the Novel*. The tale had interested not only Forster, but also two other friends of Britten who exerted a lasting influence on his interests. Britten worked from John Lehmann's British edition of *Billy Budd*, as edited by friend and future librettist William Plomer, and would have been familiar with his introductory comments. Another one of the most important and enduring literary influences on Britten was that of Auden, with whom Britten had earlier collaborated on an operetta and numerous poetical settings. Britten asserted in 1963: "I read a great deal of poetry of all sorts, ancient and modern. Of the moderns I enjoy especially the work of those poets who are my friends: Plomer, Auden, and, of course, E. M. Forster though he writes only prose" (qtd. in Schafer 122). Although *Billy Budd* was still in a comparatively early stage of republication at the time at which it was adapted as an opera, Forster had written (albeit passingly) of *Billy Budd*; Plomer had produced an edition; and Auden had dealt with the character of Billy and the novella's meaning in some depth in "Herman Melville" (1939) and *The Enchafèd Flood* (1950). Britten's close personal relationship with these writers, as well as his natural interest in intellectual argument, would have made him familiar with the interpretations offered by Forster, Plomer, and Auden. Often analysed (particularly by American critics) as a text by one of the "greatest American writers," *Billy Budd* became through Britten and his collaborators a distinctly British creation. Set on a British naval ship, created by British writers and a British composer undoubtedly influenced by British critics (and apparently reading from a British edition of the work), the great American tale of injustice and inhumanity on a corrupt naval vessel took on new implications in its performed setting at Aldeburgh.

The influence of Auden on Britten was such that, just as *The Beach of Falesá* was undoubtedly informed by the earlier adaptation of Dylan Thomas, *Billy Budd* can be considered in the light of Auden's writings both on the novella and on opera in general. Auden had been Britten's first operatic collaborator, and had expressed such strong opinions regarding the setting of words to music that many speculate that Britten never worked with Auden again because of Auden's attempt to control the operatic creation.[7] Nonetheless, Britten's correspondence indicates a constant awareness of the intellectual and artistic engagements of his former collaborator. In his earlier poem, "Herman Melville," Auden identifies in *Billy Budd* a representation of both absolute evil and absolute goodness, and evidence of Melville's own Christian revelation of the potential for humanity and redemption in a world of moral absolutes. Auden's later study of the novella in *The Enchafèd Flood* again attributes a Christian interpretation to the tale. Auden sees in *Billy Budd* Melville's treatment of "the Religious Hero and the Devil or the negative Religious Hero in their absolute form" (144). Arguing that Melville wishes Budd to represent Adam both in the sense of an innocent and perfect hero, and as the Second Adam, he isolates the paradox inherent to this dual representation, that of the sinless innocent and that of the sinless hero who "must know what sin is, or else his suffering is not redemptive" (146). Billy "becomes an aesthetic hero to admire from a distance" (147). Auden argues that although Melville recognized the necessity of transforming the "unconscious Adam" of Billy into the "conscious Christ," he could not make this transition explicit "in terms of his fable," and as a result resorted to suggesting this transition in the off-stage final interview (147). He isolates a similar difficulty in Melville's depiction of Claggart. Asserting that "the difference between God and the Devil is ... that God loves and the Devil will not love" (148), Auden nonetheless recognizes in the novella a homosexual tension between Claggart and Billy so that, although Claggart cannot admit a sexual desire, "for that would be an admission of loneliness which pride cannot admit" (149), the "motive for Claggart's behaviour, half-stated only to be withdrawn because no motive will really do, is homosexual desire" (148).[8]

Auden's isolation of a Christian focus to *Billy Budd*, his assertion of a suppressed homosexual desire in Claggart, his perception of the interview scene between Vere and Budd as thematically vital, and his awareness of the narrative difficulties and thematic contradictions in the tale have been reiterated by countless critics since the publication of *The Enchafèd Flood*. Nonetheless, that Auden took such an interest in the tale, and that he articulated this interest in a text published only a year before the performance of Britten's opera may well have influenced Britten's interest in, if not approach to, the Melville story.

Significantly, Forster differs from Auden in his admiration of *Billy Budd*. He sees in the tale the exposition of Melville's disinterested mind: "What one notices in him is that his apprehensions are free from personal worry, so that we become bigger, not smaller, after sharing them" (*Aspects of the Novel* 98). Whereas Auden's "Herman Melville" celebrates Melville for transcribing personal Christian revelation into *Billy Budd*, Forster in *Aspects of the Novel* applauds Melville for removing himself from any such preoccupations: "he has not got that tiresome little receptacle, a conscience" (98). While resisting any identification of a specific allegorical function

---

7   See H. Carpenter's biographies of both Auden and Britten for an assessment of this working relationship.

8   One of the most thorough examinations of the homosexual implications of the text is offered in Sedgwick, *Epistemology of the Closet* 91–130.

to the tale, Forster nonetheless resembles Auden in asserting Claggart's identity as representative evil. Where Auden reads Claggart as demonic, however, Forster eschews theological assumptions, labelling him only as "a real villain" (97). For Forster, Claggart effectually kills Budd, whereas for Auden, Budd conquers evil by killing Claggart and by providing redemption through his own death; Auden labels the tale "The Passion of Billy Budd" (*Enchafèd Flood* 145). Such a "passion" necessitates a society in need of saving, and by recognizing Billy as a Christ figure, Auden invites a consideration of the spiritual state of the other characters in the tale. Forster's perceived focus, however, is restricted to Claggart and Budd: "It is again the contest between Ahab and Moby Dick, though the parts are more clearly assigned" (*Enchafèd Flood* 98).

Although Forster resembles Auden in recognizing a representation of universal absolutes, he denies the tale a Christian function; it is precisely because Melville does not have the "tiresome receptacle" of a conscience that he is able to reach "straight back into the universal, to a blackness and sadness so transcending our own that they are undistinguishable from glory" (98). For Forster, it is the overall effect of Melville's tale rather than the fate of Billy that inspires transcendence. This transcendence is achieved by the reader in his or her recognition of an implicitly higher state, rather than by the characters in the tale who are exposed to what Auden implies to be Billy's Christ-like apotheosis.

According to Forster, Melville overcomes the "initial roughness of his realism" to create a universal myth of tragic importance (*Aspects* 98). Despite their differing interpretations, Forster identifies in *Billy Budd* that which Auden deems requisite to successful opera: opera's "pure artifice renders [it] the ideal dramatic medium for a tragic myth" ("Notes" 469). That Forster's assessment should express what Auden would later identify as an ideal operatic aesthetic is no doubt coincidental. Nonetheless, much of Forster's criticism of *Billy Budd* is expressed in musical terms, and it was perhaps this additional musical treatment of the narrative that aided Britten in his isolation of the novella for adaptation. Stating that "in music fiction is likely to find its nearest parallel," Forster employs musical metaphor to describe the effect of the novella: "*Billy Budd* is a remote unearthly episode, but it is a song not without words" (116, 98). Although the tale poses interpretative difficulties, its "words" demand that it "be read both for its own beauty and as an introduction to more difficult works" (98). For Forster, inherent narrative difficulties and problems of thematic or symbolic resolution do not preclude the enjoyment of *Billy Budd*. Nonetheless, this enjoyment can only be expressed in terms of musical metaphor, as music implicitly absorbs such difficulties and renders them irrelevant:

> Music ... does offer in its final expression a type of beauty which fiction might achieve in its own way. Expansion. That is the idea the novelist must cling to. Not completion. Not rounding off but opening out. When the symphony is over we feel that the notes and tunes composing it have been liberated, that they have found in the rhythm of the whole their individual freedom. (116)

Forster articulates a similar assessment of the potential musical effect of fiction in his final appraisal of *Billy Budd*: Melville "threw it in, that undefinable something, the balance righted itself, and he gave us harmony and temporary salvation" (98–9). Forster isolates the narrative from its literary context and, through analogy, "elevates" it to a musical stature; it is only in its musical status that the tale achieves for the reader the "salvation" (albeit temporary) akin to that identified by Auden in the fictional context of the narrative.

Forster unconsciously embodies in his criticism the operatic transformation which he and Britten were later to achieve in their adaptation of the tale. Nonetheless, Forster's criticism establishes a relationship between words and music that is problematic in the consideration of his libretto. *Moby-Dick* is "song," whereas *Billy Budd* is a "song not without words" (98). In other words, *Billy Budd* is more explicitly grounded within a fictional structure than is *Moby-Dick*, with its "unformulated connection[s]" (97). Forster himself wrote that he much preferred "music itself" to "music that reminds me of something," and that "music which is untrammelled and untainted by reference is obviously the best sort of music to listen to; we get nearer the centre of reality" ("Not Listening to Music" 122, 124). Forster's comments suggest his greater aesthetic appreciation of the earlier novel. He admires the "rhythm" of music over the presence of an aesthetic pattern, and equates this quality with the potential future for the novel: "We will not give up the hope of beauty yet. Cannot it be introduced into fiction by some other method than the pattern? Let us edge rather nervously towards the idea of 'rhythm'" (*Aspects* 112). Literature is most admirable when it embodies in its structure, or lack thereof, the qualities which Forster appreciates in absolute music. In the operatic transformation of *Billy Budd*, Forster may have seen an opportunity for himself to free the narrative from its aesthetic pattern.

It is intriguing to speculate that Forster may have abandoned the writing of novels out of a recognition of the impossibility of achieving, within a structured fictional context, an emotionally transcendent effect akin to that which he admired in absolute music.[9] Freed from the creation of a narrative framework by the use of a pre-existing source, Forster was enabled to explore his musical potential in the context of the creation of the opera libretto. Forster asserted to Crozier that literature stirred him up "when it [woke him] up to the greatness of the world. Galsworthy doesn't, Peter Grimes does ..." (*Letters* 2: 234). He attributes to opera the artistic importance achieved by literature. In referring to Galsworthy, Forster touches upon novelistic ground thematically similar to that of his own. With this assertion, Forster rejects the social comedy advocated by Britten, and suggests his awareness of the potential for his own creative growth in the writing of the libretto.

Despite his appreciation for absolute music, however, Forster's own task as librettist necessitates the impossibility of achieving music "untainted by reference." Impossible, that is, unless Forster can be read as attempting to blur the lines between musical composition and literary musicality. Britten's assessment in "Some Notes on Forster and Music" remains one of the most acute considerations of Forster's critical relation to music.[10] As a composer, Britten was more aware of the threat which

---

9   Furbank offers a few of many assessments of Forster's potential motives for abandoning the writing of novels (2: 131–3).

10   For a more thorough consideration of the role and assessment of music in the literary critical writings of Forster, see Hutcheon. Weatherhead examines the structure and thematic

Forster's assertions and novelistic evocations of music[11] might pose to the autonomy and artistic respectability of music. Addressing Forster's "Not Listening to Music," he contests what he identifies as Forster's insistence that "no one can listen to a piece of music from beginning to end, consistently—unless one is a 'professional critic'" (84). Britten recognizes in Forster's prose the presumption that the serious study of music is an esoteric pursuit, and argues, "No, for some reason Forster does not want to admit that knowing about music is a help" (84–5). Identifying Forster as a Romantic, Britten excuses his friend's dismissal of the intellectual capacity of music by recognizing a difference in aesthetics. What Britten fails to articulate, however, is that by denying music its artistic complexity, Forster is more easily able to assimilate music into the realm of literature. If music is not defined by its own specific techniques and can be likened to the rhetorical devices of literature, it can be both imitated and realized just as much through the written word as through musical sound.

Forster's implicit assumption of his own "musical" capability informs his early correspondence with Britten and Crozier, and reveals both his desire to dispense with subjects already treated by himself in his novels, and his need to determine the narrative interest of the opera. Forster wrote to Crozier that, although he was attracted to *Margaret Catchpole* at first, "There seems to me good reason that Ben should not yet write again about the sea" (*Letters* 2: 234). At the same time as he was making judgments about the creative direction for Britten's operas, Forster was declaring to the creative team of Britten, Pears, and Crozier: "I do not altogether agree with the three of you ... I seem to have the fear of a lot of symbolic and inexpensive scenery, whereas I want grand opera mounted clearly and grandly" (*Letters* 2: 235). Like Auden, Forster was interested in determining not only the subject of the opera, but also its operatic style. Asserting to Britten that Melville was "often trying to do what [he himself had] tried to do" (*Letters* 2: 235), Forster identifies himself with the concerns of the author, and in so doing attributes to himself a superior knowledge and interpretative authority towards the original text. In these early letters, Forster demonstrates his tendency towards Wagnerianism without the music; attempting to assimilate musical style, structure, and thematic emphasis within the realm of the libretto, Forster was already asserting for himself a creative importance not traditionally demanded or allowed the librettist.

Furthermore, in a talk at Aldeburgh, Forster gave mixed praise to *Peter Grimes* as an adaptation of Crabbe's intentions: "I knew the poem well, and I missed its horizontality, its mud ... At the second hearing ... I accepted the opera

---

emphasis of *Howards End* in terms of the described Beethoven's Fifth, considering in particular the relationship between Helen's "sexual career as chief catalyst" (251) and her reading of the symphony at the start of the novel. J. Gordon offers an examination of the role of voice in Forster's novels, and Herz considers the structural and thematic relationship between Forster's *The Longest Journey* and Wagner's *Parsifal* in the context of her assertion that an interest in Wagner was "for homosexuals, a lightly coded affirmation of sexual preference" (141). Burra's article remains the precursor to all such studies, and was one greatly appreciated by Forster himself, who included it in the 1942 Everyman edition of *A Passage to India*.

11 As discussed earlier, the Beethoven passage in *Howards End* imposes Forster's own narrative and musical values onto a hitherto absolute musical work.

as an independent masterpiece, with a life of its own" ("George Crabbe and Peter Grimes" 179). Recognizing the trend in modern opera towards the depiction of the misunderstood hero victimized by society, Forster speculates what he would have done to adapt *Peter Grimes* as an opera:

> I should certainly have starred the murdered apprentices. I should have introduced their ghosts in the last scene, rising out of the estuary, on either side of the vengeful graybeard, blood and fire would have been thrown in the tenor's face, hell would have opened, and on a mixture of *Don Juan* and the *Freischütz* I should have lowered my final curtain. (178)

Forster's operatic vision indicates his willingness to transform events into a form defined by spectacle and melodrama. This approach differs from that of Britten who, with his chamber operas *The Rape of Lucretia* and *Albert Herring*, had defined himself as a modern classicist, intent on more intimate psychological depictions. Britten himself isolated the difference in musical taste between himself and Forster: "Forster prefers music based on striking themes, dramatic happenings, and strong immediate moods, rather than on classical control and balance, beautiful melodies and perfection of detail; music which benefits from being listened to closely and from some knowledge of it" ("Notes on Forster and Music" 85). Britten recognizes in Forster a dismissal of the intellectual potential of music, while Forster in his criticism of *Peter Grimes* implicitly argues against the psychologization of characters at the expense of the original narrative and overall dramatic effect. Given these very different musical and dramatic visions, how could Forster and Britten have managed to create what continues to be one of the most enduring and respected operatic adaptations of the twentieth century?

For a possible answer, we must first turn to Melville[12] and consider the extent to which his narrative allows for either Forster's interests or Britten's modern operatic adaptation. That the original is amenable to stage setting is suggested by the existence of at least two other works derived from the narrative, a play by Coxe and Chapman, and a 1949 opera by Giorgio Ghedini.[13] Throughout the tale, the narrator usefully identifies events that he deems "germane." One identified incident is "the occurrence at the mess" (61). Signalling its importance to his tale, the narrator writes, "Not many days after the last incident narrated, something befell Billy Budd that more gravelled him than aught that had previously occurred" (62). Later, he comments, "After the mysterious interview in the fore-chains ... nothing especially germane to the story occurred until the events now about to be narrated" (73). Although the narrator also includes chapters that frequently involve digression, by specifically signalling germane incidents, he differentiates between these digressions and

---

12   Despite the many inaccuracies in the Plomer edition, all references to *Billy Budd* will be taken from that edition, as it was by Crozier's account the text from which the collaborators worked ("Writing" 12). Forster's earlier criticism of the work in *Aspects of the Novel* would have been based upon Weaver's publication.

13   Britten and his librettists became aware of the other opera only after they had undertaken their project. For a discussion of the reactions of Forster and Britten to the libretto (by Salvatore Quasimodo) and to the essential characteristics of the earlier work, see Reed, "From First Thoughts" 57–8.

the dramatic events of the plot. In so doing, he makes easy the librettist's task of identifying events for dramatization. Crozier writes that on the first afternoon of collaboration, the collaborators produced "two pages in Britten's writing, one listing all the characters in the story, the second tabulating Melville's dramatic incidents" ("Writing" 12).

Furthermore, the novella provides several instances in which the action is described in terms of a stage setting. Melville describes the imprisoned Billy, for example, as if writing stage directions: "On the starboard side of the Indomitable's upper gun-deck, behold Billy Budd under sentry lying prone in irons" (105). After his interview with Claggart, who is implicitly staged by regarding his captain "with a look difficult to render" (79), Vere determines upon a measure that "involv[es] a shifting of the scene" (80). The most extensive of these references is offered at the midpoint of the narrative, when the narrator is about to detail Claggart's hatred for Budd and thus establish the conflict which will end in the death of both characters:

> Down among the groundlings, among the beggars and rakers of the garbage, profound passion is enacted. And the circumstances that provoke it, however trivial or mean, are no measure of its power. In the present instance the stage is a scrubbed gun-deck, and one of the external provocations a man-of-war's man's spilled soup. (59–60)

The narrator's recognition of the potential to expose tragic myth through a drama involving characters of low social status mirrors Auden's similar assertion about opera: "Feelings of joy, tenderness, and nobility are not confined to 'noble' characters but are experienced by everybody, by the most conventional, most stupid, most depraved" ("Notes" 469). Stating, however, that "it is one of the glories of opera that it can demonstrate this and to the shame of the spoken drama that it cannot" ("Notes" 469), Auden claims for opera an exclusive ability to express and evoke the "passion in its profoundest" to which Melville's narrator alludes. Britten, Forster, and Crozier are implicitly invited by Melville's tale itself to see an appeal for fulfilment through stage adaptation.

That Melville himself seems to have recognized the potential for song, rather than spoken language, to express depths of emotion, is suggested throughout the novella, particularly in the narrator's careful depiction of character though the description of voice quality and tone. Billy is "a superb figure" (16). He "could sing, and like the illiterate nightingale was sometimes the composer of his own song" (26). His voice indicates his moral worth, and is "singularly musical, as if expressive of the harmony within" (27). Billy's helplessness is evoked in terms of his physical and vocal diminution: "He stood like one impaled and gagged" (82). Once he has sacrificed himself, however, Billy returns to the status of a second Adam, capable of transcending through near-song his own imminent death. His final words are "delivered in the clear melody of a singing-bird" and have a "phenomenal effect, not unenhanced by the rare personal beauty of the young sailor" (112). The narrator likens Billy's physical beauty to his musical beauty, and with this dual emphasis on the visual and aural representation of his hero, makes such a representation ideal for a staged opera.

Furthermore, Billy's influence on others is frequently represented with vocal imagery. The thought of his absence disrupts the "certain musical chime" in the voice of Captain Graveling, who is able to break the silence only with a "rueful reproach in the tone of his voice" (18–19). Later, at Billy's last words, "as if indeed the ship's populace were the vehicles of some vocal current-electric, with one voice, from alow and aloft, [comes] a resonant echo" (112). This suggestive imagery supports Auden's assertion of the class-transcending ability of song; Billy's vocal influence not only elicits sympathy for the protagonist, but disrupts boundaries of social status to unite the various classes of men on board in vocal exclamation.[14]

The narrative's presentation of dialogue seemingly reinforces the "musicality" of the text. In the interview between Claggart and Vere, the narrator notes that "throughout the interview Captain Vere's voice was far from high, and Claggart's silvery and low" (80). This description, in combination with that of the sound of the "wind in the cordage and the wash of the sea" (80), evokes operatic comparison: it emphasizes both voice quality, and the underlying, "orchestral" effect of the wind and the sea. Old Dansker asserts to Billy, "Baby Budd, *Jemmy Legs* ... is down on you." Billy immediately reiterates this phrase, exclaiming, "*Jemmy Legs*! ... what for? Why he calls me the *sweet and pleasant young fellow*." Not only does Dansker again reiterate the name, but he recognizes the influence of Claggart's voice quality rather than his words: "Ay Baby Lad a sweet voice has *Jemmy Legs*" (49). This reiteration establishes a verbal leitmotif (an effect put to great use by Britten in his setting of these phrases in the opera), and draws attention to the vocal manipulations of Claggart. Thus in the immediately succeeding chapter, after Billy has spilled his soup, Claggart speaks in "a low musical voice, peculiar to him at times" (51). The scene provides many opportunities for musical adaptation; the narrator both draws attention to Claggart's vocal quality and includes within the scene a reiteration of the pre-established vocal motif. Billy states, "There, now, who says that Jemmy Legs is down on me!" (52). This exclamation is given an extra emphasis by the narrator himself, whose reiteration of the phrase suggests an orchestral statement of the dramatic importance of the scene: "Yes, why should *Jemmy Legs*, to borrow the Dansker's expression, be *down* on the Handsome Sailor?" (53).

The novella gradually emphasizes the importance of voice quality and exclamation to evoke character, to show the effect of that character on others, and to establish a dramatic structure characterized by reiterated phrases that lend the narrative momentum and thematic emphasis. These images and exclamations culminate towards the end of the novella in what is arguably an extended operatic scene: sounds of voices mingle with others to invoke both vocal and orchestral comparisons. The scene begins with a "silence" "emphasised by the regular wash of the sea against the hull, or the flutter of sail" (115). This silence is gradually disturbed, however, "by a sound not easily to be verbally rendered": "Whoever has heard the freshet-

---

14   Song "abolishes all social and age differences" (Auden, "The World of Opera" 89). Because "we use language in everyday life, our style and vocabulary become identified with our social character as others see us ... But precisely because we do not communicate by singing, a song can be out of place but not out of character" (Auden, "Notes" 469–70).

wave of a torrent suddenly swelled by pouring showers in the tropical mountains ... whoever has heard the first muffled murmur of its sloping advance ... may form some conception of the sound now heard" (115). The description is sufficiently vague as to invite Britten's orchestral depiction without overly specifying its natural reference. Gradually, this sound is revealed to come from the men themselves, inviting a choral effect similar to that which Britten achieves in his evocation of the "murmurous indistinctness" (115) of the men.

Britten musically defines this murmur by reiterating a motif that is associated throughout the opera with discussions of mutiny and potential mass action.[15] The text enables him musically to represent the motive behind the "strategic command" that comes "with abrupt unexpectedness" (115) to suggest the unease of the ship's officers. Thus, the whistles of the Boatswain "[pierce] that ominous low sound" (115) and represent through sound the officers' ability to quash potential unrest. This unrest is not so easily defeated, however, and is again evoked in musical terms with the return of a "second strange human murmur ... blended now with another inarticulate sound proceeding from certain larger sea-fowl" who circle the burial spot "with the moving shadow of their outstretched wings and the croaked requiem of their cries" (116). This scene both evokes latent potential for mutiny in musical terms and, by affiliating the cries of nature with the death of Billy and the unrest of the sailors, implicitly validates the cause of the sailors in their protest against unnatural deeds. Again, however, the murmur is silenced through sound: the drum beat dissolves the multitude, as "the official sound of command" for the men "much resembles in its promptitude the effect of an instinct" (117). The scene concludes in what evokes a gentle operatic finale, describing both the dispersal of the final sounds and the effect of the silence that succeeds them. This passage suggests the bare stage to which Vere returns in the final scene of Britten's opera:

> The band on the quarter-deck played a sacred air. ... That done, the drum beat the retreat, and toned by music and religious rites subserving the discipline and purpose of war, the men ... dispersed ... And now it was full day. The fleece of low-hanging vapour had vanished, licked up by the sun that late had so glorified it. And the circumambient air in the clearness of its serenity was like smooth white marble in the polished block not yet removed from the marble-dealer's yard. (117–18)

This final scene is thus "operatic" in its evocation of emotion, events, and narrative affiliation through sound imagery. As such, it implicitly enforces the necessary

---

15   White offers a musicological examination of the motif as it appears throughout the opera (*Benjamin Britten: His Life and Operas* 180). Howard asserts that these notes "are used to suggest real or imagined, potential or actual mutiny." The phrase "colours references to the Spithead and the Nore ... appears as *The Rights o' Man* ... appears when the Novice attempts to trap Billy into leading a mutiny and ... becomes the expansive melodic line of the men's working song, revealing the raw material of mutiny—the cause and the justification, the incipient threat" (80–81). This motif later becomes integral to the wordless exclamations of the sailors after the hanging of Billy. As Brett notes, of course, a motif need not represent a consistent symbol; it is suggestive rather than specific, and "can reflect subtle changes of mood and meaning" (140–41).

operatic contention that passionate moments of emotion cannot be articulated sufficiently through words alone.

The work's "operatic chapter," its musical repetition of vocal exclamations, and its definition of characters according to their vocal qualities initially appeal to a composer seeking an operatically adaptable source. Furthermore, the musical details given in the narrative are always sufficiently vague as to render their musical adaptation an embellishment or explication rather than a superfluous rearticulation of written details. Despite these apparently musical qualities, however, the novella seems to resist operatic adaptation as much as invite it, primarily because it offers a conflict between extensive narrative discourse and a central fable. The narrator consistently adopts various, often conflicting tones that render the mood, interpretation, and credibility of events and characters unclear. As read by the opera's creators, the novella contained a preface that positioned the narrative in the context of a historical survey of the causes of mutiny and subsequent reform in the British Navy. The next chapter seems to ignore this preface when it launches into the narrator's "inside narrative" of the Handsome Sailor. A similar juxtaposition of narrative emphasis occurs at the start of the third chapter, when the narrator begins to contextualize the story of the ship within the history of the British Navy. He then asserts: "But with all this the story has little concernment, restricted as it is to the inner life of one particular ship and the career of an individual sailor" (29). Curiously, however, it is in this chapter that the narrator describes the events and effect of the Nore Mutiny in considerable detail. Immediately following what his earlier statement would imply to be a historical digression, the narrator calls the reader's attention to himself yet again, announcing that he is about to "err" into a literary "by-path," and that if the reader will "keep [him] company" he shall be glad: "At the least we can promise ourselves that pleasure which is wickedly said to be in sinning, for a literary sin the divergence will be" (32). This digression is both literary and historical; initiated by the narrator's poetic ruminations at the sight of Nelson's ship, it leads to a wider discussion of Nelson's actions. The following chapter continues this apparent digression so that, when the narrator resumes his tale, he denies the thematic validity of his preceding chapter and announces that on Billy's ship, "very little in the manner of the men and nothing obvious in the demeanour of the officers would have suggested to an ordinary observer that the Great Mutiny was a recent event" (36). The tale is at once realistic and removed from historical realism; ostensibly telling a tale of the inner life of a ship, the narrator nonetheless feels himself obliged by a sense of literary and historical responsibility to contextualize this inner life according to historical events. These events, he asserts, bear little influence on the events of his narrative.

That Melville's narrator recognizes and is concerned with this apparent discrepancy between historical fact and literary fable is particularly evident in his inability to maintain a consistent narrative approach. He vacillates between asserting the truth of his tale and acknowledging that this truth does not originate from the historical context which he provides in his digressions, but from his own literary imagination. At one point, for example, he leaves the reader to accept the narrative: "the resumed narrative must be left to vindicate as it may its own credibility" (57). While this credibility is allegedly founded upon the narrator's personal understanding of observed events, it is threatened by the narrator's revelation of his creative literary role. He speaks of Billy not as a person, but as a hero constructed according to literary precedent: Billy is "like the beautiful woman in one of Hawthorne's minor tales" (27). Later, defensive about the credibility of his narrative, he excuses his tale's apparent strangeness in terms of literary precedent:

> Not to invent something touching the more private career of Claggart, something involving Billy Budd, of which something the latter should be wholly ignorant ... all this, not so difficult to do, might avail in a way more or less interesting to account for whatever enigma may appear to lurk in the case. But, in fact, there was nothing of the sort. And yet the cause, necessarily to be assumed as the sole one assignable, is in its very realism as much charged with that prime element of Radcliffian romance, *the mysterious*, as any that the ingenuity of the author of the *Mysteries of Udolpho* could devise. (53)

In his literary self-consciousness, Melville's narrator manifests an inability to differentiate between his desire to present an historical tale and his urge to render that tale in literary, subjective terms.

The narrative further complicates direct adaptation by signaling the narrator's uncertainty about events and characters, and how best to represent them. At one point, he dismisses his own speculations with, the "*might have been* is but boggy ground to build on" (33). Later, though, he refers to having once spoken to an "honest scholar, my senior" (54), details the philosophical discussion which ensued, and arrives at an assessment of Claggart's character based upon this philosophy: "Now something such was Claggart" (57). Since this conclusion is based upon speculation, the narrator's subsequent description of Claggart in Miltonic terms can be attributed less to Claggart's real character than to the literary inclinations of the narrator: "what recourse is left to a nature like Claggart's, surcharged with energy as such natures almost invariably are, but to recoil upon itself, and, like the scorpion for which the Creator alone is responsible, act out to the end its allotted part?" (59). The narrator accepts his own ideas about the nature of Claggart, and articulates them both as fact and in the language of literary analogy. The apparently simple fable to which the narrator alludes is complicated by his self-exposition as interfering, ultimately inconclusive, and occasionally unwilling to differentiate between fact, subjectivity, and literary creativity.

Nowhere is the narrator's subversion of his own credibility more apparent than in the final interview scene between Budd and Vere: "Beyond the communication of the sentence what took place at this interview was never known. But, in view of the character of the twain briefly closeted in that state-room ... some conjectures may be ventured" (101). Coming as it does after Vere's uncharacteristically lengthy tirade against Billy, the scene gains a structural and thematic centrality. Nonetheless, the narrator chooses to withdraw at this point; not admitted to the scene of conference, he is apparently limited by his historical role from describing events. He has, however, detailed earlier private interviews, and in his extended character descriptions of Claggart and Vere in particular, emphasized to the reader his authorial ability to understand characters. By withdrawing from this crucial scene into conjecture, the narrator emphasizes his own creative incompetence or willed self-silencing; he is unable or unwilling to provide in his narrative the dramatic culmination of a growing conflict between two central characters. This withdrawal imposes a significant gap in the tale. The narrator fails to fulfil the dramatic conflict signalled earlier in the narrative. Furthermore, by indicating the existence of an important event without describing it, he so emphasizes his subjectivity and creative insecurities that the tale becomes just as much a narrative of literary anxiety as it does of the conflict between Vere, Claggart, and Billy.

It is difficult to determine the extent to which this narrative omission and tentative speculation were intended to draw the reader's attention to the insecurities inherent in the writing of a moral or political tale. They might just as easily result from Melville's own indecision or the partially fragmentary nature of the manuscript. No matter, the resultant narrative anxiety is an inherent part of the novella, and demands critical and adaptive attention along with the described events and the historical digressions. The extent to which the literary projects and shifting emphases of the original narrator render the tale amenable to operatic adaptation is questionable. Like *The Beach of Falesá*, *Billy Budd* is defined as much by narrative voice as it is by incident. One might conclude that the necessary operatic approach to such adaptation would be to extricate from that complex narrative a simple plot to dramatize with emotionally effective music. The opera not only adapts the "germane incidents" defined by Melville's narrator, however, but simultaneously transcribes the narrative difficulties of the original text into an operatic idiom.

The creators did not allow their enthusiasm for the original source to prevent them from asserting the necessity of changes to the original narrative.[16] These changes were made equally for the sake of operatic transformation and their own interpretations and dramatic interests. Although Vere is arguably not the centre of the original tale, his voice is constantly affiliated with that of the narrator. As a result, any faithful adaptation of the concerns of the captain to a certain extent mirrors those of the narrator. Vere could therefore be seen as a means through which an adapter might effectively translate the concerns of Melville's narrative.

In the original, Vere has "nothing of that literary taste which less heeds the thing conveyed than the vehicle"; like all those with a "serious mind of superior order," he inclines towards books "treating of actual men and events no matter of what era" which "honestly, and in the spirit of common sense, philosophise upon realities" (39). The narrator's endorsement of Vere's reading interests reflects the literary self-consciousness of the narrator himself. Like the narrator, Vere imposes his own order and creative interests on events. He takes it upon himself to end the story of Budd and transform it into a tragedy. After Billy kills Claggart, Vere contextualizes the event in terms of tragic precedent and fate: "Fated boy ... what have you done!" (84); "It is the divine judgment of Ananias! Look!" (85); "Struck dead by an angel

---

16   Curiously, these changes are frequently overlooked; as Law notes, "Commentators may note that Britten and his two librettists have departed occasionally from their text, but no one has really examined the extent to which the opera contends with Melville's text" ("'We Have Ventured to Tidy Up Vere'" 298). This might be in part a result of the frequent textual faithfulness of the libretto; Eric Walter White lists a number of the direct citations from Melville's text and drafts (*Benjamin Britten* 155), and Law expands upon this list in a footnote to his article ("'We Have Ventured to Tidy Up Vere'" 312–13). These citations notwithstanding, the libretto offers significant changes to the original text.

of God. Yet the angel must hang!" (85). This later assertion is not the statement of a careful lawyer, but of a "divine myth-making dramatist assembling his material for a tragedy" (Hamilton 44–5). Vere's language is informed by literary awareness and precedent. Unable to explain his dying motive for repeating the words "Billy Budd, Billy Budd" (120), Vere echoes the narrator who, unable to consign his tale to a specific historical or literary closure, leaves it in the hands of another creator, the foretopman of "artless poetic temperament" who writes the "Billy in the Darbies" ballad to conclude the tale (123).

The decision of the opera makers to frame their opera within the context of Vere's prologue and epilogue therefore evokes the narrative effect of the original tale. They translate the subjectivity of the narrator into Vere's opening and closing statements. At the same time, however, the operatic prologue and epilogue provide significantly more dramatic closure than the novella. The framing soliloquies of Vere echo each other both textually and musically to suggest a thematic emphasis and overriding narrative structure to the opera which contrast with the digressions and literary anxieties of Melville's narrator. If read as Vere's tale, the opera gains significantly more dramatic consistency than the original. Some critics have interpreted the opera as a subjective narration of Vere's telling so that, as with the novella, one is never sure to what extent the narrative is true, and to what extent it is tempered by the varying interests and needs of the narrator.[17] Assertions that the libretto must be read consistently as narrated from the point of view of Vere, however, pose difficulties. Why, for example, should Vere choose to modify the trial scene to his advantage, and yet not create for the audience a similarly sympathetic portrayal of himself by offering a description of the crucial interview scene? Speculation beyond the context of the opera as staged is unhelpful; to be forced to speculate as to the motives of the apparent operatic narrator suggests that that narrator is not clearly delineated in the opera.

Unlike prose narrative, which allows for the influence of the narrator on the creation and reportage of the actions, motivations, and dialogue of characters, opera does not allow for a consistent, narrative persona independent of composer and librettist. Moreover, the form of opera does not allow for a controlling narrator with an omniscient creative power; once a singer sings, that song as staged and heard comes from the singer, not the narrator. As a result, any controlling subjective voice is very difficult to evoke in either libretto or music, and depends primarily on staging for representation. Although many of Vere's vocal exclamations and musical themes are reiterated by other characters throughout the opera, they must be taken as a sign either of Vere's accumulated worldly experience, thus reinforcing his first

---

17 Law offers a thorough consideration of the opera as a subjective retelling of events through Vere, noting that Vere not only echoes Melville's phrases at some points in the libretto, but that the reiteration of phrases introduced by Vere by other characters indicates his creative influence on the drama as a whole. He asserts that "Vere's struggle in the opera is so powerful that it leads him to try to suppress the truth of his own involvement in the decision," and that only "the admission of an involvement greater than that shown in the present version of the events can explain Vere's acute sense of responsibility" ("'We Have Ventured'" 311, 309).

statement, "I am an old man who has experienced much" (7), or as an indication of the universality of the emotions and situations which he describes.

Nonetheless, the prominence granted Vere by the operatic prologue and epilogue mirrors the ultimate attempt of Melville's narrator to give events a dramatic focus. Crozier and Britten explicitly attempted to define a dramatic structure for their narrative. In a letter from the first week of collaboration, Crozier expressed this emphasis on dramatic consistency and unity: "It is going to be a stupendous opera. Like *Grimes*—with a much better story, a fine libretto, and a classical shape. Morgan says he has no gift for the theatre, but I am so thrilled by his mastery of drama and dialogue that I shall try to persuade him to write a play" (qtd. in Crozier, "Writing" 18). In keeping with this emphasis on the conventions of traditional drama, the decision to have Vere frame the narrative was a result of the interest of Crozier (and possibly Britten) in unifying the tale. Vere's narrative was originally planned as a choral device to provide structure rather than to place dramatic emphasis on Vere himself:

> It seemed a natural development that the action on board ship should be 'framed' by a prologue and epilogue of Vere as an elderly man looking back on the troubled days of his wartime command ... For operatic purposes it seemed necessary for him to live on. Forster liked this idea, and a week or so later ... enclosed the first draft of a possible opening speech, headed "Scene I. Vere as Chorus." (Crozier, "Writing" 13)

Vere's choric function is reinforced by his not entering the related narrative until the end of Act I; his apparent withdrawal after the prologue suggests that his eventual entrance is not that of a central protagonist, but of one resembling Melville's inside narrator who will "see and experience much." Forster wrote to Britten that he liked the idea of a chorus, "provided it is at the level of the half-informed Greek chorus, which was always making mistakes. The well-informed commentator, the person or personages outside time, would not here be suitable" (*Letters* 2: 235). Vere's choric figure sings of "confusion," "mist," and being "lost on the infinite sea." As a result, he seems initially to conform to Forster's demands.

While Vere is a choric figure to the extent that his words and music begin and end the opera, he is also a character in the evoked tale. Indeed, the opera is essentially defined by the actions and reactions of Vere. Vere's distanced choric effect is denied by his personal involvement in the tale. Billy dies blessing his captain, and it is Vere who is left ultimately to face his own weakness and to interpret for the audience the significance of Billy's final act. Vere is not merely an omniscient choric voice, but a central character in the opera. The opera vacillates in dramatic focus between Vere as a choric figure distanced from the action by time and perspective, and Vere as a dramatically tragic figure.[18] In so doing, of course, it mirrors the uncertainty of Melville's narrator.

This uncertainty is further dramatized by the opera's manifestation of the conflict between Forster and Britten in the interpretation of the tale. For Forster, the primary conflict was to be between Claggart and Budd, and the central interest to be Billy's

---

18   Given Crozier's perception of the collective intention of the opera's creators to unify the original work, this effect was doubtless inadvertent.

goodness. In a letter to *The Griffin* in 1950, Forster asserted, "Each adapter has his own problems. Ours has been how to make Billy, rather than Vere, the hero. Melville must have intended this; he called the story Billy Budd, and unless there is strong evidence to the contrary one may assume that an author calls his story after the chief character" (4). To Forster, perhaps, Vere's choric function provided him with an opportunity to relegate to Vere the marginal role necessary to better define the importance of Billy as protagonist: "Solely talking out of my instincts—when I think of the play, before I think of anything else I think of Billy" (qtd. in Wilkinson 167). In a later BBC broadcast, however, Forster asserted, "I don't think Billy the central figure. He names the opera, and I think I consider things from his point of view ... But I quite see the position of Vere. It's very easy to place him in the centre of the opera, because he has much more apprehension than poor Billy" (qtd. in Cooke, "Britten's *Billy Budd*" 28–9). This contradiction in Forster's understanding of the dramatic focus of the opera might be a consequence of his having had occasion to revisit his own adaptation of the work, as well as to consider the ultimate effect of the opera as a whole. At the same time as he relegates his appreciation of the primacy of Billy in the "play" to his "instincts" rather than to his perceptions, Forster seems to isolate a contradiction between the achievement of the "play," or the libretto, and that of the opera.

In keeping with his greater interest in Billy, Forster's text for the prologue emphasizes the narrative to follow rather than the character of Vere. Vere abstractly discusses the nature of good and the presence of evil in his prologue: "the good has never been perfect. There is always some flaw in it, some defect, some imperfection in the divine image, some fault in the angelic song, some stammer in the divine speech" (7). Vere does not recognize his own culpability until the final stanza, and even then, that awareness is only half-expressed: "Confusion, so much is confusion!" (7). Vere's following lines focus on his own fate: "Who has blessed me? Who saved me?" Coming as it does after an equally lengthy discourse on the nature of the presence of evil, Vere's articulated anguish is given equal, rather than prominent, textual emphasis in the prologue. This apparent diminishing of Vere's status allows the later choral exclamation of "we're all of us lost, lost for ever on the endless sea" (19) to be seen as an additional diminishing of Vere's unique status in the drama. This balance in the prologue between Vere's philosophical discourse on the nature of evil and his awareness of his own moral dilemma ensures that the libretto denies the unique and central dramatic importance of the captain as advocated by Britten.

Unlike Forster, Britten consistently argued the importance of Vere as a central character: "Billy always attracted me, of course, as a radiant young figure. I felt there was going to be quite an opportunity for writing nice dark music for Claggart, but I think I must admit that [it was] Vere, who has what seems to me the main moral problem of the whole work, round whom the drama was going to centre" (qtd. in Cooke, "Britten's *Billy Budd*" 28). Furthermore, "I think it was the quality of conflict in Vere's mind ... which attracted me to this particular subject" (qtd. in Cooke, "Britten's *Billy Budd*" 29). Forster saw Vere's prologue and epilogue as dramatic devices through which to introduce the tale and suggest the allegorical significance hinted at in the novella. Britten's initial music for Vere, however, evokes in its tonal instability and subtle word-setting the composer's immediate appreciation of the importance not merely of Vere's narrative but of his character: it grants Vere a centrality not acknowledged in the libretto. The music underlines both the themes introduced by Vere and Vere's personal articulation of those themes. The importance of this emphasis is indicated by the musical setting of the succeeding scene, when musical themes introduced by Vere (the motif of "Oh what have I done" is echoed in the sailors' "Oh heave") are rearticulated in a more pronouncedly melodic and rhythmic form to suggest the simplicity of the seamen relative to the complexity of Vere. Despite the libretto's apparently equal emphasis on the philosophy expressed by Vere and on his personal dilemma, Britten's overriding interest in the "tragedy of Vere" is such that the emotional and melodic emphasis in the prologue's music comes precisely at the point at which Vere addresses his own dilemma ("Oh what have I done?"). The first half of the setting provides "a tranquil, reflective introduction which has not much to do with the impetuous character we are to see in the narrative of the opera" (Howard 80). It is only with Vere's assertion of personal crisis that Britten introduces musical themes that will continue throughout the opera to emphasize dramatic conflict and emotion. With pronounced rhythms and subsequent melodic echoes of Vere's statement throughout the opera, Britten overcomes Forster's thematic equality to emphasize immediately the importance of Vere as character rather than choric voice.[19]

This is not to contend that Forster did not recognize the dramatic potential of Vere in the opera. Indeed, he stated that he wished to "rescue" Vere from Melville (*Letters* 2: 237). In the same letter to *The Griffin* in which he asserted Billy's primacy, he noted, "How odiously Vere comes out in the trial scene!" Arguing that Vere's "unseemly harangue arises" from "Melville's wavering attitude towards an impeccable commander, a superior philosopher, and a British aristocrat," he observed that "every now and then [Melville] doused Billy's light and felt that Vere, being well-educated and just, must shine like a star" (5). To Forster, Vere and Billy are in a state of conflict in the novella; Billy is the inarticulate handsome sailor, and Vere is the well-read official. Although "Vere is on much more to what's going on" and "really understands it" (qtd. in Cooke, "Britten's *Billy Budd*" 28–9), he is unable to do anything with that knowledge. In recognition of this perceived dilemma, Forster has Vere articulate a conflict between conscience and duty that is only half-recognized and summarily dismissed by Melville's captain. Recognizing in the opera that he is about to "destroy goodness," Vere accepts the inevitability of his necessary action as an unwilling "king of this fragment of earth, of this floating monarchy" (58).

In rendering Vere more sympathetic in the libretto by having him articulate his understanding of events and actions, Forster unwittingly compromises the centrality of his chosen protagonist. The captain gives himself up to despair at the realization of his necessary duty: "I, Edward Fairfax Vere, Captain of the *Indomitable*, lost

---

19   Vere's musical centrality can also be attributed to the fact that the role was intended for Britten's long-time partner, Peter Pears, whose presence in the production would have demanded a role that allowed him to be vocally prominent. As Britten asserted: "Almost every piece I have ever written has been composed with a certain occasion in mind, and usually for definite performers, and certainly always *human* ones" (*On Receiving the First Aspen Award* 11).

with all hands on the infinite sea" (58). By allowing Vere to articulate his suffering, Forster elevates him above Billy in terms not of education or office, but of self-awareness. As a result of this self-awareness, Vere gains the status of tragic hero, and Billy the role of naive victim.

No matter Forster's occasional acknowledgment of the importance of Vere's dilemma, his greater interest in Billy not only left more work for Britten's music in the elucidation of Vere's character, but resulted in considerable confusion as to the dramatic centre of the tale. In a letter to Crozier, Forster indicated his continuing perception of the centrality of Billy's character and influence: "As for the end, I believe that the abortive mutiny should come (if at all) *before* Billy's words. I am not sure whether it should come at all: two anti-climaxes (this & frigate chase) being too much for one drama" (qtd. in Reed, "From First Thoughts" 54). Similarly, Forster wrote to Crozier: "We shall discuss the opera's difficult end. Perhaps I am being deflected by Wagnerism from essential truth, but I do feel that the abortive mutiny might be an anti-climax, whereas Billy's last phrase ... if Ben could get it into the air as he did the last phrase in *Lucretia*, might be very fine" (Crozier, "Writing" 20). For Forster, the effect of Billy's last words on the audience must provide the final focus of the opera.

Britten and Crozier differed most notably from Forster in their interpretation of this last scene. Crozier's correspondence indicates his historical interest in the potential mutiny. Britten was primarily concerned with evoking the impact of Billy's execution (and final cry) on Vere. Furthermore, like Auden, Britten seems to have seen in the novella a suggestion of the Christian influence of Billy after his death; Britten's focus is therefore the effect of Billy's Christian blessing on Vere. These interests are most apparent in Forster's response to a letter (now lost) of Britten's:

> [Billy's last cry] was compassion, comprehension, love. Only Vere understood it, and it has the supernatural force inherent in something which only one person understands. I wish it could have been purely musical. Since we have to use words, Starry Vere seems better than Captain Vere, but the really wrong word is 'God'. Who but Billy, at such a moment, could bless? (qtd. in Reed, "From First Thoughts" 67)

Forster denies the Christian relevance of Billy perceived by Britten: Billy is "our Saviour, yet he is Billy, not Christ or Orion" (*Letters* 2: 235). Despite his firm denial of Billy's Christian function, Forster remains sufficiently ambiguous about Billy's saving role as to cause considerable confusion in the libretto and in the thematic coherence of the opera. Some have found in Billy's saving of Vere a parallel to that of Maurice by Alec Scudder in Forster's novel: "the intellectual Captain Vere is saved by the love of his handsome sailor Billy—with less reason, perhaps, and certainly more poignancy" (Brett 136). Similarly, a convincing examination of the libretto manuscripts indicates that Forster's primary interest in the tale lay in its potential for homosexual interpretation, and thus that Billy's saving role was affiliated with his potential embodiment of a sexual ideal (Hindley, "Love and Salvation in Britten's *Billy Budd*"). Nonetheless, this interpretation can be derived only from studying manuscripts of earlier libretti that were eventually discarded; the libretto as it stands is far from specific in its promotion of a consistently identifiable homosexual theme.

While assertions of Billy's homosexual appeal or of Claggart and Vere's erotic desire for Billy and their resultant need for salvation are valid interpretations of Forster's initial intentions, they are not immediately supported by the opera itself.[20]

Forster further complicates his representation of Billy by frequently invoking a Christian context to the drama. His original plan was to "start realistically, and then alter the ship and crew until they were what we wanted, and good and evil and eternal matters could shine through them" (*Letters* 2: 235). Writing to Lionel Trilling, Forster asserted that after Billy sings "Billy in the Darbies," Dansker brings in "not too obtrusively the eucharist of grog and biscuits" (*Letters* 2: 237). By invoking Christian tradition, Forster invites a Christian interpretation of Billy's significance, and in so doing neglects to establish an alternate context in which Billy's saving ability can be understood. Furthermore, when singing of Billy's archetypal role as "beauty," "handsomeness," and "goodness," Claggart alludes to and modifies the opening lines of the gospel of John: "the light shines in the darkness, and the darkness comprehends it and suffers" (32).[21] These parallels nonetheless remain vague. Recognizing his own mortality and inability to save, Billy sings to Dansker: "I had to strike down that Jemmy Legs—it's fate. And Captain Vere has had to strike me down—Fate. We are both in sore trouble, him and me, with great need for strength, and my trouble's soon ending, so I can't help him longer with his" (60). Here, Billy is merely a helpless repository of goodness. Although he echoes Christ's exhortation to the apostle John to take care of his mother in his request of Dansker, "Dansker of the *Indomitable*, help him all of you" (60), Billy does not indicate in his speech any expression of potential redemptive power. Instead, he can merely envision for himself his own reward: "I've sighted a sail in the storm, the far-shining sail that's not Fate, and I'm contented" (61). Forster simultaneously invites Christian parallels and denies their relevance in a narrative for which he refuses to offer an alternative spiritual or thematic context.

It is in his evocation of the dramatic consequences of Billy's execution that Forster most emphatically implies yet explicitly denies Billy a Christ-like status. In the novella, the description of the hanging is balanced by a consideration of the potential symbolism and meaning of Billy's apparently Christ-like death. There is no such symbolism in the libretto, and in his letter to *The Griffin*, Forster emphasized: "The hero hangs dead from the yard-arm, dead irredeemably and not in any heaven, dead as a doornail, dead as Antigone, and he has given us life" (6). Nonetheless, Vere states at the conclusion to his epilogue: "he has saved me, and blessed me, and the

---

20   The contrast between Forster's writings on the opera and the libretto itself is often ignored by critics. Hindley, for example, offers a compelling argument for the salvation of Vere through the love of Billy. His argument is founded less on the text of the libretto, however, than on Forster's critical writing. Citing the *Griffin* article, Hindley concludes, "For Forster the humanist, this gift of life means a present experience of personal self-worth and the self-affirming reality of personal relationships if not of sensual love" ("Eros in Life and Death" 154). Although Hindley reveals in a musicological analysis the close musical relationship between Billy and Vere, he relies on the critical writings of the librettist rather than on the text of the libretto itself to infer the meaning of this musical closeness.

21   "And the light shineth in darkness; and the darkness comprehended it not" (King James Version, John 1.5).

love that passes understanding has come to me" (63). Although Billy is not Christ-like, his influence is such as to grant the captain a vision of eternal peace. Vere's final assertions are expressed in distinctly Christian tones, and suggest that Vere feels himself to have experienced spiritual redemption in Billy's final exclamation of "Starry Vere, God bless you!"

Significantly, Vere does not articulate his sense of final peace until the end of the opera. Although he is an "old man who has experienced much" (7) at the beginning of the opera, Vere only achieves peace after recalling the tale of Billy; Billy's action does not bring him the vision of "the far-shining sail," but rather his own contemplation of past events. It is implicitly by watching and experiencing the events of the opera that Vere is able to achieve the peace and vision of the enigmatic "sail" which he claims for himself. Vere takes on the role of an ideal audience, transformed to inner peace and conviction through the catharsis invited by the performed drama.

This appreciation of Vere's salvation might superficially resolve the interpretative difficulties invoked by the libretto's simultaneous assertion and denial of Billy's Christian saving function. The opera is further complicated, however, by its ambiguous stance towards Claggart, alternately representing him as absolute evil and as a flawed character. Despite stating unequivocally in *Aspects of the Novel* (98) that Claggart is evil, Forster gives Claggart an extended speech in the libretto in which he bemoans having ever encountered "beauty," "handsomeness," or "goodness": "Would that I lived in my own world always, in that depravity to which I was born. ... The light shines in the darkness, and the darkness comprehends it and suffers. ... What choice remains to me? None, none! I am doomed to annihilate" (32). Forster further indicates the importance of his villain's dramatic complexity when he chastises Britten for not recognizing in the musical setting of Claggart's "self-exposition speech" the passion inherent in the text: "I want *passion*—love constricted, perverted poisoned, but nevertheless *flowing* down its agonising channel; a sexual discharge gone evil. Not soggy depression or growling remorse" (*Letters* 2: 242). Neither Melville nor Forster allows Claggart the absolutism of evil which they claim for their villain. Recognizing the order "such as reigns in Hell" which he has established in his own depravity, Melville's Claggart nonetheless "comprehends" the light "and suffers" (32). As a suffering villain, Claggart cannot be entirely evil; as Auden has noted, the Devil "cannot himself be lustful, gluttonous, avaricious, envious, slothful, or angry, for his pride will not allow him to be anything less than proud" (*Enchafèd Flood* 148). By giving a lengthy speech to Claggart, however, Forster surpasses Melville in his suggestion of the motivation and humanity of his character. While Melville's narrator provides speculation and the occasional insight into the character of Claggart, Forster's libretto allows the character himself a chance to express the passion that motivates his actions.

In Forster's speech for Claggart, therefore, Britten faced the problem of allowing his ostensible villain the prominence of a set-piece that would expose his feelings and make him susceptible to the sympathy of the audience. Forster complained of Britten's setting: "I looked for an aria perhaps, for a more recognisable form. I liked the last section best, and if it is extended so that it dominates, my vague objections may vanish" (*Letters* 2: 242). By confining his "recognisable forms" to the set-pieces of Vere and Billy (i.e., Vere's prologue and epilogue and Billy's final ballad), Britten diminishes the dramatic importance of Claggart and adheres to his own apparent vision of the drama. The last section to which Forster refers is that in which Claggart declares his status as a vengeful villain: "I, John Claggart, Master-at-arms upon the *Indomitable*, have you in my power, and I will destroy you" (33). This statement comes, like Satan's declaration of antagonism towards Adam and Eve in *Paradise Lost*, only after a prolonged assessment of his own complex motivations. By granting only this final statement a musical prominence, Britten not only furthers the dramatic action, but musically identifies his Claggart as an absolute villain, and in so doing qualifies the import of Forster's preceding text. Despite Britten's effort to nullify the potential dramatic inconsistency posed by Claggart's speech, the speech nonetheless exists in the opera. As a result, it subtly complicates the focus of the drama, and most clearly manifests a conflict between Forster and Britten.

Although the opera makers collaborated closely in planning the incidents to be dramatized, therefore, their individual interpretation of these events resulted in half-articulated dramatic and thematic emphases. While Forster was apparently concerned with evoking (rather than delineating) Billy's saving role, Britten was concerned with depicting the tragic centrality of Vere. As the designated historian and dramatic technician, Crozier concerned himself with integrating within the libretto the historical digressions of the original, and imputing to them a dramatic significance within the fictional context of the tale. The opera's incorporation of Melville's digressive descriptions of the frigate attack, the anxieties of the officers about mutiny, and their prevailing animosity towards the French to a certain extent unifies the narrative. At the same time, however, it problematizes the import of the individual dramas played out within that context.

This contrast in thematic focus is amplified by Britten's musical emphasis of the theme of mutiny and unrest on the ship. Possibly finding in mutiny a clearer potential for musical dramatization of conflict, Britten occasionally emphasizes the social and political implications of events at the expense of his dramatic focus on the motivations of the protagonists. The libretto suggests that the misunderstanding of the officers regarding Billy's farewell to *The Rights o'Man* indicates that they are "evidently a very dim lot not to realize it was the ship he was referring to and not Tom Paine's political book" (Wilcox 53). Careful attention to the score, however, reveals that Billy expresses this political threat in his music by echoing the potentially mutinous "Oh heave" motif of the sailors. The officials are justified musically for their suspicions. As a result, Billy's expressions of loyalty to Vere become somewhat complicated by his musical allegiance to the social cause of his fellow seamen.

By endorsing Vere at the end of the opera, Billy to a certain extent saves him by inviting the men with whom he has musically articulated a solidarity of social experience to recognize Vere's official status. At the same time, however, this exhortation results in subsequent rumblings of potential mutiny. By blessing Vere, Billy can be read as betraying the crew: "Billy's spiritual goodness appears not only selective, but class selective in its effectiveness" (Emslie 48). The importance of this scene as that in which Billy saves Vere is undermined by Britten's musical dramatization of potential mutiny. Coming as it does as a grand finale to the opera, this emphasis again distracts from the centrality of the relationship between Billy and Vere, lending to the scene a musical political emphasis that distances the cause of Billy from the concerns of Vere. Billy's influence as depicted in both libretto and music is thus suggested to be potentially subversive: his musical allegiance to integrated historical and social concerns complicates an interpretation of his character as an exemplar of innocent goodness.

This apparent conflict in thematic interest is not confined to a difference among the three collaborators; both Britten and Forster contradict their own declared dramatic interests throughout the opera. Forster denies his declared protagonist a Christian function, yet articulates the saving effect of Billy in the context of biblical archetypes and Christian parallels. Although Billy is his intended protagonist, Forster unwittingly allows for the usurpation of this protagonist by granting him the role of a cipher rather than a dramatic personality and by giving to Vere lines which suggest his role as tragic hero. Billy is "so innately but 'meaningfully' vague that even at the end of the opera no one is entirely sure who he really was" (Emslie 52).

Although Britten clearly considers Vere to be the center of his drama, he occasionally detracts from this centrality by musically emphasizing social unrest. Britten chooses, like Melville, to abstain from depicting the interview between Billy and Vere. The inconclusive speculations of Melville's narrator achieve some musical representation in Britten's ambiguous 34 chords. Many, including Auden, objected to this decision to evoke the scene with chords of ambiguous tonal relation rather than to provide a more traditionally operatic scene of dramatic conflict and high emotion. Britten may well have recognized in the original a deliberate avoidance of narrative responsibility, and chose at this point to remain faithful to the text. His greater interest in the captain's dilemma and the influence of Billy's death on Vere, however, renders this omission more problematic than it is in the source. It is possible that Britten recognized in this scene an opportunity to manifest absolute musical autonomy; with the absence of a text, he gained an overriding creative role. In thus "liberating" music from text and immediate narrative pattern, Britten ironically comes closest to achieving Forster's absolute music, without his librettist. Furthermore, by embodying the lack of narrative responsibility which characterizes Melville's novella, Britten faithfully adapts the inherent ambiguities of the original text within an operatic idiom.

Emslie states that *Billy Budd* "rests on strategies of evasion which, alongside an attendant ambiguity of language and imagery, mislead the spectator into believing that the material reaches some final resolution when in fact at crucial points the issue at stake is flunked and fudged" (44). This argument might equally be applied to the novella and the opera. Ultimately, the opera is just as much about doubt and confusion as it is about individual dramas or social unrest. Like that of the source, the opera's "most powerful and most modern" feature is that it "leaves the tension between personal concerns and the wider world ... teasingly unresolved" (Whittall, "'Twisted Relations'" 170).

That the opera has maintained its popularity is doubtless due to the apparent uniformity of structure and theme achieved by the framing device of Vere's prologue and epilogue, and the complex motivic and tonal structure of the score. Just as Melville's tale can be read for its "germane incidents," the opera can be appreciated for its structural emphasis on Vere, and its musical emphasis on the dramatic conflict between individuals and social classes. Although the opera lacks a consistent dramatic and thematic focus, therefore, it is sufficiently unified musically as to suggest that this inconsistency is deliberate, rather than inadvertent. While Porter is justified in his observation that the libretto "is flawed by a vagueness in the presentation of what its writers have chosen to make the central theme" ("Britten's 'Billy Budd'" 118), his assertion of a flaw can be countered with the argument that the opera successfully articulates a modern instability and uncertainty within a musically effective context: "The opera can be seen as embodying, in its formal structure, the epistemological notion of a 'gap': a key post-structuralist concept that explodes the myth of the stable and homogenous work of art" (Emslie 51–2).

By invoking archetypal conflict, political realism, and psychological complexity and subsuming these elements within a tightly structured musical score, the creators simultaneously achieve the psychological realism and complexity suggested by Melville's ambiguous and subjective narrator, and transcend that specific context by complicating the "aesthetic pattern" of their drama. In so doing, the collaborators achieve through opera what Forster asserts of Melville's original text. The opera is in effect Melville's "song not without some words"; expressing some social ideals and themes, it transcends through music critical concerns of thematic inconsistency to render staged events imminent and powerful.

Thus, whereas Jones and Hoddinott ultimately romanticize Stevenson's realistic tale of psychological development, Forster, Crozier, and Britten inadvertently transcribe the psychological complexities and ambiguities of Melville's original text into a form which allows, through its musically expressive potential, for the celebration of such inconsistencies. That *Billy Budd* is structurally and thematically more complex as an opera than *The Beach of Falesá* is not simply a result of the talents of its librettists and composer. The conscientious adaptation of a "difficult" literary work demands an audience capable of appreciating that adaptation. Britten and his librettists wrote for an audience already accustomed to the psychologically explorative operas exemplified by *Peter Grimes* and *The Rape of Lucretia*. The interest of Forster, Crozier, and Britten in the faithful transcription of a difficult literary work necessarily demanded an informedly literary audience conscious of the reinterpretative process embodied in the opera. Stephen Spender has noted in his journals the presence in the audience of "the Harewoods, the Clarks, Willie [Somerset] Maugham, Rose Macaulay, William Plomer, Joe Ackerley, John and Myfanwy Piper, Desmond Shawe-Taylor, etc." (106). Forster's earlier talk at Aldeburgh, along with those by Auden and Britten himself, defined a literary consciousness to the Aldeburgh Festival that ensured a total experience of text, music, and drama. This consciousness allowed not only complexities in libretto and music, but also a natural expectation that the audience be aware of the nature of the operatic adaptation and interpretation. The comparative conventionality of the Jones and Hoddinott opera is not necessarily attributable to any conservatism on the part of composer and librettist, but to their awareness of a difference in expectation on the part of their audience.

Forster implied in his literary criticism the need for fiction to overcome such potentially limiting aspects of narrative as structure and "aesthetic pattern." In so doing, it could better emulate the "rhythm" of music and achieve an artistic transcendence over realistic specificity. Ironically, however, it is only through its tense dialogue with the opera's source that the libretto, with its attendant ambiguities and inconsistencies, succeeds in achieving any such "transcendence." The opera ultimately manifests simultaneously Melville's "harmony and temporary salvation," Britten's "classical control and balance ... and perfection of [musical] detail," and Forster's "grand opera," deceptively mounted "clearly and grandly."

Conclusion

Dear Sir,

I have read with interest and approval your article on *An Opera of Good and Evil* in this morning's *Times*, but wish you could have managed to squeeze in a reference to Eric Crozier and myself. We did the libretto. We worked on it in Britten's house for several weeks. We might reasonably be credited with having helped to interpret his intentions and his conception of Melville's intentions. (Forster, qtd. in Crozier, "The Writing of *Billy Budd*" 26)

In his letter to the *Times*, E. M. Forster expresses his awareness of a prevailing lack of regard for the role of the librettist. Such oversight is notable, given the literary prominence of many twentieth-century British librettists, and the literary preoccupations of modern British opera. Indeed, it is incongruous not only with the concerns of the librettist, but also with those of the composer who specifically chose his librettist to adapt a recognizably literary work.

Auden, Harsent, and Forster were willing to collaborate in a form traditionally characterized by the demeaned role of the librettist. The librettists recognized in their role the potential to exert a distinctly literary influence which has yet to be consistently acknowledged. Moreover, British opera tends to assert its respectability in terms of its literary and intellectual integrity. With the interest of British opera in both critical appreciation and artistic creativity, the role and explicative credentials of the librettist have gained an increased status in British opera.

Curiously, few librettists assert this dominant status. Auden and Forster, for example, explicitly deny any such assumptions, and speak of submitting to the greater authority of the music or the composer. This music, however, must first be determined by the libretto, which not only provides a text for setting, but assumes interpretative control. Forster adopted a propriety approach towards *Billy Budd*: he was setting out to "rescue" Vere from Melville and to ensure Billy's centrality. Similarly, Hassall tried to "rescue" Cressida from Shakespeare, and Auden and Kallman hoped to rescue their source from "Gluck-y Greekiness." The librettists were concerned not merely with interpreting their source, but with either improving or returning that source to its original "purity" after earlier adaptations. By thus associating critical interpretation with instinctive literary tendencies towards reparation, the librettists associate their assumedly superior critical abilities with an equally superior literary knowledge of what has to be done in order to offer a successful improvement or rewriting of their source.

Such assumption of authority becomes even more problematic for the composer when librettists "stray" into musical concerns. Auden and Kallman differ from the other librettists examined in their articulation of the rescue of their source in terms of operatic, rather than literary, precedent. Medieval narratives have rarely been treated operatically, and contemporary prose narratives such as *The Beach of Falesá* and *Billy Budd* were too recent and obscure at the time of adaptation to have received prominent adaptive treatment. Classical sources, however, have been translated, adapted and interpreted in various works, most memorably in the visual arts and in opera. By choosing a classical source for their opera, the creators of *The Bassarids* insinuate themselves and their implied interpretative authority equally within a literary and an operatic tradition. Far from aspiring towards a literary interpretation of a literary source, Auden and Kallman attempt to dictate musical style and structure with a firm awareness of operatic precedent and the place of their creation within operatic tradition.

These operas were written in a cultural climate that witnessed the increasing involvement of literary figures in the criticism, creation, and representation of music. Thus, Forster's comments in *Aspects of the Novel* about the "song with some words" quality of *Billy Budd* cannot be ignored in the context of his later libretto. Forster is unwilling to acknowledge the independent language of musical expression. In denying the independent constructive skill required for the creation of music, Forster creates for the writer the opportunity to "muddy up the wells" in the manner identified by Margaret Schlegel in *Howards End*.

While such "muddying up" is sufficiently problematic to novelistic construction, it becomes significantly more so in the creation of an opera. Opera traditionally demands text that allows for musical expression, rather than text that embodies musical expression. Ironically, it is Auden, the one writer who speaks so emphatically of ceding creative authority to the composer, who poses the greatest threat to the creative independence of that composer. In their construction of set-pieces and their specifications of musical style, Auden and Kallman attempt to determine the musical construction of the opera. Their complex verse impedes direct musical adaptation and necessitates an appreciation of the musical construction of the libretto independent from the score. Because of the increased status of the librettist in British opera, such independent musicality in the libretto can be less easily dismissed by a contemporary composer than it might have been in a previous century. What results is a thorough literary interpretation of a source, a libretto independently musical in terms of structure, rhythm, and verse sound, and a score capable of only half-acknowledging the metrical, interpretative, and structural complexities of its libretto.

This convergence of musical and literary tendencies most intriguingly informs the approach of Tippett. Instead of asserting the independent importance of musical construction and creativity, Tippett emphasizes his own literary awareness by including literary references throughout his libretti. Furthermore, he asserts his independent intellectual status by arguing for his literary ability, an ability which he equates with the expression of ideology in text, rather than in musical language. Tippett aligns his creations with the literary dramatic tradition of Shaw, Auden, Eliot, and Fry. In so doing, he implicitly denies music the creative independence similarly ignored by Forster in *Aspects of the Novel* and by Auden and Kallman in the libretto to *The Bassarids*.

One might consider that such a "muddying up of the wells" and breaking down of the creative boundaries between literature and music is necessary for an ideal union between music and text, and thus a successful opera. As *The Bassarids* and *King Priam* reveal, however, such a breaking down frequently results in the subjugation of one art to another. It is significant that out of the operas examined in this study, *Billy Budd* seems to adhere most prominently to the concerns of its original source while doing some justice to the individual interpretative concerns of its composer and two librettists. Britten, Crozier, and Forster were sufficiently assertive in their own approaches to the opera as to avoid any "muddying up of the wells." Unlike the equally different approaches in *Gawain*, these approaches engage to some extent with each other. Where Birtwistle imposed his own musical structures without setting those of Harsent, Forster, Britten, and Crozier tended to agree on an overall structure to the libretto that would be supported in the music. Nonetheless, the perception and realization of the thematic emphasis behind that structure differed between the collaborators. The frequently disparate interpretations which result within the opera's overarching structure often contradict and undermine any central dramatic emphasis in the opera. In so doing, however, they ultimately represent the many narrative idiosyncrasies of the original source, and embody in that achievement the perceived ideals of modern British opera.

Is it coincidental that a narrative that is arguably very difficult to adapt ultimately provides the source for a successful adaptation and a successful opera? The majority of the sources for modern British operas pose notable adaptive difficulties, often because of their structure and narrative voice. While Forster, Britten and Crozier may not have initially perceived the difficulties posed by the narrative complexities of their original source, or Walton and Hassall may not have noticed the constant vacillation of narrative focus in *Troilus and Criseyde*, it is equally possible to assume that such narrative complexity has become an understood expectation, indeed criterion, of modern British opera.

In *Aspects of the Novel*, E. M. Forster praises the "unresolvable difficulties" within *Moby-Dick* which allow for the expression of "prophetic song": "Nothing can be stated about *Moby Dick* except that it is a contest. The rest is song" (97). Such an assessment arguably demeans the complexities and logic inherent in musical structure. When this view is applied to modern operas such as *The Bassarids*, *Troilus and Cressida*, or *Billy Budd*, however, this difficulty is removed. In these operas, the music advertises its presence as construction rather than inevitable expression precisely because of the conflict which exists between itself and the text of the libretto. As a result, it creates "unresolvable difficulties" and allows for the expression of Forster's "song."

Modern British opera demands by its literary emphasis a revaluation of the aesthetic criteria by which it is commonly assessed. Is it not possible that in its continuing aspiration towards literary respectability, British opera intends to inspire in its viewer, listener, and reader an appreciation for its representation of uncertainty and ambiguity in a context stabilized by the vague, yet reassuringly familiar voice of music? Indeed, instead of assessing these works in terms of the faithfulness of their adaptation, the coherence of their dramatic structure, or the transcendent effect of their music, it is perhaps more accurate to recognize in them the articulation of a constant struggle in literature and music towards the artistically undefinable. Ultimately, in their narrative vacillations, conflicting structures, and moments of occasional lyricism, modern British operas can be seen as expressing their recognition of a universal artistic desire to embody "some element of human nature, some aspect of the human condition which is of permanent concern to human beings irrespective of their time and place" (Auden, "The World of Opera" 95).

Works Consulted

Ackerman, John, ed. *Dylan Thomas: The Filmscripts*. London: Dent, 1995.

Addison, Joseph. *The Works of Joseph Addison Complete in Three Volumes: Embracing the Whole of the "Spectator," &c*. Vol. 1. New York: Harper, 1845.

Adlington, Robert. Rev. of *Gawain*, comp. Harrison Birtwistle. *The Musical Times* 135 (1994): 463.

— *The Music of Harrison Birtwistle*. Cambridge: Cambridge UP, 2000.

Adorno, Theodor W. *Philosophy of Modern Music*. Trans. Anne G. Mitchell and Welsey V. Blomster. New York: Seabury, 1973.

Albright, Daniel. *Untwisting the Serpent: Modernism in Music, Literature, and Other Arts*. Chicago: U of Chicago P, 2000.

— ed. *Modernism and Music: An Anthology of Sources*. Chicago: U of Chicago P, 2004.

Arrowsmith, William. Introduction. *The Bacchae*. Ed. Grene and Lattimore. New York: Washington Square P, 1972. 147–59.

Aschaffenburg, Walter. "Bartleby: Genesis of an Opera I." *Melville Annual 1965 Symposium: Bartleby the Scrivener*. Ed. Howard P. Vincent. Kent: Kent State UP, 1966: 25–41.

Auden, W. H. "Cav & Pag." Auden, *The Dyer's Hand*. 475–82.

—. "The Composer." 1938. *W. H. Auden: Collected Poems*. Ed. Edward Mendelson. New York: Random, 1976. 148.

—. *The Dyer's Hand and Other Essays*. London: Faber, 1963.

—. *The Enchafèd Flood, or The Romantic Iconography of the Sea*. New York: Random, 1950.

—. "The Fall of Rome." Bucknell and Jenkins, *'In Solitude'* 120–37.

—. "Herman Melville." 1939. *W. H. Auden: Collected Poems*. Ed. Edward Mendelson. New York: Random, 1976. 200.

—. "How the Libretto of the Opera 'The Rake's Progress' was Born." Trans. Mendelson from "Com'è Nato il Libretto Dell'Opera 'The Rake's Progress'." Auden and Kallman, *Libretti* 607–11.

—. "Making, Knowing and Judging." Auden, *The Dyer's Hand* 31–60.

—. "Music in Shakespeare." Auden, *The Dyer's Hand* 500–527.

—. "Notes on Music and Opera." Auden, *The Dyer's Hand* 465–74.

—. *Paul Bunyan*. Auden and Kallman, *Libretti* 3–46.

—. *Secondary Worlds*. London: Faber, 1968.

—. "The World of Opera." Auden, *Secondary Worlds* 85–116.

—. Auden, W. H. and Christopher Isherwood. *W. H. Auden and Christopher Isherwood: Plays and Other Dramatic Writings by W. H. Auden 1938–1938*. Princeton: Princeton UP, 1988.

Auden, W. H. and Chester Kallman. *The Bassarids: Opera Seria with Intermezzo in One Act based on "The Bacchae" of Euripides*. Auden and Kallman, *Libretti* 249–313.

—. *Delia*. Auden and Kallman, *Libretti* 95–126.

—. *The Rake's Progress*. Auden and Kallman, *Libretti* 47–93.

—. "Euripides for Today." *The Musical Times* 115 (1974): 833–34.

—. "Translating Opera Libretti." Auden, *The Dyer's Hand* 483–99.

—. *W. H. Auden and Chester Kallman: Libretti and Other Dramatic Writings by W.H. Auden, 1939–1973*. Ed. Edward Mendelson. Princeton: Princeton UP, 1993.

—. "Why Rewrite a Masterpiece?" Auden and Kallman, *Libretti* 705–7.

Auden, W. H. and Louis MacNiece. *Letters from Iceland*. London: Faber, 1967.

Auden, W. H. and Paul B. Taylor, trans. *The Elder Edda: A Selection*. London: Faber, 1973.

Bahlke, George W., ed. *Critical Essays on W. H. Auden*. New York: Hall, 1991.

Banfield, Stephen. "British Opera in Retrospect." *The Musical Times* 127 (1986): 205–7.

—, ed. *Music in Britain: The Twentieth Century*. Oxford: Blackwell, 1995.

Bartley, William. "'Measured Forms' and Orphic Eloquence: The Style of Herman Melville's *Billy Budd, Sailor*." *University of Toronto Quarterly* 59 (1990): 516–34.

Bell, Katherine, ed. "A Change of Heart: Six Letters from Auden to Professor and Mrs. E.R. Dodds Written at the Beginning of World War II." Bucknell and Jenkins, *W.H. Auden: 'The Map of All My Youth'* 95–115.

The Bible: Authorized King James Version. Ed. Robert Carroll and Stephen Prickett. Oxford: Oxford UP, 1998.

Birtwistle, Harrison. *Gawain: An Opera in Two Acts*. London: Universal, 1992.

—. Interview with Mark Pappenheim. *The Independent*. 8 April 1994: 21.

Blom, Eric. "The Later William Walton." *The Listener*. 20 September 1945: 333.

Bokina, John. "Eros and Revolution: Henze's *Bassarids*." *The European Legacy: Toward New Paradigms* 1.4 (1996): 1591–6.

—. *Opera and Politics: From Monteverdi to Henze*. New Haven: Yale UP, 1997.

Bowen, Meirion. *Michael Tippett*. London: Robson, 1982.

—. *Michael Tippett*. 2nd ed. London: Robson, 1997.

—. "Tippett in Interview." Bowen, *Michael Tippett* [1982] 155–67.

Boyd, Malcolm. "The Beach of Falesá." *The Musical Times* 115 (1974): 207–9.

Boyden, David D. Rev. of *Troilus and Cressida*, comp. William Walton. *The Musical Quarterly* 41 (1958): 238–41.

Bradley, Noel. "The Non-Clinical Test of a Clinical Theory: *Billy Budd*, Novel and Libretto." *International Review of Psycho-Analysis* 7 (1980): 233–49.

Bradley, Sculley, Richmond Croom Beatty, and E. Hudson Long, eds. *The American Tradition in Literature*. New York: Norton, 1956.

Braswell, William. *Melville's Religious Thought: An Essay in Interpretation*. 1943. New York: Duke UP, 1973.

Brett, Philip. "Salvation at Sea: *Billy Budd*." Palmer, *Britten Companion* 133–43.

Britten, Benjamin. *Billy Budd: An Opera in Two Acts, Op. 50*. London: Boosey, 1961.

—. *Letters from a Life: The Selected Letters and Diaries of Benjamin Britten, 1913–1976*. Ed. Donald Mitchell and Philip Reed. 2 vols. London: Faber, 1991.

—. *On Receiving the First Aspen Award*. London: Faber, 1964.

—. *The Operas of Benjamin Britten: The Complete Librettos Illustrated with Designs of the First Production.* Ed. David Herbert. New York: Columbia UP, 1979.

—. "Some Notes on Forster and Music." *Aspects of E. M. Forster: Essays and Recollections Written for his Ninetieth Birthday 1st January 1969.* Ed. Oliver Stallybrass. London: Edward Arnold, 1969: 81–6.

Brown, Marshall. "Origins of Modernism: Musical Structures and Narrative Forms." Scher 75–92.

Bucknell, Katherine and Nicholas Jenkins, eds. *'In Solitude, for Company': W. H. Auden After 1940—Unpublished Prose and Recent Criticism.* Oxford: Clarendon, 1995.

—, eds. *W. H. Auden: 'The Map of All My Youth'—Early Works, Friends and Influences.* Oxford: Clarendon, 1990.

Burgess, Anthony. *Oberon Old and New.* London: Hutchinson, 1985.

Burra, Peter. Introduction. *A Passage to India.* By E. M. Forster. London: Dent, 1942. xi–xxviii.

Byerly, Alison. *Realism, Representation, and the Arts in Nineteenth-Century Literature.* Cambridge: Cambridge UP, 1997.

Calder, Jenni. Introduction. *The Strange Case of Dr Jekyll and Mr Hyde and Other Stories.* By Robert Louis Stevenson. London: Penguin, 1979. 7–23.

—. *RLS: A Life Study.* London: Hamilton, 1980.

Caldwell, John. *The Oxford History of English Music.* Vol. 2. Oxford: Oxford UP, 1999.

Campbell, Jackson J. Introduction. *The Tragedy of Troilus and Cressida.* By William Shakespeare. *The Yale Shakespeare: The Complete Works.* New York: Barnes, 1993. 323–5.

Carpenter, Humphrey. *Benjamin Britten: A Biography.* London: Faber, 1992.

—. *W. H. Auden: A Biography.* Boston: Houghton, 1981.

Carpenter, Kevin. *Desert Isles and Pirate Islands: The Island Theme in Nineteenth-Century English Juvenile Fiction: A Survey and Bibliography.* Frankfurt: Lang, 1984.

Chaucer, Geoffrey. *Troilus and Criseyde. The Riverside Chaucer.* Ed. Larry D. Benson. 3rd. ed. New York: Houghton, 1987. 473–595.

Clark, Andrew. Rev. of *Gawain,* comp. Harrison Birtwistle. *Opera* 51 (2000): 367–70.

Clark, Robert S. "Music Chronicle." *The Hudson Review* 44 (1991): 113–17.

Clark, Thekla. *Wystan and Chester: A Personal Memoir of W. H. Auden and Chester Kallman.* London: Faber, 1995.

Clarke, David, ed. *Tippett Studies.* Cambridge: Cambridge UP, 1999.

Clements, Andrew. "'Gawain'—an Opera About People." *Opera* 42 (1991): 874–9.

—. "King Priam." *Opera* 35 (1984): 1383–5.

—. "Tippett at 80." *Opera* 36 (1985): 16–24.

Colvin, Sidney, ed. *The Works of Robert Louis Stevenson. South Seas Edition.* New York: C. Schriber's Sons, 1925.

Conacher, D. J. *Euripidean Drama: Myth, Theme and Structure.* Toronto: U of Toronto P, 1967.

Conrad, Peter. *Romantic Opera and Literary Form.* Berkeley: U of California P, 1977.

—. *A Song of Love and Death: The Meaning of Opera*. London: Chatto, 1987.

Cooke, Mervyn, ed. *The Cambridge Companion to Benjamin Britten*. Cambridge: Cambridge UP, 1999.

—. "Britten's *Billy Budd*: Melville as Opera Libretto." Cooke and Reed 27–41.

—. "Britten's 'Prophetic Song': Tonal Symbolism in *Billy Budd*." Cooke and Reed 85–110.

—. "Herman Melville's Billy Budd." Cooke and Reed 15–26.

—. "Stage History and Critical Reception." Cooke and Reed 135–49.

Cooke, Mervyn and Philip Reed, eds. *Benjamin Britten: Billy Budd*. Cambridge: Cambridge UP, 1993.

Corse, Sandra. *Opera and the Uses of Language: Mozart, Verdi and Britten*. Rutherford: Fairleigh Dickinson UP, 1987.

—. *Operatic Subjects: The Evolution of Self in Modern Opera*. London: Associated U Presses, 2000.

Cox, David and John Bishop, eds. *Peter Warlock: A Centenary Celebration*. London: Thames, 1994.

Coxe, Louis O. and Robert Chapman. *Billy Budd*. New York: Hill, 1962.

Craft, Robert. "The Poet and the Rake." Spender, *W. H. Auden* 149–55.

Craggs, Stewart R., ed. *William Walton: Music and Literature*. Aldershot: Ashgate, 1999.

Cross, Jonathan. *Harrison Birtwistle: Man, Mind, Music*. London: Faber, 2000.

Crozier, Eric. "Composer and Librettist." *Composer* 18 (1966): 2–5.

—. "Staging first productions I." Herbert 24–33.

—. "The Writing of *Billy Budd*." *Opera Quarterly* 4.3 (1986): 11–27.

Cuckston, Alan. "The Songs." Craggs 1–21.

Dahlhaus, Carl. "What is a Musical Drama?" Trans. Mary Whittall. *Cambridge Opera Journal* 1 (1989): 95–111.

Davenport-Hines, Richard. *Auden*. London: Heinemann, 1995.

Davies, Alistair and Alan Sinfield, eds. *British Culture of the Postwar: An Introduction to Literature and Society 1945–1999*. London: Routledge, 2000.

Davies, James A. *A Reference Companion to Dylan Thomas*. Westport: Greenwood, 1998.

Day, James. *'Englishness' in Music: From Elizabethan Times to Elgar, Tippett and Britten*. London: Thames, 1999.

Dean, Winton. Rev. of *Gawain*, comp. Harrison Birtwistle. *Opera* 45 (1994): 749–52.

—. Rev. of *Troilus and Cressida*, comp. William Walton. *The Musical Times* 118 (1977): 55.

Deane, Basil. *Alun Hoddinott*. [Cardiff]: U of Wales P, 1978.

Dent, Edward J. *Opera*. 1940. Harmondsworth: Penguin, 1945.

Dickinson, Peter, ed. *Twenty British Composers*. London: Chester, 1975.

Dodds, E. R. Introduction. *Euripides Bacchae*. London: Oxford UP, 1960. x–lix.

—. *The Greeks and the Irrational*. Berkeley: U of California P, 1951.

—. *Missing Persons: An Autobiography*. Oxford: Clarendon, 1977.

Douglas, Lawrence. "Discursive Limits: Narrative and Judgment in *Billy Budd*." *Mosaic* 27 (1994): 141–60.

Downs, Philip G. *Classical Music: The Era of Haydn, Mozart, and Beethoven*. New York: Norton, 1992.

Driver, Paul. "King Priam." *Opera* 36 (1985): 700–703.

Drummond, John D. "Apollo and Dionysos: The Study of an Aesthetic Idea in Wagner's *Tristan und Isolde*, Schoenberg's *Moses und Aron* and Henze's *The Bassarids*." Diss. U. of Birmingham, 1972.

Dryden, John. Preface. *Albion and Albanius. Works of John Dryden. Plays: Albion and Albanius, Don Sebastian, Amphityron*. Ed. Earl Miner. Berkeley: U of California P, 1976. 2–13.

—. Preface. *King Arthur. Works of John Dryden. Plays: King Author* [sic], *Cleomenes, Love Triumphant, Contributions to the Pilgrim*. Ed. Vinton A. Dearing. Berkeley: U of California P, 1996. 4–9.

Duncan, Edmoundstone. *Ultra-Modernism in Music: A Treatise on the Latter-Day Revolution in Musical Art*. London: Rogers, 1915.

Duncan, Ronald. "Artistic Policy of the English Stage Company." Krysia Cairns, *Ronald Duncan the Man and the Artist*. Plymouth: U of Plymouth, 1998. 108–14.

—. Introduction. *Collected Plays*. London: Rupert Hart-Davis, 1971. vii–xiii.

Eckert, Michael. "Dialogues with History—Designs for the Future: Four Centuries of European Opera." *The European Legacy: Toward New Paradigms* 1.4 (1996): 1585–90.

Eigner, E. M. *Robert Louis Stevenson and Romantic Tradition*. Princeton: Princeton UP, 1966.

Eliot, T. S. *Poetry and Drama*. London: Faber, 1951.

—. *The Waste Land. Selected Poems: T. S. Eliot*. London: Faber, 1970. 49–74.

Emslie, Barry. "*Billy Budd* and the Fear of Words." *Cambridge Opera Journal* 4 (1992): 43–59.

Euripides. *The Bacchae*. Trans. William Arrowsmith. *Euripides V*. Ed. David Grene and Richmond Lattimore. New York: Washington Square P, 1972. 147–227.

Evans, Edwin. "Modern British Composers: William Walton." *The Musical Times and Singing-Class Circular* 85 (1944): 329–32, 364–71.

Evans, Peter. "Benjamin Britten." Sadie, *The New Grove Twentieth-Century English Masters* 239–96.

—. *The Music of Benjamin Britten*. 1979. Oxford: Oxford UP, 1996.

—. "Sir William Walton's Manner and Mannerism." *The Listener* 20 August 1959: 297.

Fawkes, Richard. *Welsh National Opera*. London: Watts, 1986.

Ferris, Paul. *Dylan Thomas*. London: Hodder, 1977.

Foley, Mary. "The Digressions in *Billy Budd*." Stafford, *Melville's Billy Budd* 220–23.

Forbes, Anne-Marie H. "Celticism in British Opera: 1878–1938." *Music Review* 47.3 (1986): 176–83.

Ford, Boris, ed. *Benjamin Britten's Poets: The Poetry He Set to Music*. Manchester: Carcanet, 1994.

Ford, Andrew. *Composer to Composer: Conversations about Contemporary Music*. London: Quartet, 1993.

Foreman, Lewis, ed. *British Music Now: A Guide to the Work of Younger Composers.* London: Elek, 1975.

Foreman, Lewis. *From Parry to Britten: British Music in Letters 1900–1945.* London: Batsford, 1987.

—. "Walton's Words." Craggs 228–55.

Forster, E. M. *Aspects of the Novel and Related Writings.* 1927. London: Edward Arnold, 1974.

—. "The C Minor of that Life." 1941. Forster, *Two Cheers for Democracy* 119–21.

—. "George Crabbe and Peter Grimes: A Lecture given at the Aldeburgh Festival of 1948." 1948. Forster, *Two Cheers for Democracy* 166–80.

—. "George Crabbe: The Poet and the Man." *Peter Grimes/Gloriana.* Ed. Nicholas John. London: Calder, 1983. Rpt. From Salder's Wells Opera Book *Peter Grimes*, 1945.

—. *Howards End.* 1910. London: Edward Arnold, 1973.

—. "Letter." *The Griffin* 1 (1951): 4–6.

—. *Selected Letters of E. M. Forster.* Ed. Mary Lago and P. N. Furbank. 2 vols. Cambridge: Harvard UP, 1983–85.

—. "Not Listening to Music." 1939. Forster, *Two Cheers for Democracy* 122–25.

—. "The *Raison d'Etre* of Criticism: An Address Delivered at a Symposium on Music at Harvard University." 1947. Forster, *Two Cheers for Democracy* 105–18.

—. *Two Cheers for Democracy.* 1951. London: Edward Arnold, 1972.

Forster, E.M. and Eric Crozier. *Billy Budd: Opera in Four Acts.* London: Hawkes, 1951.

—. *Billy Budd: Opera in Two Acts.* Rev. ed. London: Hawkes, 1961.

Frantzen, Allen J. *Troilus and Criseyde: The Poem and the Frame.* New York: Twayne, 1993.

Frazer, James George. *The Golden Bough: A Study in Magic and Religion.* London: Macmillan, 1980.

Fry, Christopher. "Why Verse?" *Vogue* (March 1955): 136–7.

Fuller, John. *A Reader's Guide to W. H. Auden.* London: Thames, 1970.

—. *W. H. Auden: A Commentary.* London: Faber, 1998.

Furbank, P. N. *E. M. Forster: A Life.* 2 vols. London: Secker, 1978.

Galloway, William Johnson, M.P. *The Operatic Problem.* London: J. Long, 1902.

Giles, F. "Regionalism: Three Overlooked Poets." *Agenda* 13 (1975): 75–7.

Gilman, Todd. "*The Beggar's Opera* and British Opera." *University of Toronto Quarterly* 66 (1997): 539–61.

Goldmann, Lucien. *The Hidden God: A Study of Tragic Vision in The Pensées of Pascal and The Tragedies of Racine.* Trans. Philip Thody. London: Routledge, 1964.

Gordon, Jan B. "The Third Cheer: 'Voice' in Forster." *Twentieth Century Literature* 31 (1985): 315–28.

Gordon, R. K., ed. *The Story of Troilus.* 1964. Toronto: U of Toronto P, 1988.

Graves, Robert and Alan Hodge. *The Long Weekend: A Social History of Great Britain 1918–1939.* 1940. London: Macdonald, 1991.

Gray, Cecil. *Musical Chairs, or Between Two Stools.* 1948. London: Hogarth, 1985.

Griffiths, Paul. *Modern Music and After: Directions since 1945*. Oxford: Oxford UP, 1995.

Groos, Arthur and Roger Parker, eds. *Reading Opera*. Princeton: Princeton UP, 1988.

Hall, Michael. *Harrison Birtwistle*. London: Robson, 1984.

—. *Harrison Birtwistle in Recent Years*. London: Robson, 1998.

—. "The Sanctity of the Context: Birtwistle's Recent Music." *The Musical Times* 129 (1988): 14–16.

Hamilton, William. *Melville and the Gods*. Chico: Scholars, 1985.

Harding, James. *Ivor Novello*. London: Allen, 1987.

Harris, John. *A Bibliographical Guide to Twenty-Four Modern Anglo-Welsh Writers*. Cardiff: U of Wales P, 1994.

Harsent, David. *A Bird's Idea of Flight*. London: Faber, 1998.

—. *From an Inland Sea*. Harmondsworth: Penguin, 1985.

—. *Gawain*. London: Universal, 1991.

—. *Mister Punch*. Oxford: Oxford UP, 1984.

—. *News from the Front*. Oxford: Oxford UP, 1993.

—. *Selected Poems*. Oxford: Oxford UP, 1989.

Hartog, Howard, ed. *European Music in the Twentieth Century*. 1957. Harmondsworth: Penguin, 1961.

Hassall, Christopher, ed. *Ambrosia and Small Beer: The Record of a Correspondence between Edward Marsh and Christopher Hassall*. London: Longmans, 1964.

—. "And Now—Walton's First Opera." *Music and Musicians* 3 (1954): 12–14.

—. *Devil's Dyke with Compliment and Satire*. London: Heinemann, 1936.

—. *Edward Marsh, Patron of the Arts: A Biography*. London: Longmans, 1959.

—. *Out of the Whirlwind: A Play for Westminster Abbey June 1953*. London: Heinemann, 1953.

—. *Ivor Novello: Memorial Address*. Operetta Research Centre. 9 September 2007. <http://www.operetta-researchcenter.org/print.php?task=archart&cat=2&sub_cat=5&id=00107>

—. "To a Contemporary Poet: An Epistle." Hassall, *Devil's Dyke with Compliment and Satire* 79–86.

—. *Troilus and Cressida: Opera in Three Acts*. London: Oxford UP, 1954.

Hayford, Harrison and Merton M. Sealts Jr., ed. *Billy Budd: The Genetic Text*. Chicago: U of Chicago P, 1962.

Helm, Everett. "Current Chronicle." *The Musical Quarterly* 53.3 (July 1967): 397–415.

Henderson, Robert. "Hans Werner Henze." Sadie, *The New Grove Dictionary of Music and Musicians* 489–96.

Henze, Hans Werner. Appendix. "Open Letter to Hans Werner Henze." By Helmut Lachenmann. Trans. Jeffrey Stadelman. *Perspectives of New Music* 35 (1997): 194–99.

—. "*The Bassarids*: Psychology in Music." Henze, *Music and Politics* 147–51.

—. "*The Bassarids*: Symphony in One Act." Henze, *Music and Politics* 152–6.

—. "*The Bassarids*: Tradition and Cultural Heritage." 1966. Henze, *Music and Politics* 143–6.

—. *Bohemian Fifths: An Autobiography*. Trans. Stewart Spencer. London: Faber, 1998.

—. Interview with Paul Griffiths. "The Bassarids." *The Musical Times* 115 (1974): 831–2.

—. *Music and Politics: Collected Writings 1953–81*. Trans. Peter Labanyi. London: Faber, 1982.

Herrick, Robert. "To the Virgins, to Make Much of Time." *The Poems of Robert Herrick*. Ed. L. C. Martin. London: Oxford UP, 1965. 84.

Herz, Judith Scherer. "'This is the End of Parsival': The Orphic and the Operatic in *The Longest Journey.*" Martin and Piggford 136–50.

Herz, Judith Scherer and Robert K. Martin, eds. *E. M. Forster: Centenary Revaluations*. Toronto: U of Toronto P, 1982.

Heseltine, Philip. *The Occasional Writings of Philip Heseltine (Peter Warlock)*. Ed. Barry Smith. 2 vols. London: Thames, 1997.

Hillier, Robert Irwin. *The South Seas Fiction of Robert Louis Stevenson*. New York: Lang, 1989.

Hindley, Clifford. "Eros in Life and Death: *Billy Budd* and *Death in Venice.*" Cooke, *The Cambridge Companion* 147–66.

—. "Love and Salvation in Britten's 'Billy Budd'." *Music and Letters* 70 (1989): 363–81.

Hoddinott, Alun. *The Beach of Falesá*. Oxford: Oxford UP, 1974.

Hollander, John. *The Untuning of the Sky: Ideas of Music in English Poetry 1500–1700*. Princeton: Princeton UP, 1961.

Howard, Patricia. *The Operas of Benjamin Britten: An Introduction*. London: Barrie, 1969.

Hubbard, Tom. *Seeking Mr. Hyde: Studies in Robert Louis Stevenson, Symbolism, Myth and the Pre-Modern*. Frankfurt: Lang, 1995.

Hutcheon, Linda. "'Sublime Noise' for Three Friends: Music in the Critical Writings of E. M. Forster, Roger Fry and Charles Mauron." Herz and Martin, 84–98.

Hutcheon, Linda and Michael. *Opera: Desire, Disease, Death*. Lincoln: U of Nebraska P, 1996.

—. *Bodily Charm: Living Opera*. Lincoln: U of Nebraska P, 2000.

—. *Opera: The Art of Dying*. Harvard: Harvard UP, 2004.

Hutchinson, Stuart. "'Troilus'—Forty Years On." *Opera* 46 (1996): 16–17.

Huxley, Aldous. *Music at Night and Other Essays*. London: Chatto, 1931.

—. *On Art and Artists*. Ed. Morris Philipson. London: Chatto, 1960.

—. *Point Counter Point*. London: Chatto, 1928.

Innes, Christopher. *Modern British Drama: The Twentieth Century*. Cambridge: Cambridge UP, 2002.

Jacobs, Alan. *What Became of Wystan: Change and Continuity in Auden's Poetry*. Fayetteville: U of Arkansas P, 1998.

Jacobs, Arthur. Rev. of *Troilus and Cressida*, comp. William Walton. *Opera* 14 (1963): 419–21.

John, Nicholas, ed. *The Operas of Michael Tippett*. London: Calder, 1985.

Jolly, Roslyn. "Stevenson's 'Sterling Domestic Fiction', 'The Beach of Falesá'." *The Review of English Studies* 50 (1999): 463–82.

Jones, David. *In Parenthesis.* 1937. London: Faber, 1961.

Jones, Glyn. *The Beach of Falesá.* London: Oxford UP, 1974.

—. "Robert Jeffreys." Jones, *Welsh Heirs* 9–39.

—. *Selected Poems: Fragments & Fictions.* Ogmore-by-Sea: Poetry Wales, 1988.

—. *Welsh Heirs.* Llandysul: Gomer, 1977.

Jones, Glyn and John Rowlands. *Profiles: A Visitors' Guide to Writing in Twentieth Century Wales.* Llandysul: Gomer, 1980.

Jones, Graham. "Hoddinott's *The Beach of Falesá*." *Anglo-Welsh Review* 23 (1974): 259–61.

Jones, Richard Elfyn. *The Early Operas of Michael Tippett: A Study of The Midsummer Marriage, King Priam and The Knot Garden.* Lewiston: Mellen, 1996.

Karolyi, Otto. *Modern British Music: The Second British Musical Renaissance— From Elgar to P. Maxwell Davies.* London: Associated U Presses, 1994.

Kemp, Ian. "Michael Tippett." Sadie, *The New Grove Twentieth-Century English Masters* 201–36.

—. *Tippett: The Composer and His Music.* London: Eulenburg, 1984.

Kennedy, Michael. *Portrait of Walton.* Oxford: Oxford UP, 1989.

Kennett, Christian. "Criticism and Theory." Banfield, *Music in Britain* 503–18.

Kerman, Joseph. *Opera as Drama: New and Revised Edition.* Berkeley: U of California P, 1988.

Krenek, Ernst. "What is Called the New Music, and Why?" Albright, *Modernism and Music* 330–36.

Lachenmann, Helmut. "Open Letter to Hans Werner Henze." Trans. Jeffrey Stadelman. *Perspectives of New Music* 35 (1997): 189–93.

Lambert, Constant. *Music Ho! A Study of Music in Decline.* 1934. London: Faber, 1966.

Law, Joe K. "The Dialogics of Operatic Adaptation: Reading Benjamin Britten." *Yearbook of Interdisciplinary Studies in the Fine Arts* 1 (1989): 407–27.

—. "Linking the Past with the Present: A Conversation with Nancy Evans and Eric Crozier." *Opera Quarterly* 3.1 (1985): 72–9.

—. "'We Have Ventured to Tidy up Vere': The Adapters' Dialogue in *Billy Budd.*" *Twentieth Century Literature* 31 (1985): 297–314.

Lee, M. Owen. *A Season of Opera: From Orpheus to Ariadne.* Toronto: U of Toronto P, 1998.

Lehmann, John. *A Nest of Tigers: Edith, Osbert and Sacheverell Sitwell in their Times.* London: Macmillan, 1968.

Lewis, C. S. *The Allegory of Love: A Study in Medieval Tradition.* 1936. London: Oxford UP, 1953.

Leyda, Jay. "Bartleby: Genesis of an Opera 2." *Melville Annual 1965 Symposium: Bartleby the Scrivener.* Ed. Howard P. Vincent. Kent: Kent State UP, 1966: 42–4.

—, ed. *The Portable Melville.* New York: Viking, 1965.

Lindenberger, Herbert. *Opera the Extravagant Art.* Ithaca: Cornell UP, 1984.

—. *Opera in History: From Monteverdi to Cage.* Stanford: Stanford UP, 1998.

Lloyd, Stephen. "Film Music." Craggs 109–31.

Macqueen-Pope, W. *Ivor: The Story of an Achievement.* London: Allen, 1951.

Martin, Robert K. "Saving Captain Vere: *Billy Budd* from Melville's Novella to Britten's Opera." *Studies in Short Fiction* 23 (1986): 49–56.

Martin, Robert K. and George Piggford, eds. *Queer Forster*. Chicago: U of Chicago P, 1997.

McCracken-Flesher, Caroline. "Thinking Nationally/Writing Colonially? Scott, Stevenson and England." *Novel* 24 (1991): 296–318.

McLynn, Frank. *Robert Louis Stevenson: A Biography*. London: Random, 1993.

Mégroz, R. L. *The Three Sitwells: A Biographical and Critical Study*. Port Washington: Kennikat, 1927.

Mellers, Wilfrid. *Caliban Reborn: Renewal in Twentieth-Century Music*. London: Gollancz, 1968.

—. "Through *Noye's Fludde*." Palmer, *Britten Companion* 153–60.

—. "Tippett at the Millenium: A Personal Memoir." Clarke 186–99.

Melnick, Daniel C. *Fullness of Dissonance: Modern Fiction and the Aesthetics of Music*. London: Associated U Presses, 1994.

Melville, Herman. *Billy Budd and Other Prose Pieces*. Ed. Raymond W. Weaver. London: Constable, 1924.

—. *Billy Budd, Foretopman*. London: Lehmann, 1946.

—. *Moby-Dick; or, The Whale*. London: Penguin, 1986.

Mendelson, Edward. *Early Auden*. London: Faber, 1981.

—. *Later Auden*. New York: Farrar, 1999.

Menikoff, Barry. *Robert Louis Stevenson and 'The Beach of Falesá': A Study in Victorian Publishing*. Stanford: Stanford UP, 1984.

Milder, Robert, ed. *Critical Essays on Melville's Billy Budd, Sailor*. Boston: Hall, 1989.

—. Introduction. *Critical Essays on Melville's Billy Budd, Sailor*. Ed. Milder.

Milnes, Robert. Rev. of *Troilus and Cressida*, comp. William Walton. *Opera* 46: 355–9.

Mitchell, Donald. "A *Billy Budd* Notebook (1979–1991)." Cooke and Reed 111–34.

—. *Britten and Auden in the Thirties: The Year 1936*. Woodbridge: Boydell, 2000.

—. *The Language of Modern Music*. 1963. Rev. 1976. London: Faber, 1993.

—. "More off than on *Billy Budd*." *Music Survey* 4 (1952): 386–408.

—. Rev. of *Troilus and Cressida*, comp. William Walton. *The Musical Times* 96 (1955): 36.

—. "'Troilus and Cressida': Two Further Opinions." *Opera* 6 (1955): 88–91.

Mitchell, Donald and Hans Keller, eds. *Benjamin Britten: A Commentary on His Works From a Group of Specialists*. London: Rockcliff, 1952.

Mitchell, Jerome. *More Scott Operas: Further Analyses of Operas Based on the Works of Sir Walter Scott*. Lanham: U Press of America, 1996.

—. *The Walter Scott Operas: An Analysis of Operas Based on the Works of Sir Walter Scott*. Alabama: U of Alabama P, 1977.

Mordden, Ethan. *Opera in the Twentieth Century: Sacred, Profane, Godot*. New York: Oxford UP, 1978.

Morgan, Robert P. *Twentieth-Century Music*. New York: Norton, 1991.

Muldoon, Paul. *Bandanna*. London: Faber, 1999.

Müller, Paul. "'Troilus and Cressida': Two Further Opinions." *Opera* 6 (1955): 91–2.

Myers, Rollo H., ed. *Twentieth Century Music*. London: Calder, 1968.

Norris, Leslie. *Glyn Jones*. Rev. ed. Cardiff: U of Wales, 1997.

O'Connor, Patrick. "Music for the Stage." Banfield, *Music in Britain* 107–24.

Orga, Ates. "Sir William Walton: Some Thoughts." *Composer* 68 (1979): 11–14.

Ottaway, Hugh. "William Walton." Sadie, *The New Grove Twentieth-Century English Masters* 175–97.

Paglia, Camille. *Sexual Personae: Art and Decadence from Nefertiti to Emily Dickinson*. London: Yale UP, 1990.

Palmer, Christopher, ed. *The Britten Companion*. London: Faber, 1984.

—. "Towards a Geneology of Death in Venice." Palmer, *Britten Companion* 250–67.

Parker, Hershel. *Reading "Billy Budd"*. Evanston: Northwestern UP, 1990.

Piper, Myfanwy. "Writing for Britten." Herbert 8–21.

Poizat, Michel. *The Angel's Cry: Beyond the Pleasure Principle in Opera*. Trans. Arthur Denner. Ithaca: Cornell UP, 1992. Trans. of *L'opéra, ou le cri de l'ange: essai sur la jouissance de l'amateur d'opéra*. 1986.

Pollard, Rowena and David Clarke. "Tippett's *King Priam* and 'The Tragic Vision'." Clarke 166–85.

Porter, Andrew. "Britten's 'Billy Budd'." *Music and Letters* 33 (1952): 111–18.

—. "Saved." *Music of Three More Seasons: 1977–1980*. New York: Knopf, 1981: 230–36.

Porter, Peter. "Composer and Poet." Palmer, *Britten Companion* 271–85.

Price, Scott. "'A Lost Child': A Study of the Genesis of *Troilus and Cressida*." Craggs 182–208.

Price, T. R. "A Study in Chaucer's Method of Narrative Construction." *PMLA* 2 (1896): 307–22.

Rebellato, Dan. *1956 and All That: The Making of Modern British Drama*. London: Routledge, 1999.

Reed, Philip. "From First Thoughts to First Night: A *Billy Budd* Chronology." Cooke and Reed 42–73.

—. "The 1960 Revisions: A Two-Act *Billy Budd*." Cooke and Reed 74–84.

Rees, David. "Britten in the Darbies: Benjamin Britten." Rees, *Words & Music* 15–39.

—. "Slightly Dotty, Rather Messianic: Michael Tippett." Rees, *Words & Music* 143–54.

—. *Words & Music*. Brighton: Millivres, 1993.

Rickards, Guy. *Hindemith, Hartmann and Henze*. London: Phaidon, 1995.

Rilke, Rainer Maria. *Letters to a Young Poet*. Trans. M. D. Herter Norton. New York: Norton, 1962.

Rollins, Hyder E. *The Troilus-Cressida Story from Chaucer to Shakespeare*. New York: Haskell, 1972.

Rosen, Charles. "Public and Private." Spender, *W. H. Auden: A Tribute*. 218–19.

Rosenthal, Harold. Rev. of *Troilus and Cressida*, comp. William Walton. *Opera* 28 (1977): 101–3.

Rosmarin, Léonard. *When Literature Becomes Opera: Study of a Transformational Process*. Amsterdam/Atlanta: Rodopi, 1999.

Routh, Francis. *Contemporary British Music: The Twenty-Five Years from 1945 to 1970*. London: Macdonald, 1972.

Ruttenburg, Nancy. "Melville's Handsome Sailor: The Anxiety of Innocence." *American Literature* 66 (1994): 83–103.

Rye, Matthew. "Music and Drama." Banfield, *Music in Britain* 343–401.

Sacks, Oliver. "Dear Mr A. . . ." Spender, *W.H. Auden: A Tribute*. 187–95.

Sadie, Stanley, ed. *The New Grove Dictionary of Music and Musicians*. Vol. 8. London: Macmillan, 1994.

—, ed. *The New Grove Twentieth-Century English Masters: Elgar, Delius, Vaughan Williams, Holst, Walton, Tippett, Britten*. New York: Norton, 1986.

Samuel, Rhian. "Birtwistle's *Gawain*: An Essay and a Diary." *Cambridge Opera Journal* 4 (1992): 163–78.

Schafer, Murray. *British Composers in Interview*. London: Faber, 1963.

Scheppach, Margaret A. *Dramatic Parallels in Michael Tippett's Operas: Analytical Essays on the Musico-Dramatic Techniques*. Lewiston: Mellen, 1990.

Scher, Steven Paul, ed. *Music and Text: Critical Inquiries*. Cambridge: Cambridge UP, 1992.

Schmidgall, Gary. *Literature as Opera*. New York: Oxford UP, 1977.

—. *Shakespeare and Opera*. New York: Oxford UP, 1990.

Scorza, Thomas J. *In the Time Before Steamships: Billy Budd, the Limits of Politics and Modernity*. Dekalb: Northern Illinois UP, 1979.

Scott, Cyril. *The Philosophy of Modernism (In its Connection with Music)*. London: Kegan, 1917.

Searle, Humphrey and Robert Layton. *Twentieth-Century Composers. Vol. III Britain, Scandinavia and the Netherlands*. London: Weidenfeld, 1972.

Sedgwick, Eve Kosofsky. *Epistemology of the Closet*. Berkeley: U of California P, 1990.

Shakespeare, William. *The Tragedy of Troilus and Cressida*. Ed. Jackson J. Campbell. *The Yale Shakespeare: The Complete Works*. Ed. Wilbur L. Cross and Tucker Brooke. New York: Barnes, 1993. 320–64.

Shaw, George Bernard. *Bernard Shaw: Music in London 1890–94: Criticisms Contributed Week by Week to The World in Three Vols. The Works of Bernard Shaw*. Vols. 26–28 London: Constable, 1931.

Sinfield, Alan. *Literature, Politics and Culture in Postwar Britain*. Oxford: Blackwell, 1989.

Sir Gawain and the Green Knight, Ed. J. R. R. Tolkien and E. V. Gordon. 2nd ed. Ed. Norman Davis. Oxford: Oxford UP, 1967.

Sitwell, Edith. *English Eccentrics*. London: Faber, 1933.

—. *Façade and Other Poems, 1920–1935*. London: Duckworth, 1950.

—. *Selected Letters of Edith Sitwell*. Ed. Richard Greene. London: Virago, 1997.

Sitwell, Osbert. *Laughter in the Next Room: An Autobiography*. London: Macmillan, 1949.

Smith, Janet Adam, ed. *Henry James and Robert Louis Stevenson: A Record of Friendship and Criticism*. London: Hart-Davis, 1948.

Smith, Patrick J. *The Tenth Muse: A Historical Study of the Opera Libretto*. New York: Knopf, 1970.

—. "Viewpoint: Henze's *Bassarids.*" *Opera News* 55.8 (Jan. 6, 1991): 6.

Smith, Vanessa. *Literary Culture and the Pacific: Nineteenth-Century Textual Encounters.* Cambridge: Cambridge UP, 1998.

Spears, Monroe K. *Auden: A Collection of Critical Essays.* Englewood Cliffs: Prentice, 1964.

—. *The Poetry of W. H. Auden: The Disenchanted Island.* New York: Oxford UP, 1963.

Spender, Stephen. *Journals 1939–1983.* Ed. John Goldsmith. London: Faber, 1985.

—. "Valediction." Spender, *W. H. Auden: A Tribute.* 244–8.

—, ed. *W. H. Auden: A Tribute.* London: Weidenfeld, 1975.

—. *World Within World.* 1948. New York: Harcourt, 1951.

Spenser, Edmund. *The Faerie Queene Books I to III.* Ed. Douglas Brooks-Davies. London: Dent, 2000.

Stafford, William T., ed. *Melville's Billy Budd and the Critics.* 2nd ed. Belmont: Wadsworth, 1969.

—. "The New *Billy Budd* and the Novelistic Fallacy: The Chicago Text." Stafford, *Melville's Billy Budd* 3–9.

Stein, Erwin. "Billy Budd." Mitchell and Keller 198–210.

Stern, Milton R., ed. *Typee and Billy Budd.* London: Dent, 1963.

Sternfeld, Frederick and David Harvey. "A Musical Magpie: Words and Music in Michael Tippett's Operas." *Parnassus: Poetry in Review* (1982): 188–92.

Stevenson, Robert Louis. *The Beach of Falesá.* 1892. *The Strange Case of Dr Jekyll and Mr Hyde and Other Stories.* Ed. Jenni Calder. London: Penguin, 1979.

—. *The Letters of Robert Louis Stevenson.* Ed. Bradford A. Booth and Ernest Mehew. Vol. 7. New Haven: Yale UP, 1995.

Stradling, Robert and Meirion Hughes. *The English Musical Renaissance 1860–1940: Construction and Deconstruction.* London: Routledge, 1993.

Stravinsky, Igor. "The Maker of Libretti." Stravinsky, *Themes and Conclusions* 284–90.

—. *Stravinsky: Selected Correspondence.* Ed. Robert Craft. Vol. 1. New York: Knopf, 1982.

—. *Themes and Conclusions.* London: Faber, 1972.

Stubbs Smith, Kathryn. "*Moby-Dick* in Forster's *Howards End.*" *Explicator* 46 (1987): 20–22.

Sutcliffe, James Helme. "The Infinite Sea." *Opera News* 48.15 (1984): 16–18, 43.

Sutcliffe, Tom. "British Journal." *Opera News* 56 (1991): 45–7.

—. "British Journal." *Opera News* 59 (1995): 38–9.

Thomas, Dylan. *The Beach of Falesá.* 1959. New York: Stein, 1963.

—. *The Collected Letters of Dylan Thomas.* Ed. Paul Ferris. London: Dent, 1985.

Thomas, M. Wynn. *Internal Difference: Twentieth-Century Writing in Wales.* Cardiff: U of Wales P, 1992.

Tierney, Neil. *William Walton: His Life and Music.* London: Hale, 1984.

Tippett, Michael. "At Work on 'King Priam'." *The Score: A Music Magazine* 28 (January 1961): 58–68.

—. "The Birth of an Opera." Tippett, *Moving into Aquarius* 47–63.

—. "A Child of Our Time: T. S. Eliot and *A Child of Our Time.*" Tippett, *Music of the Angels* 117–26.

—. *King Priam*. London: Schott, 1962.

—. *The Knot Garden: An Opera in Three Acts*. London: Schott, 1969.

—. "Love in Opera." Tippett, *Music of the Angels* 210–21.

—. *The Midsummer Marriage*. London: Schott, 1954.

—. *Moving into Aquarius*. London: Routledge, 1959.

—. "Music in England—A Personal View by Sir Michael Tippett." Dickinson 1–6.

—. *Music of the Angels: Essays and Sketchbooks of Michael Tippett*. Ed. Meirion Bowen. London: Eulenberg, 1980.

—. *New Year*. London: Schott and Co., 1989.

—. "Opera Since 1900." Tippett, *Music of the Angels* 199–200.

—. "The Resonance of Troy: Essays and Commentaries on *King Priam*." Tippett, *Music of the Angels* 222–34.

—. *Those Twentieth Century Blues: An Autobiography*. London: Hutchinson, 1991.

Tomlinson, Gary. *Metaphysical Song: An Essay on Opera*. Princeton: Princeton UP, 1999.

Trend, Michael. *Heirs and Rebels of the English Musical Renaissance: Edward Elgar to Benjamin Britten*. London: Weidenfeld, 1985.

Trilling, Lionel. *The Middle of the Journey*. 1947. New York: Avon, 1976.

Vianu, Lidia. "Poetry is a Way of Life: Interview with David Harsent." *Desperado Literature*. 13 August 2004. <http://www.lidiavianu.go.ro/David%20Harsent.htm>

Vincent, Howard. P., ed. *Twentieth Century Interpretations of Billy Budd: A Collection of Critical Essays*. Englewood Cliffs: Prentice, 1971.

Wagner, Richard. *The Ring*. Trans. Andrew Porter. Kent: Dawson, 1976.

Wahl, William. B. "My Impressions of W. H. Auden: His Last Interview." *Poetic Drama Interviews: Robert Speaight, E. Martin Browne and W.H. Auden. Poetic Drama and Poetic Theory*. Ed. James Hogg. Salzburg: Institut für Englische Sprache und Literatur 1976. 93–107.

Walton, Susana. *William Walton: Behind the Façade*. Oxford: Oxford UP, 1988.

Walton, William. Interview with Hans Keller. "Contemporary Music: Its Problems and Its Future." *Composer* 20 (1966): 2–4.

—. *Troilus and Cressida: Opera in Three Acts*. London: Oxford UP, 1954.

Warnaby, John. "Anticipating *Gawain*." *Musical Opinion* 114 (1991): 155–6.

Warrack, John. "Walton's 'Troilus and Cressida'." *The Musical Times* 95 (1954): 646–9.

Weatherhead, Andrea K. "*Howards End*: Beethoven's Fifth." *Twentieth Century Literature* 31 (1985): 247–64.

Webb, Paul. *Ivor Novello: A Portrait of a Star*. London: Stage Directions, 1999.

Weisstein, Ulrich, ed. *The Essence of Opera*. 1964. New York: Norton, 1969.

—. "The Libretto as Literature." *Books Abroad* 35 (1961): 16–22.

Wellesz, Egon. *Essays on Opera*. Trans. Patricia Kean. London: Dobson, 1968.

—. "The Idea of the Heroic and Opera." Wellesz, *Essays on Opera* 140–144.

—. "Three Lectures on Opera." Wellesz, *Essays on Opera* 90–139.

White, Eric Walter. *Benjamin Britten: His Life and Operas*. Berkeley: U of California P, 1970.

—. *A History of English Opera*. London: Faber, 1983.

—. *Tippett and His Operas*. London: Barrie, 1979.

—. *The Rise of English Opera*. London: Lehmann, 1951.

Whittall, Arnold. "British Music in the Modern World." Banfield, *Music In Britain* 9–26.

—. "'Byzantium': Tippett, Years and the Limitations of Affinity." *Music and Letters* 74 (1993): 383–98.

—. "'Is There a Choice at All?' *King Priam* and Motives for Analysis." Clarke 55–77.

—. *The Music of Britten and Tippett: Studies in Themes and Techniques*. 1982. Rev. ed. Cambridge: Cambridge UP, 1990.

—. *Music Since the First World War*. New York: St. Martin's, 1977.

—. "'Twisted Relations': Method and Meaning in Britten's *Billy Budd*." *Cambridge Opera Journal* 2 (1990): 145–71.

—. "A War and a Wedding: Two Modern British Operas." *Music and Letters* 55 (1974): 299–306.

Wilcox, Michael. *Benjamin Britten's Operas*. Bath: Absolute, 1997.

Wilkinson, L. P. "The Later Years." *E. M. Forster: Interviews and Recollections*. Ed. J. H. Stape. New York: St. Martin's, 1993. 166–8.

Williams, C. K. *The Bacchae of Euripides: A New Version*. New York: Noonday, 1990.

Winn, James Anderson. *Unsuspected Eloquence: A History of the Relations Between Poetry and Music*. New Haven: Yale UP, 1981.

Winnington-Ingram, R. P. *Euripides and Dionysus: An Interpretation of the Bacchae*. London: Cambridge UP, 1948.

Wolf, Werner. *The Musicalization of Fiction: A Study in the Theory and History of Intermediality*. Amsterdam: Rodopi, 1999.

Woolf, Virginia. *Between the Acts*. London: Hogarth, 1941.

"The Younger Generation: Alun Hoddinott." *The Musical Times* 101 (1960): 148.

Index